China Mutual Funds 2017

Charles Chaw

Published by
China Knowledge Press Pte Ltd
119 Genting Lane
HB@119 Genting #01-00
Singapore 349570
T: (65) 6743 1823 Singapore
T: (86) 21 6607 5535 Shanghai
URL: www.chinaknowledge.com
Email: info@chinaknowledge.com

Mutual Fund Website: fund.chinaknowledge.com

ISBN: 978-981-11-0895-2

Publisher & Managing Director
Charles Chaw C Loong

Research and Content Contributors
David Diao Junwei, Kevin Chen Yulan, Jessica Hu Jiafeng, Ching Hon Siong, Edward Rushton, Kent Chen Binbin, Cheryl Gan

Editorial
Michael Edward, Dr George Eli, Ang An Rui, Cheryl Gan

Designer / Graphics
Rosy Gao Ying

Public Relations
Lina Lyu Na

Photographers
Rosy Gao Ying, David Diao Junwei, Edward Rushton

Database
Edward Teng Junping, Jia Dian

FOREWORD

Within the last two decades China's mutual funds market size has grown from USD 800 million to almost USD 1.4 trillion as at Feb 2017 – that is, by more than 1,700 times. Though the first so-called mutual fund was launched in 1991, the market's phenomenal growth began in 1998, when regulators set out to develop China's stock markets.

Today some 1,300 licensed fund managers can invest in a wide array of behemoth domestic financial markets. As of March 2017, China's stock market capitalization was almost USD 10 trillion, second in the world after the U.S, and its fixed income market size was about USD 9 trillion. Other financial markets, like publicly available trust products, exceed USD 2.3 trillion and China's red hot commodities trading averages RMB 1 trillion a day. China's financial markets and trading volumes are world class.

To share key insights and investment themes with our readers, we capture and follow the country's growth and abundant opportunities on the One Belt One Road (OBOR) initiative, Industrialization 4.0, the upgrading of manufacturing to high-value output, the shift to a consumerism-centric growth model and the government's greater emphasis on and support for hi-tech sectors including bio-technology, robotics, aerospace, aviation and new materials.

During the current term (from 2013 to 2022), China's leaders and top officials are committed to tapping these opportunities, welcoming foreign investors and maintaining a moderate to moderately high GDP growth rate of about 6% to 6.5%.

Most important is the country's gradual opening of its financial markets. With the RMB as part of the IMF's basket of reserve currencies, a larger investment quota for Qualified Foreign Institutional Investor (QFII), further deregulation and new financial products entering the financial industry, the mutual fund market could see increasing participation of foreign monies.

Domestically, because retail investors are gradually turning to fund managers, where the proportion is still about 4:1, the variety of products is increasing and Chinese financial markets are becoming mature and sophisticated, mutual fund size under management could see strong, sustainable double-digit growth.

It has been more than 12 years since we last published a guide on China's mutual funds industry and followed up with a series of biweekly newsletters. In 2007, the country's financial market reforms and opening to global markets were greatly disrupted due to the U.S subprime crisis and its effects on the stability of global financial markets.

No economy could ever be free from financial mishaps, black swan events, or volatile and turbulent swings. These are natural occurrences, and surviving them is part of the journey to a better-managed system.

I am thankful to the many fund managers who agreed to be interviewed in person or by phone or email. I am also thankful for the assistance of my analysts, whose views and comments have given our readers some interesting and unique insights into China's mutual market industry.

To provide our readers real-time data and most up-to-date information, we offer our readers six months of free access to a dedicated website that provides detailed information on more than 6,100 mutual funds. There are also analytics, customizable league tables and rankings of top performing funds, funds by sector, managers, and many other variations and functions. We hope readers will find these valuable tools useful in their quest to deepen their understanding of China's mutual funds.

Charles Chaw C Loong
Publisher, Managing Director
China Knowledge Press Pte Ltd
Singapore
23rd March 2017

ACRONYMS AND ABBREVIATIONS

CDs: Certificate of Deposits

TNA: Total Net Asset

YTD: Year-to-Date

AUM: Asset under Management

NAV: Net-Asset Value

ETF: Exchange Traded Fund

LOF: Listed Open-ended Fund

CCDC: China Central Depository & Clearing Co., Ltd.

CSRC: China Securities Regulatory Commission

CBRC: China Banking Regulatory Commission

PBoC: People's Bank of China

QFII: Qualified Foreign Institutional Investors

RQFII: RMB Qualified Foreign Institutional Investors

SSE: Shanghai Stock Exchange

SZE: Shenzhen Stock Exchange

ICI: Investment Company Institute

QDII: Qualified Domestic Institutional Investor

ICBC: Industrial and Commercial Bank of China

CCB: China Construction Bank

ABC: Agricultural Bank of China

BOC: Bank of China

BoCoM: Bank of Communications

CIB: China Industrial Bank

SPDB: Shanghai Pudong Development Bank

CITIC: CITIC Securities

CDB: China Development Bank

CICC: China International Capital Co., Ltd.

PART ONE:

CHINA MUTUAL FUNDS INDUSTRY DEVELOPMENT

Figure 1.1 Development of China Mutual Fund Products

1998: March 23
The first two closed-end securities investment funds, Jin Tai Fund and Kai Yuan Fund, launched on the SSE and SZE respectively under the Interim Measures, commencing the operation of China's investment funds.

2001: September 4
HuaAn Fund Management Co., Ltd. launched China's first open-end fund, Huaan Innovation Fund.

2002: July 25
The first domestic open-end bond fund, South Baoyuan Bond Fund, was established.

2002: December 2
The first open-end index fund, SSE 180 Index Fund, was established.

2003: December 30
The first money market fund, HuaAn Fuli Cash Fund, was founded.

2004: November 29
The first exchange-traded fund (ETF), China 50 ETF, was launched. It was considered for breakthrough in China's fund industry.

2005: August 31
ICBC Credit Suisse Asset Management launched its first fund, the ICBCCS Core Value Equity Fund.

2006: November 2
HuaAn International Balanced Fund is the first independent asset management firm to secure a QDII license, with an investment quota of US$ 500 million.

2007: September 2
The first QDII mutual fund, China Southern International Select Allocation Fund, was incepted.

2008: March 28
CIB Fund Management Co., Ltd. launched CIB Fund Management Social Responsibility Investment Fund, the nation's first social responsibility fund. This marks a milestone in the development of Socially Responsible Investment (SRI) in China's financial markets.

2008: September 9
Fullgoal Asset Management Co., Ltd. launched the first closed-end bond fund – Fullgoal Tianfeng Surging Income Bond Fund.

2010: March 8
The first industry index fund, UBS SDIC CSI 300 Financial and Property (LOF), was allowed to raise capital and issue shares.

2010: March 22
Guotai Nasdaq 100 ETF, the first domestic ETF based on an overseas index,

commenced operations.

2015: December 18
The China Securities Regulatory Commission officially registered the first three mutual funds in Hong Kong and Hong Kong's securities and futures commission also officially registered the first four mainland mutual funds.

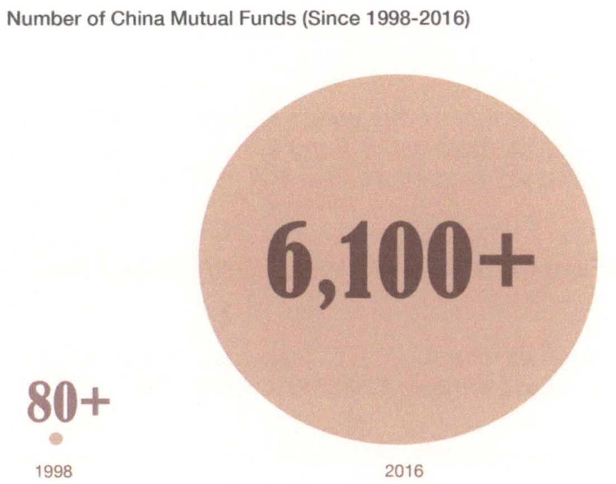

Figure 1.2 Development of China Mutual Fund Market

1997: November 14
The State Council issued the Interim Measures on the Administration of Securities Investment Fund that laid the legal framework for the development of China's investment funds industry.

1998: February 24
ICBC is the first Chinese bank to obtain custody qualification for securities investment funds upon the approval of CSRC and the PBoC.

1998: March 5
The first two asset management companies, China Southern Asset Management Co., Ltd. and Cathay Pacific Fund Management Co., Ltd., were established and licensed by CRSC.

1999: November 12
The Interim Provisions on Qualifications for Securities Practitioners was implemented.

1999: December 29
CSRC promulgated the Securities Investment Fund Industry Convention.

2000: October 8
CSRC launched the Pilot Program for Open-End Securities Investment Fund.

2001: August 28
The Securities Investment Fund Committee was founded.

2001: October 11
The Pilot Project for Open-End Securities Investment Fund was officially launched, with the objective of strengthening the investment fund management framework.

2002: June 3
CSRC issued the Rules on Establishment of Securities Companies with Foreign Equity Participation and Rules on Establishment of Fund Management Companies with Foreign Equity Participation that will take effect from 1 July 2002.

2002: December 4
The first Securities Investment Fund Committee was established in Shenzhen.

2002: December 27
The first Sino-foreign fund, China Merchants Fund, was established as a joint venture between ING Investment Management, China Merchants Bank and China Merchants Securities.

2004: June 1
The Securities Investment Fund Law of the People's Republic of China was officially implemented.

2004: July 1
Both the Administrative Measures on Sales of Securities Investment Funds and Administrative Measures on the Operations of Securities Investment Funds were officially implemented.

2004: September 16
CSRC announced the administrative Measures on the Securities Investment Fund Management Companies and the Administrative Measures on the Securities Investment Fund Industry Senior Management Personnel.

2005: February 20
The Pilot Project for Establishment of Fund Management Companies by Commercial Banks was implemented, signifying a milestone for commercial banks entry into the fund industry.

2005: April 28
ICBC is the nation's first commercial bank approved to set up an asset management company.

2005: June 7
ICBC Credit Suisse Asset Management Co., Ltd. was formally established. It is the first joint-venture asset management company sponsored, founded and controlled by a state-owned commercial bank.

2005: September 29

CSRC, the PBoC and the Ministry of Finance released the Administrative Measures for Securities Investors Protection Fund.

2007: July 30
Two more asset management companies, China Asset Management Co., Ltd. and China Southern Fund Management Co., Ltd. obtains the ODII license.

2007: October 9
Harvest Overseas Fund, the first domestic QDII fund that focuses on H shares, commenced operations.

2007: December 1
CSRC announced the Pilot Measures for the Asset Management Services of Fund Management Companies for Specific Clients.

2009: March 17
CSRC amended the Guiding Opinions on Administration of Investment Management Personnel of Fund Management Companies, and the revised edition will be implemented from April 1, 2009.

2009: April 21
CSRC promulgated the Guidance on Participation in Stock Index Futures Trading by Securities Investment Funds.

2009: November 6
CSRC released the Interim Measures for Evaluation of Securities Investment Funds.

2010: November 1
CSRC released the Revised Draft of Administrative Measures on Sales of Securities Investment Funds.

2011: August 9
CSRC promulgated the amended Administrative Measure on Sales of Securities Investment Funds.

2011: August 25
CSRC announced the Pilot Measures for the Asset Management Services of Fund Management Companies for Specific Clients.

2012: June 7
The industry's first self-regulatory committee, Asset Management Association of China, was established.

2012: September 20
CSRC promulgated the Administrative Measures on the Securities Investment Fund Management Companies.

2012: October 29
CSRC released the Interim Measures for Management of Subsidiaries of Securities Investment Fund Management Companies.

2013: May 15

China Asset Management Co., Ltd. launched a fund enquiry service on its public WeChat account, becoming the first fund company to implement a WeChat finance Service.

2013: June 1
The newly revised Securities Investment Fund Law of the People's Republic of China came into effect.

2013: June 28
CSRC released the revised versions of the administrative Measures of Asset Management Services of Fund Management Companies and Detailed Implementation Rules of Collective Asset Management Business of Securities Companies. It also amended conflicting terms in the Securities Investment Fund Law to ensure legal consistency.

2014: July 11
A registration system was set up for mutual funds product review to increase the efficiency of fund product issuance.

2015: July 1
The Interim provisions of Mainland-Hong Kong Mutual Recognition of Funds Scheme was launched.

2015: August 8
The new fund operation management approach required that stocks should make up a minimum 80% of equity funds portfolio.

2016: January 7
China has suspended its stock market circuit breakers, only four days after introducing them.

2016: June 17
China may be allowed to invest in mutual fund-of-funds later this year after the release of a consultation paper from CSRC.

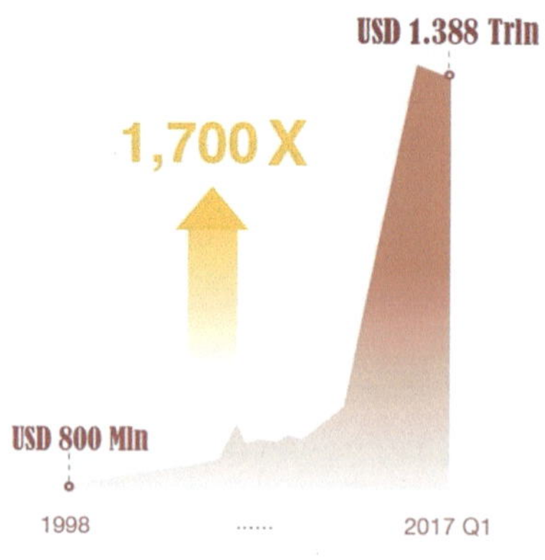

Figure 1.3 Growth History of Mutual Funds

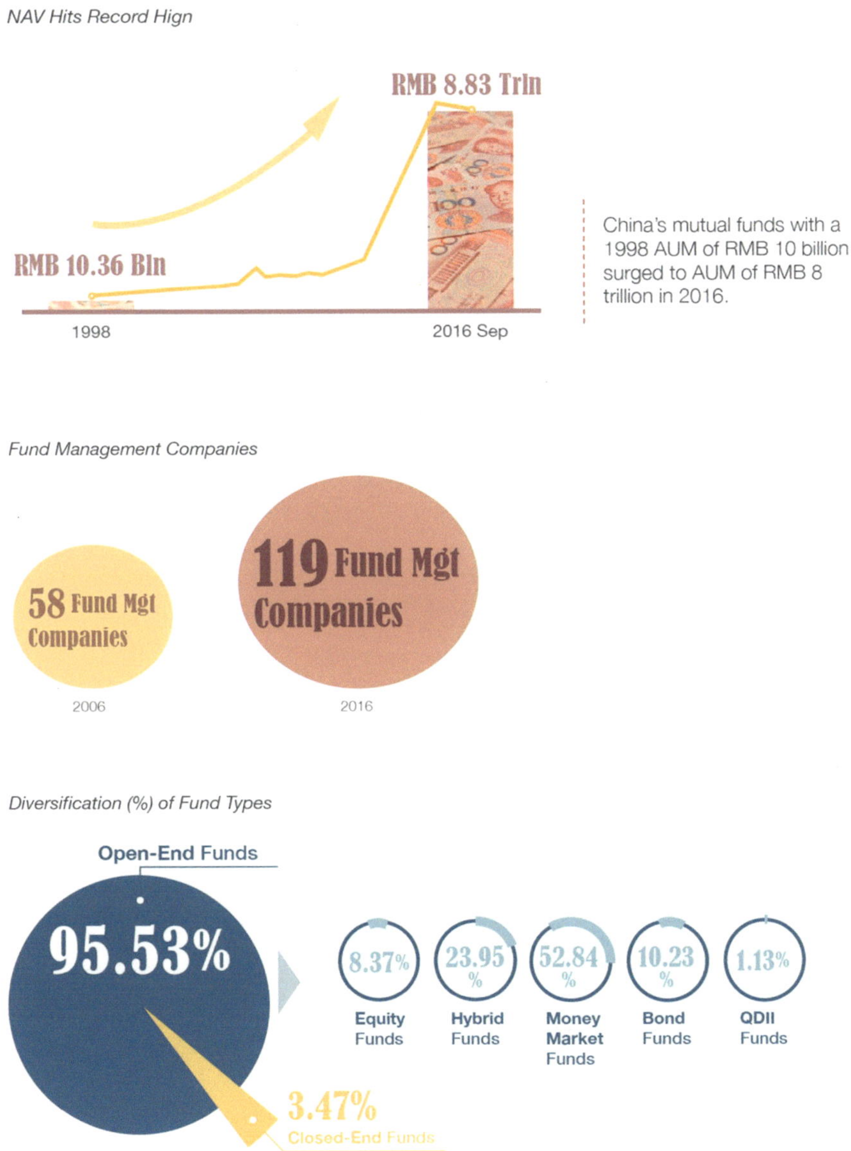

Large Increase in China Mutual Funds Industry

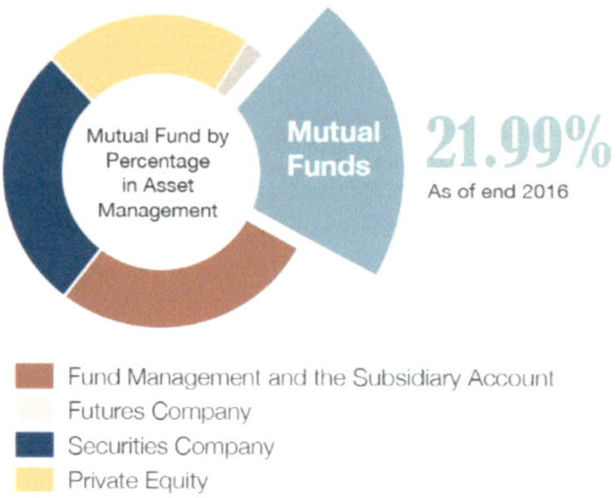

China mutual funds industry plays a significant role in macroeconomic economy, finance and financial markets to maintain capital market stability.

New Funds Launched (Shares Bln)

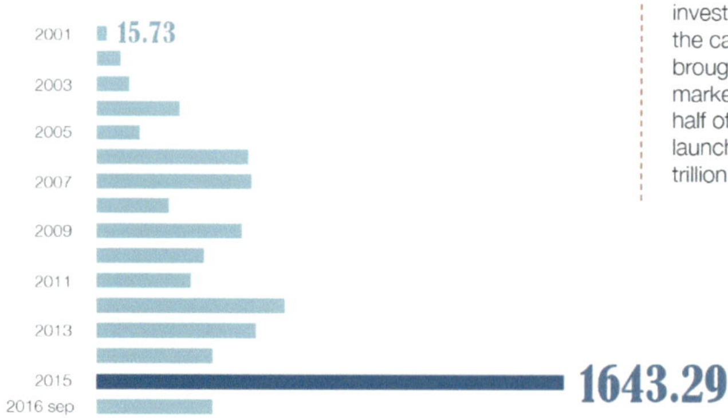

The enthusiasm of the investors and money effect the capital market has brought the mutual fund market prosperity. In the first half of 2015, the new funds launched hit astonishing 1.64 trillion shares.

Source: Asset Management Association of China, China Knowledge Mutual Funds Database

1.1 THE INDUSTRY PAST, PRESENT AND FUTURE

1.1.1 BEFORE 1997: THE UNREGULATED MARKET

The birth of China's fund management industry took place at the end of 1990 not long after the establishment of a centralized stock trading system and the opening of stock exchanges in Shanghai and Shenzhen.

In October 1991, the Wuhan Branch of the People's Bank of China (PBoC) launched China's first securities investment fund, the Wuhan Securities Investment Fund, and raised RMB 10 million (US$ 1.88 million). One year later, in October 1992, the first specialized fund management company, the Shenzhen Investment Fund Management Co., Ltd. was established. China's fund management industry entered its first boom at that point, and 37 funds were established with the approval of the various branches of the PBoC and other organizations within a year.

Following approval by head office of the PBoC, the Zibo Township Enterprises Fund listed on Shanghai Stock Exchange and became China's first public-listed fund. By the end of October 1997, China had 72 closed-end investment funds with total capital raised reaching RMB 6.6 billion (US$ 0.79 billion).

China's fund management industry remained unregulated during this period. Neither an efficient regulatory system nor standard regulations governed this emerging industry. Fund promoters came from various institutions, from banks, trust & investment companies, securities firms, insurance companies, to corporations, among others. Trust & investment companies and securities firms respectively accounted for about 51% and 20% of the total fund promotion. Most funds were approved either by various branches of the PBoC or by local governments. It was not uncommon for some funds, the fund management company, custodian company, and promoter to be part the same organization.

Funds in the 1990s were generally small, with each fund's average assets under management for amounting to RMB 80 million (US$ 9.66 million). For example, the biggest fund at the time, the Tianji Fund, was just RMB 580 million (US$ 70.05 million). By 1997, the market cap of tradable shares in China's domestic stock markets reached RMB 520.4 billion (US$ 62.85 billion). In spite of this growth, total fund assets under management accounted for only 1.27% of the market cap of tradable shares in 1997.

Due to a lack of clear investment strategies and poor performance, investment decisions made by fund managers on funds had a limited impact on the overall markets.

As relevant government agencies begin to realize how a properly managed fund management industry could lead to a prosperous capital market, they tried to rectify this problem.

In November 1997, the State Council released a set of prescriptions known as the "Provisional Measures for Managing Securities Investment Funds". These were the first national regulations governing securities investment funds and provided standard guidelines for the growth of China's fund management industry. The measures clarified and standardized the structures of funds as well as the obligations of fund managers, custodian institutions and investors. At the same time, the measures also designated the China Securities Regulatory Commission (CSRC), a ministerial-level public institution directly under the State Council, as China's official approval, regulatory and supervisory authority over investment funds.

With the measures in place, 1998 has often been referred to as the birth year of China's fund management industry. Many view the year as the beginning of China's fund management industry, rather than in 1991 when the first fund launched. To make a distinction between funds formed before and after the release of the Measures, the former were known as "old" funds.

1.1.2 1998-2002: ENTERING A NEW STAGE OF DEVELOPMENT

In March 1998, the establishment of China Southern Fund Management Co., Ltd. and Guotai Asset Management Co., Ltd. marked the beginning of China's "new" fund management industry. They were soon followed by three other fund management companies: Boshi Fund Management Co., Ltd., China Asset Management Co., Ltd. and HuaAn Fund Management Co., Ltd.

Figure 1.4 First Five Fund Management Companies (Established in 1998)

China Southern Fund Management Co., Ltd.

Guotai Asset Management Co., Ltd.

Bosera Asset Management Co., Ltd.

China Asset Management Co., Ltd.

HuaAn Fund Management Co., Ltd.

Source: China Knowledge Mutual Funds Database

According to the Province Measures for Managing Securities Investment Funds, only securities firms, trust & investment companies, and other non-bank financial institutions were permitted to promote fund management companies. As China's regulatory units began to rectify the rampant irregular corporate operations, it became apparent that few companies were qualified to be promoters. Consequently, only six fund management companies were in business by the end of 1998, the aforementioned five funds as well as a sixth, the Penghua Fund Management Co., Ltd.

In April 1998, the Kaiyuan Fund listed on the Shenzhen Stock Exchange, and the Jintai Fund listed in Shanghai. Issued by China Southern Fund Management Co.,Ltd. and Guotai Asset Management Co.,Ltd. respectively, they were the first regularized closed-end funds in China.

By the end of 1998, the first five fund companies had issued one closed-end fund each with a total value worth RMB 2 billion (US$ 0.24 million). These companies, then considered "newcomers" to the scene, were not welcomed by market participants, many of whom were manipulators who were active at that time. It thus became common that once these fund managers purchased certain stocks, manipulators would avoid exposure to them. Due to the strong influence of these manipulators, the prices of such stocks inevitably plunged. It is no surprise that these fund managers also fell out of favor with listed companies because of their effect on stock prices.

On the other hand, fund management companies won favor with another constituency, government regulators. During the early developmental stages of China's securities market, price manipulation was rife. Because of the limited number of "professional" investment institutions, many of them worked closely with market manipulators, and the securities market was highly vulnerable to such manipulations. Hence, regulators initially viewed fund management as a good tool to counter the rampant price manipulation.

Regulators adopted a series of measures to nurture these fund management companies still in their infant stages of growth. One of the most effective measures was to allocate 20% of all newly offered shares to fund management companies (stock IPOs were still considered as guaranteed returns in 1998). By the end of 1998, the total net asset value of these five "new" funds hit RMB 10.4 billion (US$ 1.25 billion). In 1999, the number of fund management companies increased to 10 while the number of funds reached 22. At the end of the year, total NAV reached RMB 57.5 billion (US$ 6.95 billion), and the ratio of total NAV to the market cap of tradable shares jumped from 1.81% in 1998 to 7.00% the following year. The influence of fund management in China's securities markets grew.

As the "new" funds grew, regulators began to restructure "old" funds issued before 1997. In 1999, 10 "old" funds were consolidated into four "new" funds. In 2000, regulators' focal point shifted to the restructuring of "old" funds, and no new fund management companies were established. As the issuance of new funds came to a halt, "old" funds found themselves restructured into "new" funds. By the end of 2000, there were 34 "new" funds with RMB 84.7 billion (US$ 10.24 billion) of assets under management. At the same time, the success of fund managers in picking up technology shares improved their profile among general investors, marking an improvement in China's fledging securities markets.

Table 1.1 Industry Statistics,1998-2002

	1998	1999	2000	2001	2002
No. of Fund Management Companies in Operation	6	10	10	15	21
No. of Funds	5	22	34	51	71
No. of Closed-end Funds	5	22	34	48	54
No. of Open-end Funds	0	0	0	3	17
Total No. of Funds (Billion)	10	50.5	56.2	80.4	131.9
NAV of Funds (RMB Biliion)	10.4	57.5	84.7	80.9	118.6
Ratio of NAV of Funds to Market Cap of Tradable Shares	1.81%	7.00%	5.27%	5.59%	9.50%

Source: China's Securities and Futures Markets

Figure 1.5 Gradual Expantion of China's Fund Management Industry (1998-2002)

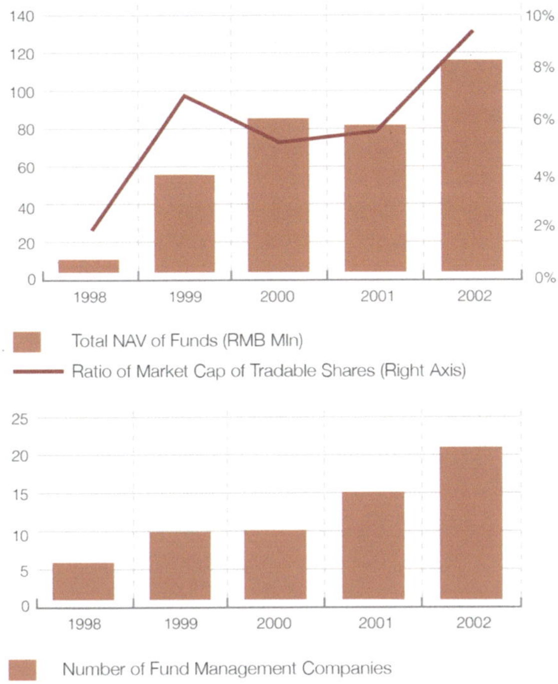

Source: China's Securities and Futures Markets

Faced with the irresistible lure of huge returns as a result of market manipulation, some fund management companies soon began to rig the market as well. Based on the statistical data from the Shanghai Stock Exchange, Zhao Yugang, an employee at the SSE, wrote two internal research reports on the irregular operations in fund management. Having closely monitored fund trading between August 1999 and April 2000, Zhao noted in his study that many fund managers manipulated the prices of their holdings. He also detailed various methods of collusion between funds under the same fund management company as well as between different fund management companies.

After these two reports leaked to the public, Caijing Magazine published an article in October 2000 entitled, "The Inside Story of the Fund Management Industry". This fallout from this incident led to the most serious crisis the nascent industry had ever experienced, sending the booming industry into a temporary ebb. Regulators quickly stepped in to rectify the situation. CSRC singled out 10 fund management companies for investigation, and eight of them were found guilty of price manipulation, including big players such as the Bashi Fund Management Co., Ltd. CSRC censured these companies and imposed administrative sanctions on some employees. Fund management companies were advised to appoint independent directors, and subsequent cleanup proved beneficial to the long-term development of fund management. The pace of maturation in the industry has since accelerated.

The HuaAn Creative Fund was established in September 2001 as the first open-end securities investment fund in China. Many viewed its creation as a revolutionary step in the progress of China's fund management industry. Because the shares of closed-end funds were fixed, fund managers to some extent were less concerned with these funds because they did not face redemption pressures from investors.

The establishment of open-end funds forced fund managers to become more market-oriented. Since they are open ended, investors can redeem their shares if they are unsatisfied with the performance of particular funds. Open-end funds soon won favor with investors, and closed-end funds found themselves marginalized. In September 2002, the Yinfeng Fund, the 54th and last closed-end fund, listed on Shanghai Stock Exchange. By comparison, 17 open-end funds had launched by the end of 2002.

1.1.3 2003-2007: MUTUAL FUNDS EXPERIENCE EXPLOSIVE GROWTH

Often referred to as the year of Chinese fund management, 2003 marked an important step in the development of the industry. Fast growing open-end funds contributed to the acceleration of innovative new products. After the first fixed income fund, the CSFMC Baoyuan Fund, launched in September 2002, and the first index fund, Hua'an 180 Index Fund, was established in November 2002, more new products were created in 2003 than ever before.

Funds'outstanding performance in 2003 lured more retail and institutional investors alike to buy them. Meanwhile, China's fund management industry continues to be viewed as an important element in the restructuring of the investment environment in China's securities markets. On January 31, 2004, the State Council released the nine-point "Guidelines on Promoting Reform, Opening-up and Steady Development of China's Capital Market that serves as a blueprint for the development of China's stock market. It explicitly endorsed China's fund management industry by stating that institutional investors represented by investment funds and insurers should overtake retail investors as the major participants in the stock markets. This prompted regulators to ease the approval of fund sales and product innovations.

Over the past few years, the funds industry has quickly developed. As a result of the Chinese government's efforts, what started out as a small, unorganized funds industry transformed into a major driving force behind China's capital markets.

On June 1, 2004, China implemented the Securities Investment Fund Law, laying the foundation for the open-end fund industry's development. By mid-2007, individual investors made up 90% of open-end fund holders. Individual investors joined in the mutual funds market, which led to a significant change in the structure of fund holders. After its decade-long development process, these funds have become one of the most effective investment channels and have spiked in popularity among individual investors. Prior to this, funds relied on interest from institutional investors such as insurance companies. By the end of 2006, the number of open-end fund accounts surpassed 10 million, and just a year later at the end of 2007, individual investors made up more than 90% of open-end equity fund holders.

The year 2006 proved to be a milestone in the history of China's fund industry. Securities investment funds achieved stellar yields relative to the stock market's performance, and became the main investment channels of choice for investors seeking lucrative returns. This led to the fund industry's rapid growth, hitting records for new funds numbers and initial capital raised. On December 7, 2006, the Harvest Strategic Growth Fund raised RMB 41.9 billion (US$ 5.37 billion) within a day after it launched. The 89 new open-end funds set up in 2006 alone reached half the number of funds established in the five years prior. The assets under management of these 89 funds reached RMB 388.8 billion (US$ 49.85 billion) in total, four times the net AUM of 62 companies in the previous year.

The rapid development of fund management companies can be attributed to three primary factors:

(1) The High Growth of Joint Venture Fund Companies

In 2002, the promulgation of "Rules on Establishment of Fund Management Companies with Foreign Equity Participation" by CSRC opened the floodgates to foreign investment.

At the end of 2002, the China Merchants Fund became the first domestic joint venture fund company. ING Bank and China Merchant Securities were the major foreign and domestic stakeholders, holding 30% and 40% stakes, respectively.

At the end of 2004, the maximum stake limit that foreign investors held increased from 33% to 49%, leading to the establishment of more joint venture funds companies such as the First State Cinda Fund Management Co., Ltd. and Lord Abbett & Co. LLC.

In 2007, 28 joint venture fund management firms accounted for 47.5% of all funds companies in China. Assets under management by joint venture fund companies accounted for 40.5% of the total industry AUM, with 9 venture funds companies managing more than RMB 100 billion (US$ 12.99 billion) in assets. Of these, 3 fund companies managed assets that exceeded RMB 200 billion (US$ 25.97 billion). While such mammoth fund sizes demonstrated the significant growth of the fund industry, the presence of these huge funds was beneficial because they added stability and reduced industry risk.

Implementation of the "Pilot Project for Establishment of Fund Management Companies by Commercial Banks"on February 20, 2005, marked commercial banks' foray into the securities business. Their entrance significantly altered the competitive landscape of the Chinese fund industry. With their extensive experience and large customer base, commercial banks exercised an absolute advantage relative to fund companies, which adapted to the increased competition by improving their existing business models. This resulted in the fission, differentiation and integration of numerous funds.

(2) Changes in Regional Structure

From 2004 to 2007, the funds industry mainly operated in three regions: Shanghai, Beijing and Shenzhen. Although Shanghai and Beijing markets grew, the Shenzhen market did not perform so well. It maintained a market capitalization above 40% but could not sustain a dominant role in the industry. Instead, its capitalization dropped to 30-40% in 2007, on par with Beijing. In contrast, Shanghai Fund Management Industry fared better. With the exception of a 15% decline in 2003, Shanghai's market capitalization has always maintained a level of 30-40% and at times even surpassed 50%. Other markets were much smaller. Out of the 59 Chinese firms nationwide, just 3 were based in Guangzhou and 1 was in Tianjin.

(3) A More Competitive Industry

By 2004, China had 6 fund management companies whose AUM exceeded RMB 10 billion (US$ 1.21 billion). China Asset Management Co., Ltd. was the largest, with AUM worth RMB 16.2 billion (US$ 1.96 billion). The fund industry at the time was highly concentrated with the nation's top 5 companies holding 42.6% of the total market share and the top 10 companies more than 70% of market share.

The situation changed by the end of 2004, with larger companies managing more assets. The combined market share of the top 10 companies dropped to around 60%. A total of 12 fund management companies had AUM that exceeded RMB 10 billion (US$ 1.45 billion). China Southern Asset Management took over as market leader with AUM of RMB 36.1 billion (US$ 5.23 billion). The top 10 companies managed RMB 298 billion (US$ 43.2 billion) worth of net assets, dominating 58.27% of the entire industry's AUM.

By the end of 2006, the funds industry grew to RMB 490.3 billion (US$ 62.86 billion). It remained concentrated with AUM of the top 10 fund management companies or 57.25% of the whole industry.

At the end of 2007, a total of 58 fund management companies managed 363 securities investment funds and RMB 3.28 trillion (US$ 419.87 billion) worth of fund assets. China Asset Management Co., Ltd. reassumed its market leader position with 18 funds under management with a total NAV of RMB 248 billion (US$ 31.79 billion). The top 10 fund management companies collectively managed RMB 16.31 billion (US$ 2.09 billion) worth of assets making up 49.78% of the market's AUM. Although differing regional performance suggested increasing market concentration, in reality, the industry decentralized.

The fund industry has done exceptionally well in diversifying fund products throughout its history to cater better to investors'demands. From 2004 to 2007, it significantly expanded its product range with new, innovative offerings and improving existing products. Investment styles became more varied, and product lines diversified with increasingly apparent differentiation. In addition to traditional investment styles such as growth, blend and value funds, the industry also introduced original offerings like index funds, money market funds, and Qualified Domestic Institutional Investor funds.

In 2007, 66 new funds launched. These included 2 innovative closed-end funds, 4 QDII funds, 19 closed-end funds converted to open-end funds, 3 guaranteed open-end funds, 5 short-term debt restructuring funds, and 33 open-end funds.

Meanwhile, the newly formed funds encouraged product diversification. China Southern Fund Management Co., Ltd. issued a RMB 3.56 billion (US$ 0.43 billion) exchange-traded fund on December 24, 2004, the first pure equity ETF listed in China. This listed open-end fund greatly reduced the cost of fund sales and enhanced the convenience of mobility, subscription and redemption, helping solve some drawbacks of open-end mutual funds.

On December 30, 2004, the first Exchange Traded Fund China 50 ETF was established. The China 50 ETF, which quickly reached RMB 5.43 billion (US$ 0.66 billion), is now an efficient investment instrument that enables investors to trade all the constituent stocks of the Shanghai Stock Exchange 50 Index (the SSE 50 Index) with the ease of one stock transaction. The China 50 ETF offers institutional investors trading flexibility and enables them to enter and exit the stock market quickly, incurring lower transaction costs and enhancing investment portfolio management and efficiency.

Overview of the China 50 ETF

The China 50 ETF is based on a typical ETF model that tracks an index with good liquidity and allows in-kind creation and redemption. In addition, it can be subscribed to with cash or a combination of cash and stocks. Unit creation and redemption use the same trading and settlement mechanisms as stocks transactions, making the China 50 ETF appealing to domestic Chinese investors.

Table 1.2 Product Overview

Name of Fund	China 50 Exchange Traded Open-End Index Securities Investment Fund (China 50 ETF).
Unit Par Value	RMB 1.00
Unit Net Asset Value	Prior to trading in the market, unit net asset value of the fund is converted to about 1/1000 of the SSE 50 Index.
Dividend Policy	Dividends may be distributed when accumulated returns exceed 1% of index returns in the same period, and satisfies the time-frame requirements of dividend distribution.
Fund Manager	China Asset Management Co., Ltd.
Technical Advisor	State Street Global Advisors and State Street Bank and Trust Company.

Source: China Knowledge Mutual Funds Database

Table 1.3 China Exchange Traded Funds Overview (2004-2007)

	No. of Funds	ETF Fund Size (RMB Bln)	Market Share (%)
2004	1	5.4	1.67
2005	1	6.6	1.41
2006	5	14.04	1.64
2007	5	32.12	1.01

Source: China Knowledge Mutual Funds Database

ETFs are a positive development in China's Fund Industry. First, they improve the structure of China's fund products. Second, they can meet the needs of long-term investors in the stock market. Finally, ETFs in the secondary market can attract many small and medium investors to participate, thereby enhancing the capital market liquidity.

QFII and QDII

Qualified Foreign Institutional Investors (QFII) is a program launched in 2003 where overseas institutional investors seek approval from CSRC to invest in China's securities market. These QFIIs obtain an investment quota from the State Administration of Foreign Exchange (SAFE) to invest in products within a specified investment scope. CSRC looks to attract long-term investors in China rather than speculative ones.

Table 1.4 Pre-requisites for QFII Application

Eligible Investors	Business Experience	Capital	Assets under Management
Asset Management Companies*	2 years	N/A	≥ US$ 500 million
Insurance Companies	2 years	N/A	≥ US$ 500 million
Securities Companies	5 years	≥ US$ 500 million of net assets	≥ US$ 5 billion
Commercial Banks	10 years	≥ US$ 300 million of tier 1 capital	≥ US$ 5 billion
Other Institutions	2 years	N/A	≥ US$ 500 million

- **Notes:** According to CSRC, private equity investment institutions may apply for QFII qualifications under Asset Management Companies, but hedge funds are not allowed since they are not seen as long-term investors.

Source: National Debt Assosiation of China

Key Parties

There are several parties involved in the QFII investment process. CSRC is the regulatory body that considers and assesses the qualifications of QFII applicants while SAFE is in charge of approving investment quotas and repatriations. QFIIs also require the help of a qualified custodian bank that represent them in the application of the license and quotas. QFIIs need to enlist the help of investment advisors for recommendations on asset allocation and individual investments. Moreover, Chinese domestic brokers have to be engaged in order for QFIIs to execute domestic securities trading activities. Finally, an accounting firm must be hired to handle repatriations and tax considerations.

Figure 1.6 Procedures

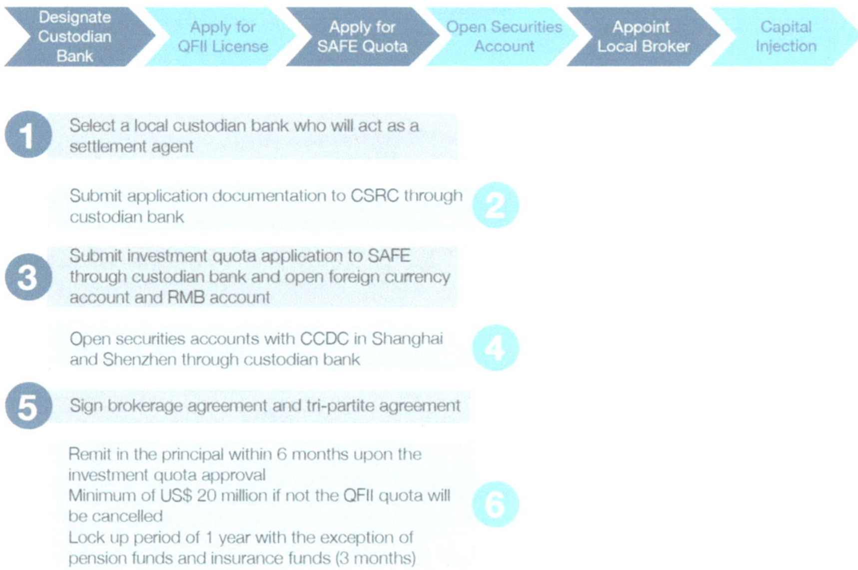

Source: China Knowledge Mutual Funds Database

QFII Quotas and Regulations

QFII Quotas

- The minimum application size is US$ 50 million.
- Generally speaking, asset management companies are typically granted quotas between US$ 100 million and US$ 300 million.

Regulations

- The "Administrative Measures for Domestic Securities Investments by Qualified Foreign Institutional Investors" policy was jointly issued by CSRC, the PBoC and SAFE in 2006.
- The "Foreign Exchange Administrative Provisions for Domestic Securities Investments by Qualified Foreign Institutional Investors" was issued by SAFE in 2012.

Recent Major Changes

Table 1.5 Relaxed QFII Qualifications

QFII Applicants	2006	2012
Asset management institutions, Insurance institutions, foundations, sovereign funds, pension funds, etc	Experience: above 5 years Most recent securities assets under management: above US$ 5 billion	Experience: above 2 years Most recent securities assets under management: US$ 500 million
Securities Firms	Experience: above 30 years Paid-in capital: Min US$ 1 billion Most recent securities assets under management: above US$ 10 billion	Experience: above 5 years Most recent securities assets under management: above US$ 5 billion
Commercial Banks	Experience: Within top 100 world ranking in the latest year Most recent securities assets under management: above US$ 10 billion	Experience: above 10 years Tier 1 capital above US$ 300 million Most recent securities assets under management: above US$ 5 billion

Source: China Knowledge Mutual Funds Database

Table 1.6 Greater Investment Range

2006	2012
QFII may invest in: • Stocks listed in the securities exchange • Bonds listed in the securities exchange • Securities investment fund • Warrants listed in the securities exchange • Other financial instruments approved by CSRC	QFII may invest in: • Stock, bonds, warrants listed in the securities exchange • Fixed-income investments listed in the inter-bank bond market • Securities investment fund • Stock futures • Other financial instruments approved by CSRC

Source: China Knowledge Mutual Funds Database

Meanwhile, QDII plays a dominant role in overseas trading. It can help open RMB trading overseas up to China's domestic capital overseas and boost the RMB's global clout. In November 2006, the first mutual QDII fund, Hua An International, was established. By 2007, 4 QDII funds launched with assets totaling RMB 108.18 billion (US$ 14.79 billion). Compared with modest growth in the bank savings and insurance markets, the funds market expanded six-fold between 2003 and 2007. By the end of 2007, the total net assets of mutual funds reached RMB 3.28 trillion (US$ 0.45 trillion), 13% higher than the insurance market's RMB 2.9 trillion (US$ 0.40 trillion) in total assets. For the first time, China's mutual funds asset value surpassed that of the insurance market.

Table 1.7 The Development of China's Fund Industry, Insurance Industry and Bank Savings

Year	Bank Savings		Insurance		Fund Industry	
	Size (RMB Bln)	Growth Rate	Size (RMB Bln)	Growth Rate	Size (RMB Bln)	Growth Rate
2003	10,400	10.28%	861.9	32.72%	171.6	44.69%
2004	11,955.5	14.96%	1,185.4	37.53%	324.6	89.16%
2005	14,105.1	17.98%	1,522.6	28.45%	469.1	44.52%
2006	16,661.6	18.12%	1,973.1	29.59%	856.5	82.58%
2007	17,253.2	3.55%	2,900.4	47%	3,275.6	282.44%

Source: China Knowledge Mutual Funds Database

1.1.4 2008-2014: DIVERSIFIED STAGES OF GROWTH

The Development of China's Fund Industry, Insurance Industry and Bank Savings

The fund industry in China has developed steadily over the past 16 years. Its regulated operations have experienced sustainable growth and momentum. The fundamental principles of "independent operation, portfolio investment, mandatory custody and public disclosure" that serve as the benchmark for the asset management industry in China have helped ensure that the industry's develops soundly. A sophisticated regulatory system for fund supervision has already taken shape, with China's Securities Investment Fund Law acting as the core regulations and rules governing various procedures such as institutional administration, investment operations, asset custody, product distribution and information disclosure, among others. The country also established a unified fund supervision system with CSRC and its regional offices, industry associations and exchanges. On July 7, 2007, CSRC publicly promulgated the "Measures for the Pilot Scheme of Securities Investments in Overseas Made by RMB Qualified Domestic Institutional Investors" and the "Fund Management Company Specific Customer Asset Management Business Pilot Measures"on January 1, 2008. These marked the start of the development period of diversified asset management in China's fund industry. Since 2008, the number of Chinese funds increased significantly to a total of number of 441 funds by 2008, and 561 funds by 2009. A new fund classification approval system was implemented in 2010, giving fund management companies the ability to issue new funds more easily. As a result, by 2014, the number of funds grew to 1,952.

Despite the launched of more funds, their total net assets did not increase noticeably until 2014. Between 2008 and 2014, the net asset size was (year over year): RMB 1.94 trillion (US$ 0.27 trillion); RMB 2.68 trillion (US$ 0.40 trillion); RMB 2.52 trillion (US$ 0.37 trillion); RMB 2.19 trillion (US$ 0.34 trillion); RMB 2.8 trillion (US$ 0.44 trillion); RMB 3.01 trillion (US$ 0.49 trillion); and RMB 4.55 trillion (US$ 0.74 trillion).

Figure 1.7 The Size of Fund NAV (RMB Bln)

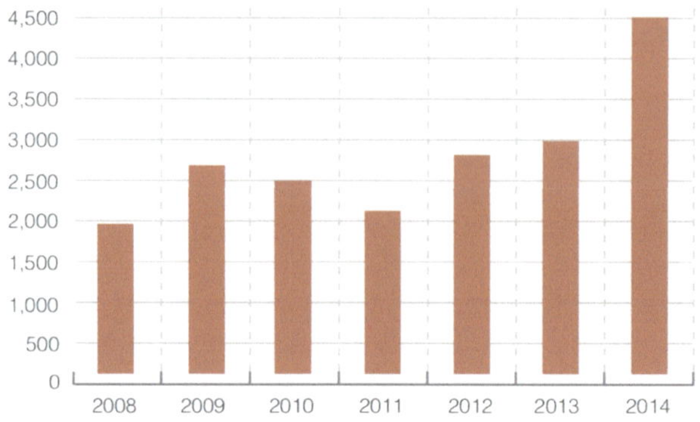

Source: China Knowledge Mutual Funds Database

By the end of May 2014, there were 91 fund management companies, 69 subsidiaries of fund management companies specializing in the management of specific client assets, and 3 asset management institutions qualified to manage mutual funds. These firms collectively managed 1,680 funds totaling RMB 7.25 trillion (US$ 1.17 trillion) AUM. A subset of funds under management, mutual fund AUM, reached RMB 3.92 trillion (US$ 0.63 trillion) in 2014, and broke the previous record of RMB 3.3 trillion (US$ 0.42 trillion) set in 2007. By 2014, China ranked tenth among the mutual fund markets worldwide, the highest since its inception. The role of professional institutional investors in the process has created a steady long-term and excess return for fund holders. Estimates indicated that in the past nine years, the annualized average excess return of equity-oriented funds across the industry stood at 5.87%, when compared with the China A-Share Index.

Playing a key role in the management of market-based and professional pension fund investments, fund management companies have contributed greatly to facilitating pension funds' participation in the capital markets and realizing the maintenance and appreciation of their value. Meanwhile, fund management companies enrich financial service channels for the public, propelling the growth of China's asset management industry and improving the investment structure of capital markets.

Since 2008, the market capitalization of shares held by mutual funds has remained between 5.5% and 7.8% of the total market capitalization of the A-share market. By the end of 2013, the market capitalization of shares held by mutual funds stood at RMB 1.3 trillion (US$ 0.17 trillion), accounting for approximately 50% of the market capitalization of total shares held by professional institutional investors on the A-share market. In addition, securities investment funds are also among the most active professional institutional investors participating in China's bond markets.

Funds have played an active role in improving the governance of listed companies, facilitating the smooth operation of capital markets; reforming the split share structure, a new share offering system, social security system and financial system; promoting direct financing; and optimizing the allocation of financial resources. Following the release of its Opinions on Innovation, CSRC will devote itself to promoting the development of the fund industry by reinforcing the role of institutional investors in advocating a long-term investment market philosophy, exploiting the positive role of fund management companies in pricing IPOs, and serving as a check on the improper governance practices of listed companies.

1.1.5 MUTUAL FUNDS INDUSTRY PERFORMANCE IN 2015

In 2015, China's mutual funds industry surpassed Japan to become the second largest in the Asia region with US$1.3 trillion in AUM. The overall East Asia mutual funds industry had an impressive run at the time that saw regional assets in the industry grow to US$ 4.2 trillion or 11% of the total global mutual funds market. In fact, with China's mutual funds industry leading the way, the East Asia market doubled in the last four years from US$ 2.3 trillion in AUM.

Figure 1.8 The Asset Scale of Different Types of Funds (RMB Bln)

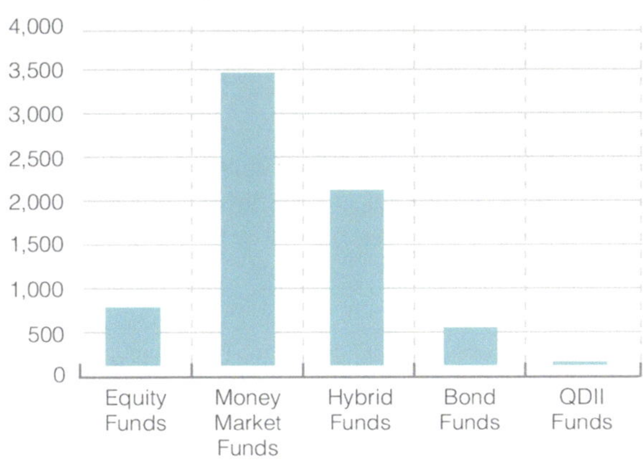

Source: China Knowledge Mutual Funds Database

Chinese money market funds have experienced substantial growth since the second half of 2013, driven in particular by demand for e-commerce money market funds. In 2015, the total assets scale of Chinese money market funds accounted for 50% of all mutual funds, reaching RMB 3.4 trillion (US$ 0.52 trillion). These were followed by hybrid funds with RMB 2.15 trillion (US$ 0.33 trillion) in assets; equity funds, RMB 758.05 billion (US$ 116.79 billion); bond funds, RMB 573.47 billion (US$ 88.35); and QDII funds, RMB 60.55 billion (US$ 9.33 billion). So many equity funds converted to hybrid funds that by the end of 2015, the total assets of hybrid funds had reached RMB 3.58 trillion (US$ 0.55 trillion). The growth scale of hybrid funds surged RMB 1.55 trillion (US$ 0.25 trillion) or 257.32%, far more than equity funds. Although many equity funds became hybrid funds, assets at the remaining equity funds declined just slightly to RMB 556.154 billion (US$ 90.36 billion) by the end of 2014.

The asset management scale of 30 fund management companies more than doubled. Assets at the largest company, the Western Leadbank Fund Management Co., Ltd., soared 41.16 times to RMB 9.37 billion (US$ 1.44 billion). On the other hand, the asset management scale at 10 other fund management companies' actually declined. Changsheng Fund Management Co., Ltd. in particular shrank by RMB 15.56 billion (US$ 2.4 billion).

As of September 30, 2016, there were 109 mutual fund management companies managing 3,369 mutual funds with assets totaling RMB 8.53 trillion (US$ 1.2 billion), a record high.

In the third quarter of 2016, the average fund had a positive yield. Among these, QDII funds were the most profitable with an eye-catching average yield of 6.33%.

In the last part of this book, we will analyze annual performance of the market in 2016.

China's booming mutual fund market is attracting more foreign companies to take part in local business. Eight fund management joint ventures have already been established in China with two more on the way, but the market has plenty of room for further expansion.

China's mutual fund market is expected to experience increasing growth as China encourages the development of its mutual fund market and helps cultivate institutional investors in the securities market. The ongoing Chinese stock market correction and money supply tightening may cast a cloud over new mutual fund IPOs in the short term, but fund managers are still optimistic about the future and should proceed with their expansion plans.

1.2 REGULATORY AND LEGAL FRAMEWORK

1.2.1 THE DEVELOPMENT AND CHANGES IN REGULATION FOR CHINA'S FUND INDUSTRY

The roots of China's fund industry date back to the early 1990s. The change in economic priorities during this period led to the gradual reform of government regulation and China's transition from a planned economy towards the free market. The fund industry today reflects the complex relationship between the government and market realities.

The government had a firm grip on the industry in its early stages, controlling resources ranging from fund issuers to fund managers, capital sources, and investment directions. As a result, funds were set up to suit the specific aims of financial sector development reforms.

Heavily regulated by the government, the fund industry initially had a difficult time shifting to free market mechanisms. The lack of protocol paired with its rapid expansion led to many bottlenecks in its development and unregulated investing behavior by fund managers who failed to act in the best interests of investors. This created chaos within the industry, hurting its credibility.

The establishment of a central regulatory body, China Securities Regulatory Commission (CSRC), in 1997, and the measures it subsequently issued, laid the legal framework for the fund industry, paving the way to healthy development. However, the laws promulgated at the time were still heavily influenced by government intervention that was not in tandem with market sentiment.

After 2004, CSRC gradually emphasized administration and transparent supervision. This led to the industry's second transition from direct to indirect regulation. CSRC supported the free market mechanism and as the industry matured, it slowly opened, and product innovation initially driven by governmental guidance shifted to one prompted by market demand. This environmental transformation significantly improved the industry.

The Industry's Behavior in the Absence of a Central Regulatory Body (Before 1998)

The beginnings of China's mutual funds industry can be traced back to four main events:

First, rapid economic development driven by the government's economic reforms led to the market's voracious demand for funds.

Second, the consecutive establishment of the Shanghai and Shenzhen Stock Exchanges led to the opening of many local securities trading centers.

Third, China began to open to the world, and its financial market became increasingly receptive to and embraced foreign financial products and investing styles. Extensive financial regulation resulted in the approach of widespread pilot testing within the domestic market.

Fourth, Chinese government supported solutions that restricted excessive speculation.

In this phase, government dominated the industry. Free market forces were too weak, and the industry lacked a uniform set of rules and regulations. Its development adhered to the government's objectives, which defeated the fundamental purpose of the fund industry – to put investors' interests first. In 1992, the Shenzhen Investment Trust Management Interim Provisions issued by the PBoC explicitly stated that funds should be established to meet market demand and develop the nation's economy, with no focus on protecting investors' interests. The lack of uniform regulations resulted in the industry's unstructured and disorganized development. Investment opportunities were restricted. Real estate funds accounted for a disproportionately large segment of the industry, and problems like small fund sizes, low quality funds, low liquidity and low profitability arose. In addition, there was no effective governance of the industry's administration. Issuers, custodians and management were unregulated, and fund embezzlement ensued. Listed funds were frequently under speculative attacks, leading to chaos in the stock markets.

By September 1996, 73 out of the 75 approved funds were established with a total value of RMB 5 billion (US$ 0.6 billion). At that time, the industry lost its bullish progression. It developed very slowly. Moral hazards were high, and there was no regard for protecting investors' interests.

Phase of Intensive Regulation (1998-2003)

Without the presence of a uniform set of rules, the chaos of the fund industry indicated to the government that a clear, centralized regulatory body was necessary to restore order for healthy development.

Consequently, the Interim Measures for Management of Securities Investment Fund was implemented in September 1997.

On April 1998, CSRC became the first centralized regulatory organization in the national securities and futures market. It took steps to build a legal framework that would form a stable foundation for the industry and set up 36 offices in different cities to control and regulate the industry better.

(1) Regulation of Practitioners

In 1999, CSRC officially imposed qualification requirements on fund practitioners. Executive committee members and board directors needed to be audited or approved by the commission.

(2) The government dictating the direction the industry's growth resulted in the failure of market forces.

In 2001, CSRC proposed an unconventional position regarding institutional investors. It unleashed a raft of new policies regarding the establishment of new fund management companies and joint-venture firms. Meanwhile, it permitted fund management companies to engage in bond purchases, bond trading and repo in the inter-bank market.

In October 1999, insurance funds could enter the securities market through securities investment funds. In December 2001, CSRC allowed the nation's Social Security Fund to invest in securities investment funds and stocks, with a maximum capital ratio of no more than 40%. In June 2002, it permitted the establishment of joint-venture funds.

Rapid Strengthening of the Regulatory Phase (2004-2009)

On June 1, 2004, the Securities Investment Fund Law was formally implemented. Incorporated with six other official measures, the law laid the jurisdiction groundwork for the industry. Compared to the previous pilot phase, the industry experienced a loosening of controls during this period. However, the underlying theory of increasing supervision remained in effect.

(1) Regulatory Framework

CSRC issued "Guidelines for the Supervision and Management of Securities Investment Funds" to establish the basic framework for regulatory agencies still in effect. Different regulatory duties are delegated to separate agencies while CSRC oversees the daily supervision of the fund management companies and their regional branches. Meanwhile, the fund department is responsible for major policy research, drafting rules, administrative licensing as well as providing guidance, coordination and supervision within the industry. The securities exchange is in charge of regulating investment activities and information disclosure of listed funds, and the Securities Association of China (SAC) enforces and upholds self-disciplinary standards among industry personnel.

(2) Internal Control Supervision

According to the "Administrative Measures on Management of Securities Investment Funds", CSRC has taken a three-prong approach to managing firms. It will conduct site inspections, certify independent third-party inspections, and monitor a firm's internal controls in tandem with site inspections. Accounting firms will also be assigned to conduct internal checks and evaluations before publishing annual audit reports.

(3) Investment Supervision

The aim of supervising investments is to regulate unfair, abnormal and risky trading behavior. Regulatory authorities try to monitor and control funds' conduct by intensifying the BRLX information disclosure procedure. This allows CSRC to regulate better unfair trading behavior, analyze the fairness of fund transactions, and investigate abnormal situations. Under such circumstances, CSRC will request an explanation from the management class before conducting site inspections in order to boost compliance standards within the industry.

Deregulation After 2009

The mutual funds industry faced both internal and external obstacles to its development by 2009.

Internally, the industry had become less attractive. Its failure to align the welfare of investors and employees hurt investors' interests. This was coupled with strong internal competition in a highly homogenous industry, a lack of diversified development, and the monopolization of sales channels by China's five major commercial banks. It indicated the lack of integrity compliance is still present within the industry.

Meanwhile, competition intensified in the external environment. Other wealth management institutions developed rapidly as commercial banks, trust companies, insurance companies and private equity funds launched their own sets of financial products. These attractive alternatives led to the decline in popularity of funds, dealing a serious blow to the fund industry's dominant position at the time. In 2007, funds'total net asset value accounted for 25.8% of net market value. By 2008 and 2009, respectively, funds' NAV tumbled to 20.2% and 12.7%.

The faltering fund industry led to the outflow of talent to other wealth management institutions. To curb this 'brain drain', the regulatory authorities offered deregulatory measures.

(1) Implementing Deregulation

a. Simplifying fund assessment process

The various assessment processes for fixed-income funds like money market funds and bond funds, as well as index funds, were removed in 2009. They were replaced with a single evaluation procedure for mature fixed-income fund products.

b. Implementing classification audits, increasing approval channels

Beginning in 2010, CSRC established several channels for funds approval. This accelerated the entry of new funds into the market and allowed fund companies to launch different product offerings suitable for various market situations.

(2) Building a Self-regulatory Industry

Self-regulation stems from industry and regulatory developments and is crucial for mature industries. In 1998, industry insiders established an unofficial fund association that was later dubbed an independent organization and shut down by the SAC.

Fund industry characteristics and regulations significantly differed from the overall securities industry. Fundamentally, the fund management companies and securities companies were buyers and sellers in the marketplace respectively. Hence, over time, conflict of interests arose. SAC imposed restrictions on the industry management, and called for the formation of an independent association.

In 2009, CSRC established the China Securities Investment Association as a step toward increasing the industry's self-regulation.

1.2.2 SUPERVISION ORGANIZATION OF CHINA MUTUAL FUNDS INDUSTRY

The China Securities Regulatory Commission, with authority granted by the State Council, performs a unified regulatory function over the securities and futures market of China, maintaining an orderly securities and futures market order and ensuring a legal operation of the capital market per relevant laws and regulations.

Based in Beijing, CSRC has one appointed chairman, four vice chairmen, one secretary of the Disciplinary Inspection Commission and three assistants to the chairman. It has eighteen functional departments, one inspection division and three centers. In accordance with Article 14 of the Securities Law of the People's Republic of China, CSRC has set up a public offering review committee, which is comprised of commission professionals and invited experts. CSRC has thirty-six established securities regulatory bureaus in China's provinces, autonomous regions, Central Government-administered municipalities, the Shanghai Commissioner Office and Shenzhen Commissioner Office, and cities specifically designated in the State Plan.

Basic Functions of CSRC

(1) To establish a centralized supervisory system for securities and futures markets and assume direct leadership over securities and futures market supervisory bodies.

(2) To strengthen supervision over securities and futures businesses, stock and futures exchange markets, listed companies, fund management companies securities investing, securities and futures investment consulting firms, and other intermediaries involved in securities and futures businesses; to raise the standards of information disclosure.

(3) To increase China's ability to prevent and handle financial crises.

(4) To organize the drafting of laws and regulations for securities markets; to study and formulate the principles, policies and rules related to securities markets; to formulate development plans and annual plans for securities markets; to direct, co-ordinate, supervise and examine matters related to securities in various regions and relevant departments; to direct, plan and coordinate operations within the futures market.

(5) To exercise centralized supervision of the securities business.

Major Responsibilities of CSRC

(1) Study and formulate policies and development plans for the securities and futures markets; draft the relevant laws and regulations on the securities and futures markets as well as put forward suggestions for the formulation or modification of said laws and regulations; and work out the relevant rules, regulations and measures for the securities and futures markets;

(2) Exercise vertical administration over domestic securities and futures regulatory institutions and conduct a unified supervision of the securities and futures markets; and perform a regulatory supervision of management and the managerial officials of relevant securities companies;

(3) Supervise the issuance, listing, trading, custody and settlement of stocks, convertible bonds, bonds of securities companies, and bonds and other securities under the charge of CSRC as assigned by the State Council; supervise the securities investment bonds; approve the listing of corporate bonds; and supervise the trading of the listed treasury bonds and corporate bonds;

(4) Supervise the securities market behaviors of the listed companies and ensure that their shareholders fulfill the relevant obligations according to relevant laws and regulations;

(5) Supervise the listing, trading and settlement of domestic contract-based futures; and monitor the overseas futures businesses of domestic institutions in accordance with the relevant regulations;

(6) Supervise the securities and futures exchanges as well as their senior managerial personnel in accordance with the relevant regulations; and supervise the securities and futures associations in the capacity of a competent authority;

(7) Supervise securities and futures business institutions, securities investment fund management companies, securities depository and clearing corporations, futures clearing institutions, securities and futures investment consulting institutions, and securities credit rating institutions; examine and approve the qualifications of fund custodian institutions, and supervise their fund custody businesses; formulate and implement measures on the qualifications of senior management for relevant institutions; and guide the Securities Association of China and the Futures Association of China in the administration of the qualifications of personnel engaged in securities and futures businesses;

(8) Supervise the direct or indirect issuance and listing of shares overseas by domestic enterprises as well as the listing of convertible bonds by companies listed overseas; oversee the establishment of securities and futures institutions overseas by domestic securities and futures business institutions; and supervise the establishment of securities and futures institutions in China by overseas institutions for securities and futures businesses;

(9) Supervise the communication of securities and futures information; and take charge of the management of the statistics and information resources for the securities and futures markets;

(10) Work with the relevant authorities in the examination and approval of qualifications of the accounting firms, the asset evaluation institutions and their personnel for securities and futures intermediary businesses; and supervise the law firms, the lawyers and the eligible accounting firms, the asset appraisal institutions and their personnel in their securities and futures business activities;

(11) Investigate and penalize activities in violation of the relevant securities and futures laws and regulations;

(12) Administer the foreign exchanges and international cooperation affairs of the securities and futures sector in the capacity of a competent authority; and

(13) Perform other duties as assigned by the State Council.

Asset Management Association of China

The Asset Management Association of China (AMAC) was founded on June 6, 2012, per the provisions of Securities Investment Funds Law (Funds Law) and Regulations on the Registration and Administration of Social Organizations. It is a national, industry-oriented, and non-profit social organization incorporated voluntarily by the several organizations in the securities investment funds industry. AMAC is subjected to the operational guidance, supervision, and administration from the operational competent authority, the China Securities Regulatory Commission and Ministry of Civil Affairs of the People's Republic of China. Currently, AMAC is a member of International Investment Funds Association (IIFA).

Membership in the AMAC is classified into three types: general members, associate members, and special members. Its scope covers funds management companies, banks, local equity associations, insurance companies, trusts, QFIIs, and private equity firms, among others.

Figure 1.9 AMAC Membership Structure

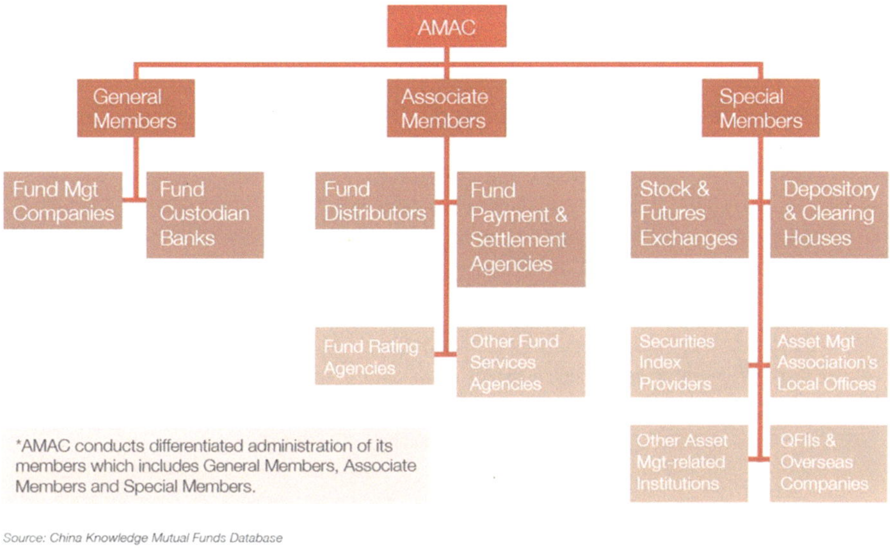

The Objectives of the AMAC

(1) To provide services for the industry by encouraging communication, innovation, professionalism, and competitiveness;

(2) To provide a communication platform between the government and industry by safeguarding the legitimate rights and interests of the industry, promoting public understanding, and enhancing industry public relations;

(3) To exercise industry self-regulation, compliance operations, and industry integrity;

(4) To supervise fulfillment of fiduciary duties and social responsibilities, while also ensuring the sustainable and healthy growth of the industry.

The Duties and Responsibilities of AMAC

(1) Safeguarding members' legitimate rights and interests, reporting suggestions and requirements of the members to the regulators and government sectors.

(2) Providing services to its members, organizing investor education programs, conducting industry research, industry promotion, members' communications and international exchanges and cooperation, encouraging innovation and development.

(3) Formulating and implementing self-regulatory rules, supervising and examining members' practices, maintaining industry order, mediating disputes among members or between members and their clients, promoting industry integrity, building the philosophy of compliance management, and imposing disciplinary actions for violations of laws, regulations or the Articles of Association of the AMAC.

(4) Formulating standards of practice and business specifications; administering professional qualifications and examinations; organizing training programs; and executing other duties and responsibilities as conferred by laws, regulations and delegated by CSRC.

1.2.3 FUND MANAGEMENT COMPANIES AND FUND CUSTODIANS

Under the Investment Fund Law, only fund management companies approved by CSRC may establish and manage investment funds. A fund management company must meet the following criteria:

(1) The company must have registered capital of RMB 100 million (US$ 12 million) or more (and the registered capital must be actual paid money capital).

(2) The principal shareholder(s) of the company must be in the business of securities management, securities investment consulting, trust asset management or other financial asset management.

(3) Each principal shareholder must have registered capital of no less than RMB 300 million (US$ 36 million).

Certain restrictions are imposed upon fund management companies to minimize conflicts of interest. For example, a fund management company must show fairness when managing different funds under its management. The company may not commingle in the investment its own assets and the funds under its management.

Commercial banks licensed by CSRC may act as fund custodians. Fund custodians are responsible for safeguarding fund assets, opening and maintaining bank accounts, executing the investment instructions of fund managers, and handling transaction settlement and clearance. Fund custodians also assume the task of monitoring the investment activities of fund managers. For example, a custodian must refuse to execute a fund manager's investment instructions if they violate the law or the terms of a fund contract and must report such instances to CSRC.

The Investment Fund Law prohibits a fund management company and a fund custodian from owning equity interests in each other.

1.3 FUNDRAISING AND DISTRIBUTION OF MUTUAL FUNDS

Fundraising

Fundraising is typically a four-step process that involves application, approval, sale and signing of a contract.

In the beginning, fund companies had no single defined sales channel and had to sell their products on a commission basis in bank branches and securities companies where investors concentrate. Although these companies have established more legitimate sales channels since then, banks still serve as effective sales vehicles.

Mutual funds are co-managed by fund promoters, managers and custodians. Administrative measures clearly define each party's required qualifications and duties, and emphasize that fund managers and custodians must act independently. Currently, newly established funds appoint securities firms and trusts companies as fund promoters and commercial banks as fund custodians. This structure mitigates the risk of conflict of interests by separating fund managers from tangible securities.

Fundraising Process

(1) Application

In order to obtain CSRC approval, new funds must submit a series of legal documents that include the application form, drafts of the fund contract, custody agreement, and prospectus, as well as related documents.

(2) Raising Capital

After obtaining CSRC approval, fund management companies may raise capital through their own sales channels or through a qualified sales agency.

(3) Investment Management

Investment management determines fund performance and is the most important segment in fund management and operation. Fund management companies must act in accordance with the provisions stated in the fund contract and prospectus and abide by the stipulated investment scope, investment ratio and decision-making procedures.

(4) Management System

A management system should be in place to ensure that mutual funds are properly and efficiently managed. It also serves to clarify the management process and specific roles of related departments. A fair and sound management system is essential to a healthy mutual funds industry.

The structure chart of fund management companies below depicts the five stages of the fund investment management process: research, execution, tracking and feedback, verification, and supervision.

Figure 1.10 Fund Investment Management Structure

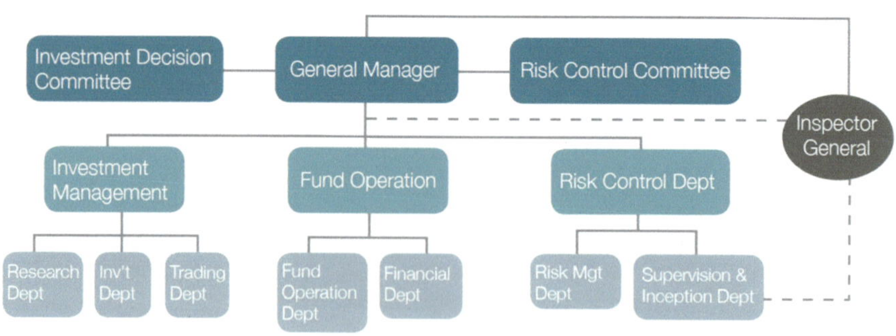

Source: China Knowledge Mutual Funds Database

(5) Information Disclosure

Public disclosure of mutual fund information to investors must be carried out in accordance with the provisions of Chinese laws and regulations and include the disclosure of all industry news such as fundraising, market transactions and investment operations. Mandatory protocol permits greater transparency and builds trust between various industry stakeholders. This is a common administration practice of securities markets worldwide, and the Chinese mutual fund market is no exception.

Differences between Public Mutual Funds and Private Mutual Funds

Public and private mutual funds differ in several aspects. These are listed below for comparison:

(1) Methods of Raising Capital and Issuing Shares

Public mutual funds are open for the public to invest in and have a minimum quota of 200 investors. Private mutual funds, on the other hand, are exclusively limited to a few select investors. In China, public funds usually pool the funds of many small, individual investors while private funds target only a few institutional investors with large AUMs, a wealth of experience or sound investment strategies.

(2) Information Disclosure

Public mutual funds must abide strictly to information disclosure policies and release fund details in a timely manner such as its investment portfolio, investment objectives and investment returns. Private mutual funds face far less stringent disclosure requirements. They are often more secretive and specialized investments and are only obliged to disclose fund details semiannually or annually. Furthermore, private funds have a more attractive incentive mechanism closely tied to fund managers' personal interests.

(3) Investment Management

Public mutual funds need to operate based on predetermined investment tools and portfolio structure, and fund managers are more restricted in terms of the control they hold over fund structure and direction of investments. Public funds treat every investor equally and will not work in the interest of specific investors. Investment decisions hinge upon the general investment strategy adopted by the fund management company.

(4) Compensation Structure

Currently, public mutual funds adopt a fixed management fee revenue model where they charge investors a flat percentage of AUM in lieu of performance fees. Conversely, most private mutual funds explicitly receive compensation from fund performance and do not charge management fees. The main goal of public funds is to expand and scale their fund size. Fund performance is merely a metric for ranking purposes for public funds, whereas it serves as the basis of compensation for private funds. Hence, while public funds seek to maximize scale, private funds focus on maximizing returns.

(5) Assessment System

Unlike their private counterparts, public fund managers are subject to quarterly assessments as well as a final major assessment at the end of each year. Their scores are ranked against those of other public fund managers. This system creates a myopic thought process whereby public fund managers are more likely to pick stocks that will perform well in the short term.

Table 1.8 Major Differences between Public Mutual Funds and Private Mutual Funds

	Public Mutual Funds	Private Mutual Funds
Type of Investors	General public	Select few investors, usually HNWIs and institutional investors
Method of Raising Capital	Public issuance	Private issuance
Information Disclosure	Extremely strict, obliged to release timely reports of fund activity and returns	High degree of secrecy
Investment Restrictions	Many restrictions, have to operate according to predetermined investment tools and portfolio structure	Fully dependent on fund agreement
Compensation Structure	No performance incentives, only management fees	Usually only charges performance fees, no management fees

Source: China Knowledge Mutual Funds Database

1.4 MARKET PERFORMANCE

1.4.1 MARKET SCALE AND DEVELOPMENT

Change in Fund Assets Over Time

As of June 30, 2016, the total size of the mutual funds industry stood at RMB 8 trillion (US$ 1.2 trillion), a decline of RMB 400 billion (US$ 57.57 billion) since the end of 2015. Conversely, the number of funds increase. A total of 410 new funds launched since the start of 2016, bringing the total number of funds in the industry to 3,110. Thus, the average size of each fund shrunk by an average of more than 15%.

Figure 1.11 Change in Fund Size

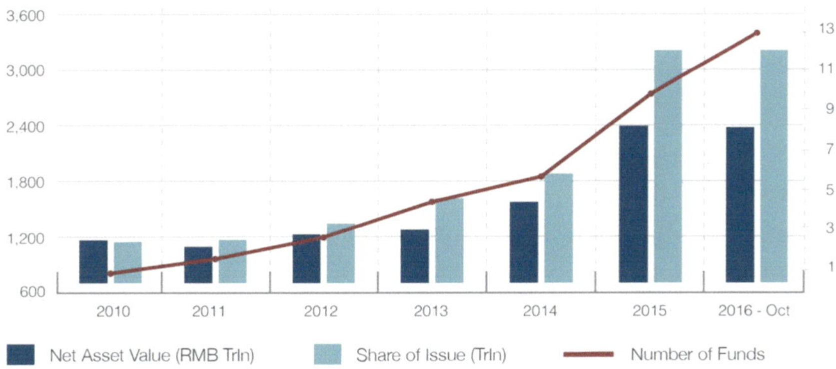

Source: Asset Management Association of China, China Knowledge Mutual Funds Database

The Proportion of Fund Types Over Time

In the third quarter of 2016, open-end funds accounted for 96% of the total net asset value in the industry. The NAV of open-end funds dropped 73.98% from 2010 to RMB 2.13 trillion (US$ 306.55 billion) in 2015. Closed-end funds' NAV decreased 49.16% from 2010 to RMB 62.73 billion (US$ 9.66 billion) in 2015.

Figure 1.12 Net Asset Value of Open-End and Closed-End Funds

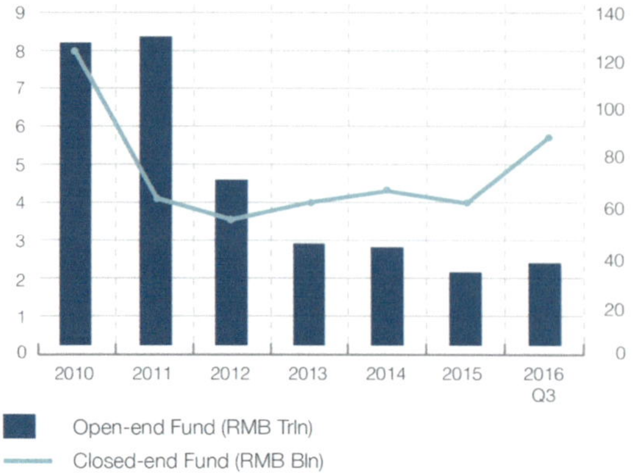

Source: Asset Management Association of China, China Knowledge Mutual Funds Database

In the third quarter of 2016, money market funds accounted for 53% of the total open-end fund market share with a NAV totaling RMB 4.43 trillion (US$ 664.2 billion). The NAV of hybrid, bond, and equity funds accounted for 46%. Hybrid funds totaled RMB 2 trillion (US$ 299.87 billion), or 24%; bond funds held RMB 1.15 trillion (US$ 172.42 billion) or 14%, and equity funds had RMB 716.13 billion (US$ 107.37 billion) or 8% of the total net value. The NAV of QDII funds totaled RMB 93.26 billion (US$ 13.98 billion) and accounted for about 1% of the fund industry's total net value.

The number of money market, hybrid, and bond funds has increased exponentially since 2012, with growth rates of 307%, 602% and 184%, respectively, in just four years. China currently has 248 money market funds, 1,531 hybrid funds and 641 bond funds. Equity and QDII funds have increased too, albeit at a slower pace. The number of QDII funds grew by 67% to 112 funds, while equity funds increased by 19% to 636.

Figure 1.13 Net Asset Value of Public Funds (RMB Trln)

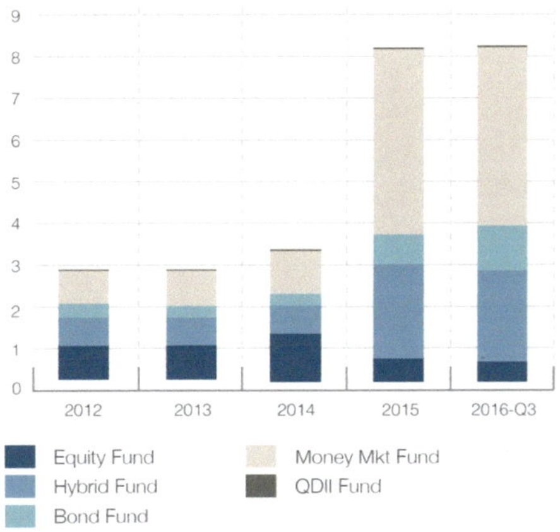

Source: Asset Management Association of China, China Knowledge Mutual Funds Database

Scale of Fund Companies

(1) Change in Volume of Fund Managers Over Time

As public mutual funds rapidly gained popularity, the number of fund companies and fund managers recorded the largest increase in nine years. In 2015, there were 13 newly established companies and a total of 107.

Figure 1.14 Total Number of Fund Companies

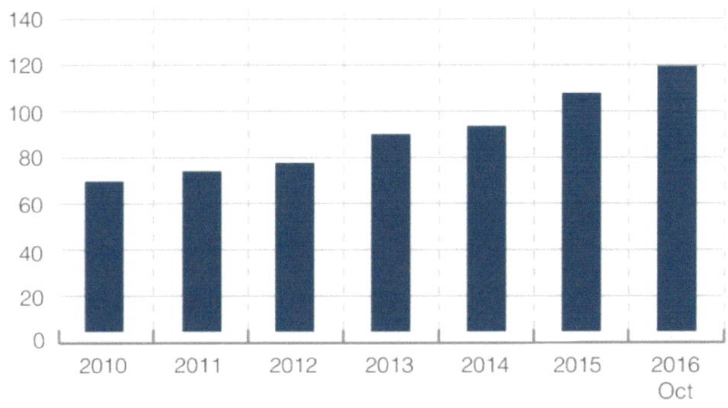

Source: China Knowledge Mutual Funds Database

The public mutual funds industry now faces a problem – a talent shortage. There were 221 new fund managers in 2015, bringing the industry total to 1,247. However, this 22% increase is insufficient to keep up with mutual funds' 85% growth rate. The average utilization rate of these managers in 2015 was 288%, the equivalent to 3 funds per manager.

Figure 1.15 Number of Fund Manager and Average Utilization Ratio of Fund Managers

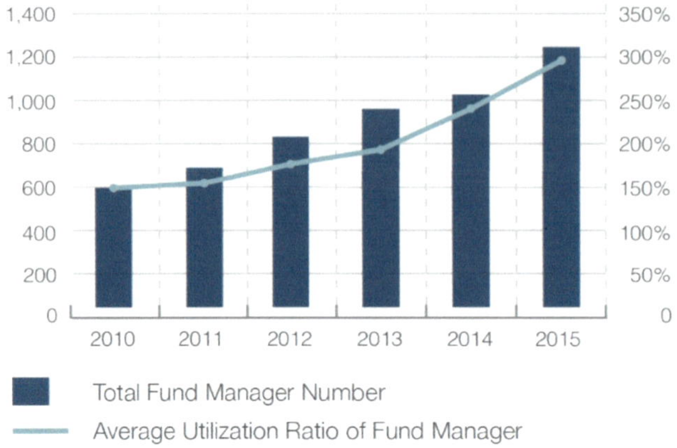

Source: China Knowledge Mutual Funds Database

Fund Management Fees

In 2015, the total operating costs of public mutual funds increased significantly by 59.28% year over year to RMB 93.54 billion (US$ 14.02 billion). This includes RMB 47.34 billion (US$ 7.1 billion) in management fees, RMB 9.65 billion (US$ 1.49 billion) in custodian fees, RMB 5.71 billion (US$ 879.71 million) in sales service fees, RMB 21.79 billion (US$ 3.36 billion) in transaction fees, RMB 8.01 billion (US$ 1.23 billion) in interest fees and RMB 1.05 billion (US$ 161.77 billion) in miscellaneous fees.

Figure 1.16 Components of Fund Expenses

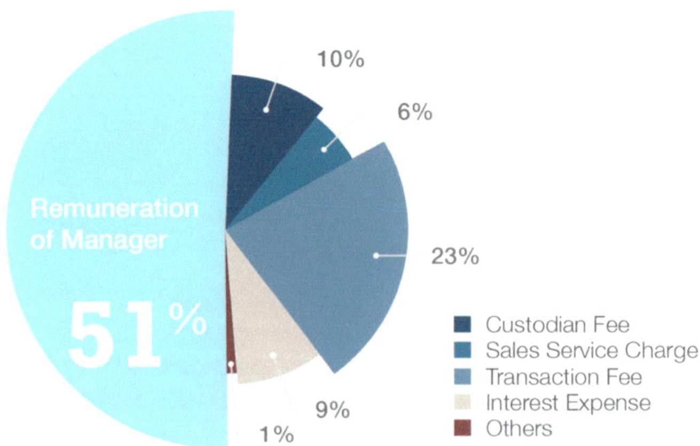

Source: China Knowledge Mutual Funds Database

Funds' operating expenses are determined by their total expense rate and overall assets under management. The NAV of funds has been steadily increasing over the past three years, contributing to their mounting operating expenses. In 2015, funds' operating expenses reached RMB 93.5 billion (US$ 14.41 billion), a 60% increase from the previous year.

Nevertheless, high operating expenses have a low correlation with funds' net profit. In 2015, the industry's total profit hit RMB 680.2 billion (US$ 104.8 billion), a 35% growth year over year. During the bull market of 2007, mutual funds were the market's best performers, with returns totaling RMB 1.06 trillion (US$ 163.31 billion).

Figure 1.17 Relationship between Operating Expense and Total Profits

Source: China Knowledge Mutual Funds Database

Over the past 2 years, custodian and management fees have remained relatively constant at about 60% of total costs. Due to market fluctuations in 2015, transaction and sales service fees increased, with the latter rising to more than 6% of total costs. Interest fees fell in direct proportion to the decrease in fund repurchases. Miscellaneous costs remained constant at about 1%.

Figure 1.18 Trend of Cost Components

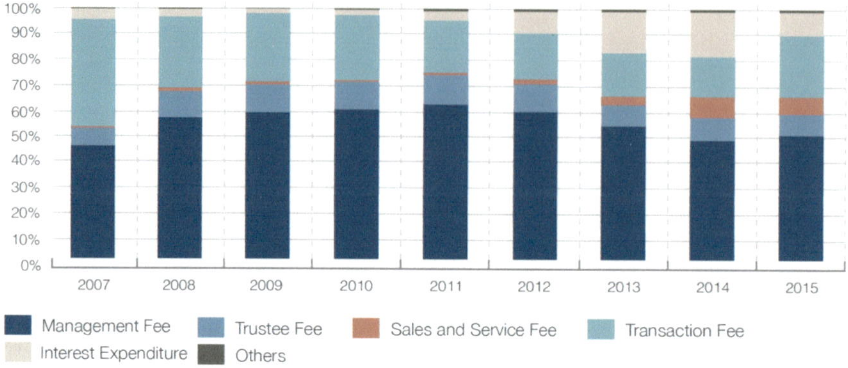

Source: China Knowledge Mutual Funds Database

As of June 30, 2016, fund management firms and banks accounted for 64.96% of the total fund costs. Fund management firms received RMB 23.57 billion (US$ 3.55 billion) in fund management fees, and banks received RMB 5.28 billion (US$ 794.45 million) in custodian fees. The five largest custodian banks managed 66% of total fund NAV, down 2% from 2015.

The collection of custodian fees remains highly concentrated. Six banks dominated the sector with an 81% market share. In addition, China CITIC Bank and China Merchant Bank made up another 13% and 5%, respectively. The five largest banks received 73% of the industry's total custodian fees, notwithstanding the next 8% incurred by China CITIC Bank.

Figure 1.19 Proportion of Custodian Fees

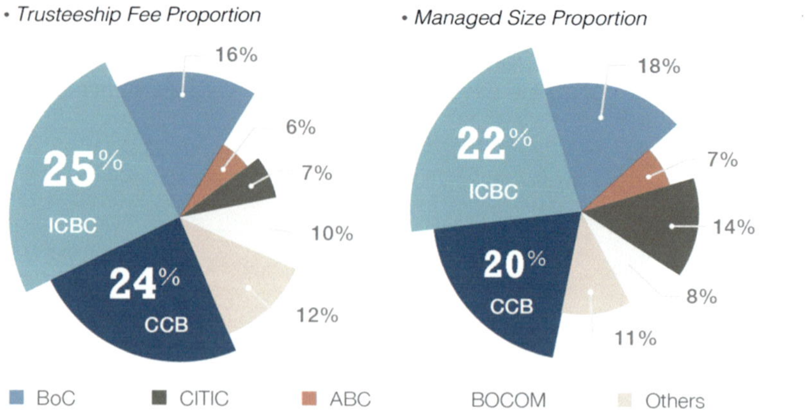

Source: China Knowledge Mutual Funds Database

Analyzing the Structure of Public Fund Holders

The number of institutional investors in public funds surpassed individual investors for the first time at the end of 2015. Although the percentage dipped slightly to 54.77% on June 30, 2016, institutional investors still make up majority of public fund holders.

In recent years, through their professional investment skills and quality service, public mutual funds have earned recognition in the Chinese market. Armed with ample liquidity in an asset-scarce environment, Chinese investors have increasingly turned to public mutual funds to earn profits.

Institutional investors generally raise the fund investors'proficiency levels and look at investments with a longer-term perspective. However, they are more sensitive to market movements compared with individual investors. This often leads to higher volumes of share purchases and redemptions, resulting in greater market volatility.

Figure 1.20 Proportion of Mutual Fund Holdings from Individual and Institutional Investors

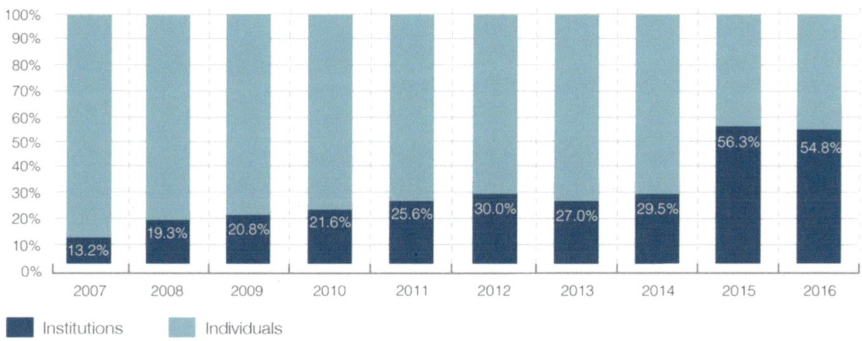

1.4.2 COMPARISON BETWEEN THE UNITED STATES AND CHINA (2015)

Total Size of Fund Industry

Figure 1.21 Fund Conditions in the United States & in China

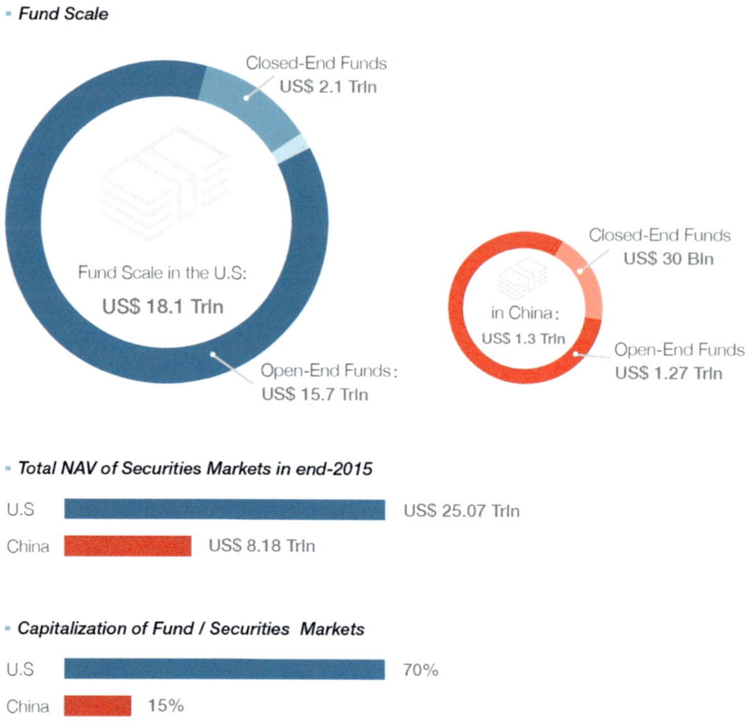

Source: ICI, Asset Management Association of China, China Knowledge Mutual Funds Database

Comparing the United States' and China's fund market capitalizations to stock market capitalization ratio, institutional investors make up a much smaller proportion of securities market stakeholders relative to other countries.

Fund Investment Direction

Figure 1.22 Proportion of Mutual Fund Types in the United States & in China

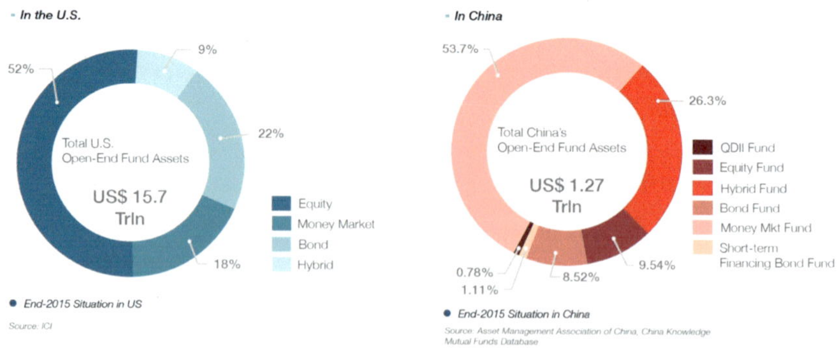

More than 50% of funds in the United States are equity funds, while in China the total is only 9.54%. Assuming that China's stock market development remains stable retail investors continue to mature, equity funds have an immense potential for future growth.

Investors in China are evidently more inclined to purchase low-risk investments, as evidenced by the fact that money market funds comprise more than 50% of China's funds versus just 18% in the United States. This is a result of high returns in the Chinese money market as well as the explosive popularity of Alibaba's online money market fund, Yu'E Bao.

Fund Holder Composite

Figure 1.23 Number of Fund Holders in the United States & in China as of end-2015

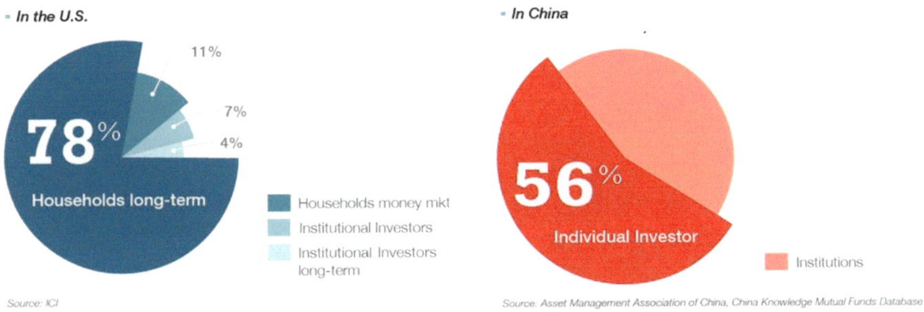

More than 75% of fund holders in the United States are families who invest through their pension funds. Individual Chinese investors once made up more than 70% of fund holders, but after the implementation of new regulations in 2015, institutional investors emerged as funds' primary investors.

In an asset-scarce environment, financial institutions such as banks, insurance firms and unit trusts actively seek stable yields. With their professional investment research capabilities and attractive product structures, mutual funds are a desirable investment vehicle for institutions.

Ratio of Index Funds in Total Equity Fund Asset

Figure 1.24 Share of Equity Index Funds in the United States & in China

In the United States, the ratio of U.S. index equity mutual funds has grown steadily since 2000, reaching 22% in 2015.

- *In the U.S.*

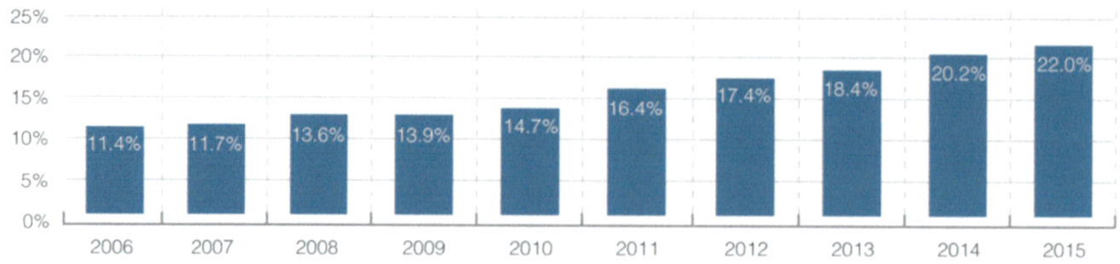

Source: ICI

By the end of 2015, index equity mutual funds totaled RMB 290 billion (US$ 44.68 billion), or 4.5% of equity funds.

- *In China*

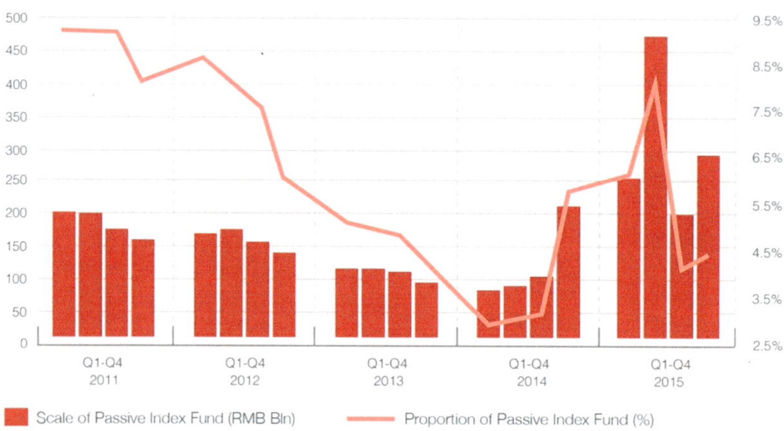

Source: Asset Management Association of China, China Knowledge Mutual Funds Database

Index funds are passive investments that reflect standard market returns, offer lower risk and diversified portfolio of fixed investments, and operate with a low-cost structure. Thus, they are increasingly popular with investors. While index funds make up to 22% of total passive funds in other market, China's index funds industry is still small and has ample room to develop.

Fund Investor Ratio

Figure 1.25 Proportion of Mutual Fund Ownership among Different Age Group in the United States & in China

Fund investors in the United States mainly fall between 35 and 70.

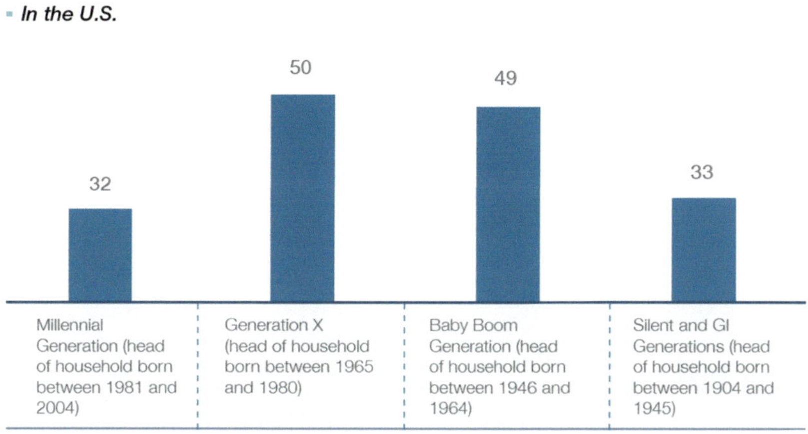

Source: ICI

Chinese investors generally fall between 30 and 50 years of age, followed by a substantial number of investors under the age of 30.

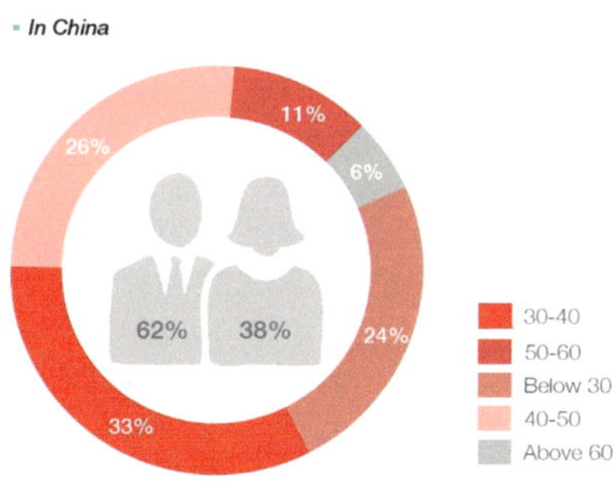

Source: Asset Management Association of China

Differences in Investment Purposes

Figure 1.26 Investment Purposes of Individual Fund Investors in the United States & in China

People in the United States invest mainly for retirement, emergency, and tax reduction purposes.

▪ *In the U.S.*

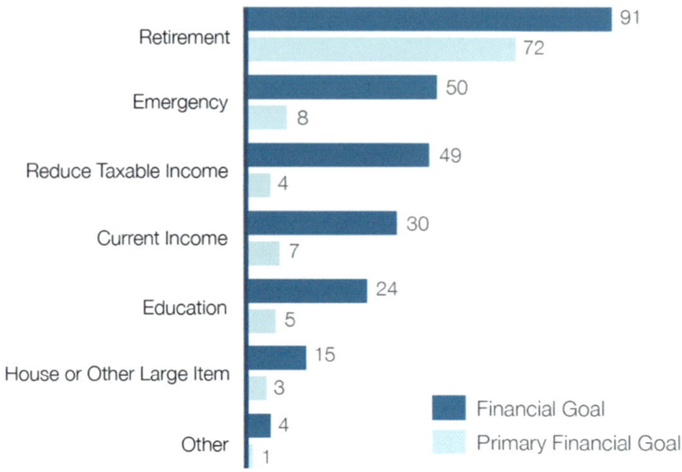

Source: ICI

Meanwhile, Chinese investors' primary investment objectives of are profits, diversification and saving for education and retirement.

▪ *In China*

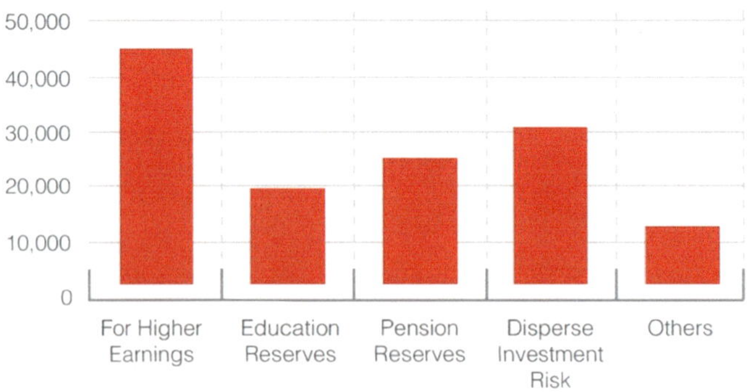

Source: China Knowledge Mutual Fund Database

PART TWO:

FUND MANAGEMENT COMPANIES

The content includes information on the fund management company's ranking, asset management size, profile, and return on equity. As of the third quarter of 2016, there were 119 fund management companies (FMC) in operation. Among these, 44 were joint ventures. According to the China Knowledge database, 110 of 119 FMCs have disclosed their figures.

2.1 RANKING OF PERFORMANCE, SIZE AND ROE

Table 2.1 Ranking of Total Net Asset under Management (Q1-Q3, 2016)

TNC Ranking	Company Name	All TNC (RMB Bln)	Change	% Chg	Share (RMB Bln)	Share Ranking
1	Tianhong Asset Mgt.	832.09	1,581.61	23.47	831.59	1
2	ICBC Credit Suisse Asset Mgt.	561.13	1,182.76	26.71	557.97	2
3	China Asset Mgt.	530.07	-476.75	-8.25	491.22	3
4	E Fund Mgt.	434.75	-1,312.08	-23.18	414.94	4
5	China Southern Fund Mgt.	383.71	570.84	17.48	361.04	5
6	GF Fund Mgt.	356.64	301.58	9.24	338.42	6
7	Harvest Fund Mgt.	312.95	-210.90	-6.31	297.94	7
8	China Universal Asset Mgt.	303.60	522.50	20.79	284.54	8
9	Bosera Fund Mgt.	290.28	849.01	41.34	281.36	10
10	CCB Principal Asset Mgt.	287.91	-265.66	-8.45	280.15	11
11	Bank of China Investment Mgt.	286.77	89.59	3.22	282.70	9
12	China Merchants Fund Mgt.	272.90	228.36	9.13	274.13	12
13	Penghua Fund Mgt.	243.01	703.34	40.73	243.74	13
14	Fullgoal Fund Mgt.	215.57	233.63	12.15	205.94	14
15	Yinhua Fund Mgt.	182.35	303.47	19.96	171.68	15
16	HuaAn Fund Mgt.	165.71	108.18	6.98	146.08	16
17	Fortune SG Fund Mgt.	154.10	-283.91	-15.56	142.53	17
18	Aegon-Industrial Fund Mgt.	140.08	270.20	23.90	120.68	18
19	Lion Fund Mgt.	111.22	134.57	13.76	105.28	20
20	CIB Fund Mgt.	110.91	374.28	50.94	107.13	19
21	China International Fund Mgt.	102.48	-141.94	-12.17	102.47	21
22	Rongtong Fund Mgt.	98.32	-0.20	-0.02	97.53	23
23	Dacheng Fund Mgt.	97.29	-332.38	-25.46	97.55	22
24	Invesco Great Wall Fund Mgt.	94.76	174.29	22.54	91.46	24
25	Guotai Asset Mgt.	87.08	-108.25	-11.06	84.28	25
26	Great Wall Fund Mgt.	85.76	160.39	23.00	82.62	26
27	Huatai-Pinebridge Fund Mgt.	84.40	-437.18	-34.12	70.51	29
28	Zhong Ou Asset Mgt.	84.12	77.67	10.17	76.02	27
29	Minsheng Royal Fund Mgt.	79.71	47.55	6.34	75.04	28
30	Bank of Communications Schroder Fund Mgt.	73.52	-96.91	-11.65	69.29	31
31	UBS SDIC Fund Mgt.	70.65	-249.06	-26.07	70.25	30
32	ABC-CA Fund Mgt.	68.06	-284.77	-29.50	63.85	32
33	China Post Fund Mgt.	65.25	-136.82	-17.33	55.69	36
34	Chang Xin Asset Mgt.	63.20	143.07	29.26	54.01	38

TNC Ranking	Company Name	All TNC (RMB Bln)	Change	% Chg	Share (RMB Bln)	Share Ranking
35	Xingyin Fund Mgt.	61.48	-107.84	-14.92	60.96	33
36	Ping An Uob Fund Mgt.	58.42	199.58	51.89	58.69	34
37	Huashang Fund Mgt.	58.27	-38.40	-6.18	45.66	43
38	China Life AMP Asset Mgt.	58.26	14.83	2.61	58.00	35
39	Citic-Prudential Fund Mgt.	55.30	81.32	17.24	54.20	37
40	BOSC Asset Mgt.	52.52	89.65	20.58	52.16	39
41	Changsheng Fund Mgt.	52.13	31.78	6.49	49.73	41
42	First Seafront Fund Mgt.	51.01	285.93	127.54	50.65	40
43	Baoying Fund Mgt.	50.17	-291.61	-36.76	47.52	42
44	Everbright Pramerica Fund Mgt.	46.63	-279.17	-37.45	41.87	46
45	AXA SPDB Investment Managers	45.26	104.53	30.03	43.46	45
46	Bank of Beijing Scotiabank Asset Mgt.	42.24	247.55	141.55	41.49	47
47	MANULIFE TEDA Fund Mgt.	42.07	62.79	17.54	40.53	49
48	SWS MU Fund Mgt.	41.35	-80.66	-16.32	44.30	44
49	HFT Investment Mgt.	40.65	-62.60	-13.34	35.45	53
50	Orient Securities Asset Mgt.	39.51	119.87	43.55	36.39	51
51	Zhonghai Fund Mgt.	38.50	81.97	27.05	40.73	48
52	Zhongrong Fund Mgt.	37.85	-12.83	-3.28	38.71	50
53	GTJA Allianz Fund Mgt.	37.69	-62.84	-14.29	36.23	52
54	Galaxy Asset Mgt.	36.06	-256.78	-41.59	32.88	54
55	New China Fund Mgt.	32.92	-14.37	-4.18	29.55	56
56	Wanjia Asset Mgt.	31.65	53.86	20.50	28.25	57
57	Morgan Stanley Huaxin Fund Mgt.	31.23	101.42	48.10	24.33	59
58	Essence Fund Mgt.	31.18	53.44	20.68	31.50	55
59	Orient Fund Mgt.	28.55	1.66	0.58	25.68	58
60	Franklin Templeton Sealand Fund Mgt.	25.75	0.11	0.04	24.31	60
61	Tebon Fund Mgt.	24.16	-0.59	-0.24	24.11	61
62	Xinyuan Asset Mgt.	23.65	95.19	67.39	22.45	64
63	Founder Fubon Fund Mgt.	23.22	139.83	151.31	23.28	62
64	Gfund Mgt.	22.84	-12.29	-5.11	22.62	63
65	Golden Eagle Asset Mgt.	22.55	114.44	103.06	22.00	65
66	Caitong Fund Mgt.	20.52	148.90	264.59	19.88	66
67	Hongde Fund Mgt.	17.93	74.63	71.32	16.79	67
68	HSBC Jintrust Fund Mgt.	14.84	44.42	42.72	11.18	74
69	Harfor Fund Mgt.	14.17	-92.57	-39.51	13.22	69
70	Caitong Securities Asset Mgt.	13.83	N.A.	N.A.	13.80	68
71	First State Cinda Fund Mgt.	12.92	21.83	20.33	12.67	71
72	Truvalue Asset Mgt.	12.71	82.85	187.34	12.38	72
73	Soochow Asset Mgt.	12.37	33.63	37.34	12.71	70
74	Taiping Fund Mgt.	11.92	119.02	93,534.26	11.92	73
75	Qianhai Alliance Asset Mgt.	10.76	-26.60	-19.82	10.76	75

TNC Ranking	Company Name	All TNC (RMB Bln)	Change	% Chg	Share (RMB Bln)	Share Ranking
76	JYAH Asset Mgt.	9.47	-26.54	-21.89	9.47	76
77	Goldstate Capital Fund Mgt.	9.02	76.29	548.47	8.43	80
78	China Fund Mgt.	9.02	32.74	57.01	8.91	77
79	Zheshang Fund Mgt.	8.69	34.75	66.66	7.93	82
80	JT Asset Mgt.	8.59	6.88	8.70	8.88	78
81	Dongxing Securities	8.56	80.79	1,684.27	8.62	79
82	Golden Trust Sinopac Fund Mgt.	8.38	69.63	490.54	7.90	83
83	Maxwealth Fund Mgt.	8.17	-30.90	-27.44	8.17	81
84	Taikang Asset Mgt.	7.43	41.15	123.97	7.31	85
85	Western Leadbank Fund Mgt.	7.37	-20.02	-21.36	7.34	84
86	First-trust Fund Mgt.	5.90	-60.36	-50.58	6.44	86
87	Beixin Ruifeng Fund Mgt.	5.56	21.21	61.76	5.47	87
88	BOC International (China) Limited	5.41	N.A.	N.A.	5.37	88
89	China Great Asset Mgt.	4.31	N.A.	N.A.	4.31	89
90	Changan Fund Mgt.	4.29	-22.35	-34.27	4.21	90
91	Shanxi Securities	4.10	12.91	45.94	4.07	91
92	Nuode Asset Mgt.	3.97	22.46	130.58	3.42	92
93	CR Yuanta Fund Mgt.	3.17	-8.06	-20.28	2.89	94
94	China Nature Asset Mgt.	3.04	-21.77	-41.70	3.41	93
95	Jiangxin Fund Mgt.	3.02	1.02	3.49	2.87	95
96	Fuanda Fund Mgt.	2.91	-15.97	-35.43	2.02	98
97	CICC Fund Mgt.	2.83	-23.11	-44.95	2.84	96
98	Yimin Asset Mgt.	2.02	-7.91	-28.17	2.75	97
99	Hongta Hotland Mgt.	2.01	-1.53	-7.07	1.82	100
100	Yingda Asset Mgt.	1.91	-31.38	-62.16	1.86	99
101	CDBS Cathay Asset Mgt.	1.79	6.13	51.89	1.69	102
102	CS Richland Fund Mgt.	1.78	N.A.	N.A.	1.78	101
103	Sinvo Fund	1.32	-9.30	-41.38	1.32	104
104	Zheshang Securities Asset Mgt.	1.15	-2.46	-17.60	1.41	103
105	Huarong Securities	0.58	-11.30	-65.90	0.61	105
106	JX Asset Mgt.	0.31	N.A.	N.A.	0.30	106
107	Donghai Fund Mgt.	0.21	-0.52	-19.61	0.25	107
108	Hotland Innovation Asset Mgt.	0.18	-0.06	-3.33	0.19	108
109	Guodu Securities	0.16	-2.19	-57.21	0.16	109
110	Mirae Asset Mgt.	0.02	-0.19	-50.84	0.02	110

Source: China Knowledge Mutual Funds Database

Bosera Asset Management Co., Ltd. ranked first in terms of the number of funds under management with 148 funds, followed by Penghua Fund Management Co., Ltd. with 136 funds, GF Fund Management Co., Ltd., with 113 funds, and China Southern Fund Management Co., Ltd., with 112 funds.

In terms of net asset value, four FMCs amassed more than RMB 400 billion in assets, including Tianhong Asset Management Co., Ltd., ICBC Credit Suisse Asset Management Co., Ltd., China Asset Management Co., Ltd., and E Fund Management Co., Ltd. Tianhong, which runs the well-known online wealth management service Yu'ebao with China's largest payment service provider, Alipay, ranked first with RMB 832.09 billion (US $124 billion) in assets under management. By the end of 2015, the number of Yu'ebao users rose 42 percent year over year to 260 million, for a total value of RMB 620.7 billion (US $92.64 billion).

Tianhong's record suggests that there may be no limit to an asset management company's development prospects and that the industry is entering a new era marked by deeper integration between the Internet and financial services.

Yu'ebao launched in June 2013, in order to make it easier for Alipay users to invest their idle cash in their Alipay accounts at a higher interest rate than a bank savings account.

In the first three quarters of 2016, total AUM of the top 10 fund management companies reached RMB 4.3 trillion or 48.4% of the total fund industry. The top 12 fund management companies accounted for 69.7% with RMB 6.2 trillion in AUM.

Among the top 10 fund management companies, only two fund management companies were joint ventures. This showed that traditional domestic companies were still a dominant force in the market.

Table 2.12 Net Asset Value and Fund Numbers of Each FMCs

Name of FMCs	Total NAV (RMB Bln)	Total No.of Funds	No.of Funds Units (Bln)	No.of Open-end Funds	No.of Closed-end Funds
Tianhong Asset Mgt.	832.09	49	831.59	48	1
ICBC Credit Suisse Asset Mgt.	561.13	94	557.97	88	6
China Asset Mgt.	530.58	82	433.27	82	0
E Fund Mgt.	434.75	107	414.78	98	9
China Southern Fund Mgt.	383.71	112	361.00	108	4
GF Fund Mgt.	357.69	113	339.47	111	2
Harvest Fund Mgt.	312.95	101	297.94	97	4
China Universal Asset Mgt.	303.27	69	284.91	68	1
Bosera Asset Mgt.	290.48	148	281.36	143	5
CCB Principal Asset Mgt.	287.91	77	280.15	73	4
Bank of China Investment Mgt.	286.77	71	282.70	71	0
China Merchants Fund Mgt.	272.90	110	273.63	100	10
Penghua Fund Mgt.	243.01	136	243.79	117	19
Fullgoal Fund Mgt.	215.57	85	204.21	75	10
Yinhua Fund Mgt.	182.35	74	171.98	63	11
HuaAn Fund Mgt.	165.71	86	146.08	81	5
Fortune SG Fund Mgt.	154.10	49	142.33	47	2
Aegon-Industrial Fund Mgt.	140.08	18	120.68	17	1
Lion Fund Mgt.	111.22	53	105.28	52	1
CIB Fund Mgt.	110.91	34	107.13	34	0
China International Fund Mgt.	102.48	50	102.47	50	0
Rongtong Fund Mgt.	98.32	58	97.43	55	3
Dacheng Fund Mgt.	97.29	77	97.55	74	3
Invesco Great Wall Fund Mgt.	94.76	59	91.46	59	0
Guotai Asset Mgt.	87.08	72	84.26	66	6
Great Wall Fund Mgt.	85.76	38	83.20	36	2
Huatai-PineBridge Fund Mgt.	84.40	40	70.52	40	0
Zhong Ou Asset Mgt.	84.33	47	76.23	46	1
Minsheng Royal Fund Mgt.	79.71	34	75.04	34	0
Bank of Communications Schroder Fund Mgt.	73.84	64	69.61	57	7
UBS SDIC Fund Mgt.	70.65	64	70.25	60	4
ABC-CA Fund Mgt.	68.26	35	64.05	35	0
China Post & Capital Fund Mgt.	65.25	28	55.69	28	0
Chang Xin Asset Mgt.	63.20	44	54.01	43	1
Xingyin Fund Mgt.	61.48	11	60.96	11	0
Ping An Uob Fund Mgt.	58.42	25	58.69	24	1
Huashang Fund Mgt.	58.27	36	45.66	36	0
China Life AMP Asset Mgt.	58.26	25	58.00	24	1

Name of FMCs	Total NAV (RMB Bln)	Total No.of Funds	No.of Funds Units (Bln)	No.of Open-end Funds	No.of Closed-end Funds
Citic-Prudential Fund Mgt.	55.30	60	54.19	50	10
BOSC Asset Fund Mgt.	52.52	4	52.16	4	0
Changsheng Fund Mgt.	52.13	60	49.72	54	6
First First Seafront Fund Mgt.	51.01	42	50.91	40	2
Baoying Fund Mgt.	50.17	22	47.52	21	1
Everbright Pramerica Fund Mgt.	46.63	29	41.87	29	0
AXA SPDB Investment Managers	45.47	24	43.67	24	0
Bank of Beijing Scotiabank Asset Mgt.	42.24	10	41.49	9	1
MANULIFE TEDA Fund Mgt.	42.07	42	40.53	41	1
SWS MU Fund Mgt.	41.65	34	44.51	26	8
Fortis Haitong Investment Mgt.	40.65	40	35.45	40	0
Orient Securities Asset Mgt.	39.51	25	36.39	20	5
Zhonghai Fund Mgt.	38.50	34	40.73	33	1
Zhongrong Fund Mgt.	37.85	24	38.69	20	4
GTJA Allianz Fund Mgt.	37.69	34	36.23	33	1
Galaxy Asset Mgt.	36.06	36	32.88	34	2
New China Fund Mgt.	32.92	41	29.55	39	2
Wanjia Asset Mgt.	31.65	33	28.25	32	1
Morgan Stanley Huaxin Fund Mgt.	31.23	24	24.33	24	0
Essence Fund Mgt.	31.18	29	31.60	28	1
Orient Fund Mgt.	28.55	38	25.68	38	0
Franklin Templeton Sealand Fund Mgt.	25.75	29	24.31	27	2
Tebon Fund Mgt.	24.16	18	24.11	17	1
Xinyuan Asset Mgt.	23.65	17	22.78	15	2
Founder Fubon Fund Mgt.	23.22	8	23.28	7	1
Gfund Mgt.	22.84	11	22.62	9	2
Golden Eagle Asset Mgt.	22.52	26	22.00	26	0
Caitong Fund Mgt.	20.52	11	19.88	8	3
Hongde Fund Mgt. Co.,Ltd	17.93	11	16.79	11	0
HSBC Jintrust Fund Mgt.	14.84	16	11.18	16	0
Harfor Fund Mgt.	14.17	27	13.22	27	0
Caitong Securities Asset Mgt.	13.83	2	13.80	2	0
First State Cinda Fund Mgt.	12.92	15	12.67	15	0
Truvalue Asset Mgt.	12.71	22	12.38	22	0
Soochow Asset Mgt.	12.64	26	12.98	25	1
Taiping Fund Mgt.	11.92	2	11.92	2	0
QianHai Alliance Asset Mgt.	10.76	2	10.76	2	0
China Fund Mgt.	10.07	11	9.96	11	0
JYAH Asset Mgt.	9.47	2	9.47	2	0
Goldstate Capital Fund Mgt.	9.02	11	8.43	11	0

Name of FMCs	Total NAV (RMB Bln)	Total No.of Funds	No.of Funds Units (Bln)	No.of Open-end Funds	No.of Closed-end Funds
Zheshang Fund Mgt.	8.89	13	8.13	12	1
JT Asset Mgt.	8.59	10	8.88	10	0
Dongxing Securities	8.56	5	8.62	5	0
Golden Trust Sinopac Fund Mgt.	8.38	6	7.90	6	0
Maxwealth Fund Mgt.	8.17	5	8.17	5	0
Taikang Asset Mgt.	7.43	10	7.31	10	0
Western Leadbank Fund Mgt.	7.37	14	7.34	13	1
First-Trust Fund Mgt.	5.90	19	6.44	18	1
BeiXin RuiFeng Fund Mgt.	5.56	11	5.47	11	0
BOC International Securities	5.41	2	5.37	2	0
Changjiang Securities (Shanghai) Mgt.	4.31	2	4.31	2	0
Changan Funds Mgt.	4.29	6	4.21	6	0
Shanxi Securities	4.10	3	4.07	3	0
Nuode Asset Mgt.	3.97	12	3.42	11	1
CR Yuanta Fund Mgt.	3.17	10	2.89	10	0
China Nature Asset Mgt.	3.04	10	3.41	10	0
Jiangxin Fund Mgt.	3.02	5	2.87	5	0
Fuanda Fund Mgt.	2.90	7	2.01	7	0
CICC Fund Mgt.	2.83	6	2.84	6	0
Yimin Asset Mgt.	2.02	7	2.75	7	0
Hongta Hotland Fund Mgt.	2.01	6	1.82	6	0
Yingda Fund Mgt.	1.91	5	1.86	5	0
CDBS Cathay Asset Mgt.	1.79	2	1.69	2	0
CS Richland Asset Mgt.	1.78	2	1.78	2	0
Sinvo Fund Mgt.	1.32	2	1.32	2	0
Zhejiang Zheshang Securities Asset Mgt.	1.15	4	1.41	4	0
Huarong Securities	0.58	3	0.61	3	0
Jinxin Fund Mgt.	0.31	4	0.30	4	0
Donghai Fund Mgt.	0.21	3	0.25	3	0
Hotland Innovation Asset Mgt.	0.18	2	0.19	2	0
Guodu Securities	0.16	1	0.16	1	0
Mirae Asset Mgt.	0.02	1	0.02	1	0

Source: China Knowledge Mutual Funds Database

Figure 2.1 NAV Comparison of Top 40 Fund Management Companies (As of end-Sep 2016) (RMB Bln)

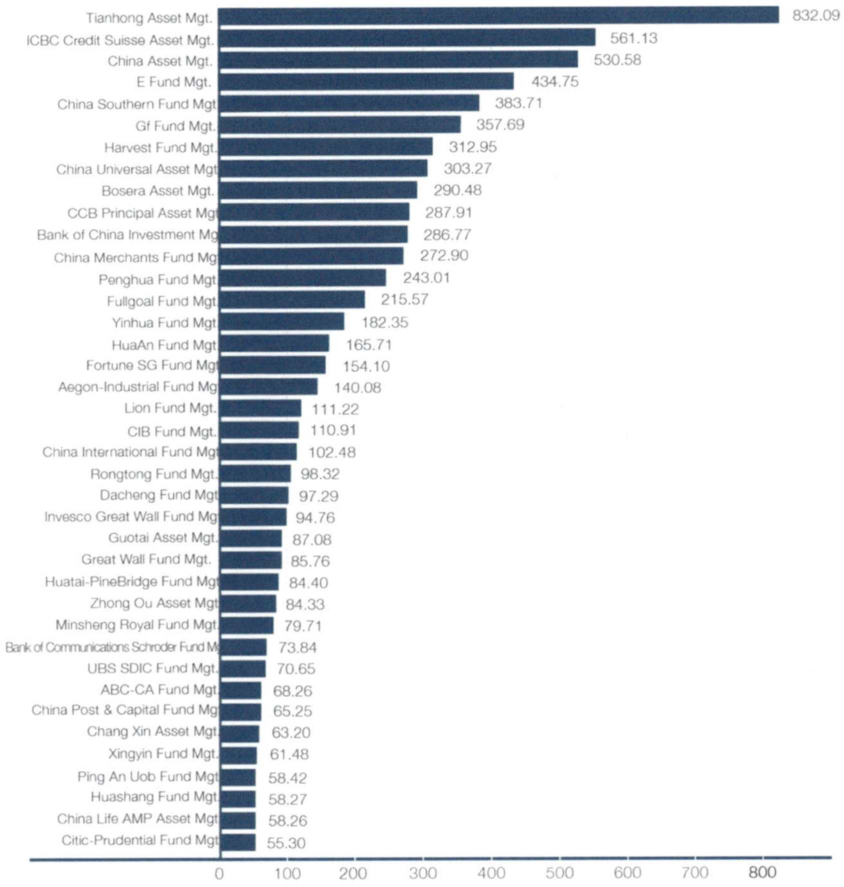

Source: China Knowledge Mutual Funds Database

There is a huge difference between the larger and smaller companies. For example, the size of Tianhong Asset Mgt Co., Ltd. the largest FMC, was more than 16 times that of Citic-Prudential Fund Mgt Co.,Ltd., which was at the bottom of the rankings. As of end-Sep 2016, the five biggest fund management companies accounted for 15% of total NAV, the top 10 accounted for 23% of total NAV, while the top 15 made up 29%. The top 20 companies took up 33% of the total.

Figure 2.2 Concentration of Fund Management Industry (as end of Sep 2016)

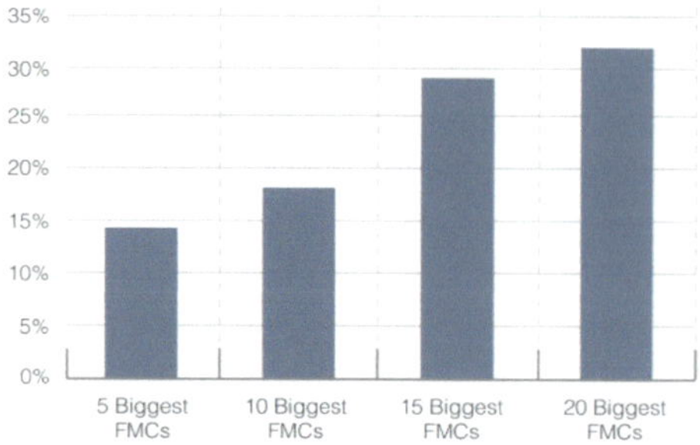

Source: China Knowledge Mutual Funds Database

Table 2.3 Ranking of Closed-end Funds (Q1-Q3, 2016)

TNC Ranking	Company Name	Closed-end TNC (RMB Bln)	Closed-end Share (RMB Bln)	Share Ranking
1	Harvest Fund Mgt.	17.71	16.35	6
2	Caitong Fund Mgt.	12.15	11.86	7
3	Orient Securities Asset Mgt.	11.32	1.69	8
4	Penghua Fund Mgt.	4.08	23.16	3
5	Bosera Fund Mgt.	3.67	3.75	16
6	Galaxy Asset Mgt.	3.35	0.39	17
7	UBS SDIC Fund Mgt.	3.01	4.56	14
8	Citic-Prudential Fund Mgt.	2.73	6.17	10
9	Yinhua Fund Mgt.	2.73	19.32	4
10	E Fund Mgt.	2.69	4.99	12
11	Baoying Fund Mgt.	2.24	0.20	20
12	Great Wall Fund Mgt.	2.13	0.29	19
13	Bank of Communications Schroder Fund Mgt.	2.00	2.62	18
14	Ping An Uob Fund Mgt.	1.32	1.32	24
15	HuaAn Fund Mgt.	1.32	3.76	15
16	China Merchants Fund Mgt.	1.22	26.44	2
17	Guotai Asset Mgt.	1.11	0.63	11
18	Dacheng Fund Mgt.	1.01	1.52	22
19	CCB Principal Asset Mgt.	0.64	1.88	21
20	Bank of Beijing Scotiabank Asset Mgt.	0.25	0.17	36

Source: China Knowledge Mutual Funds Database

For the first three quarters of 2016, Harvest Fund Management reached RMB 17.7 billion in AUM, ranking first amongst 110 other closed-end fund companies. Among China's 10 largest fund companies in terms of total assets, Harvest Fund Mgt, Bosera Fund Mgt., E Fund Mgt. and CCB Principal Asset Mgt. are among the 20 fund companies which released their closed-end fund assets, with AUM of RMB 17.71 billion (US$ 2.66 Bln), RMB 3.67 billion (US$ 550.25 mln), RMB 2.69 billion (US$ 403.32 Mln) and RMB 641.05 million (US$ 96.11 Mln) respectively. In the first three quarters of 2016, Harvest Fund Mgt., Caitong Fund Mgt. and Orient Securities Asset Mgt. are the top three fund companies in terms of closed-end funds, amounting to 53.71% with total amount of RMB 41.18 billion (US$ 6.17 Bln).

Table 2.4 Ranking of Open-end Funds (Q1-Q3, 2016)

TNC Ranking	Company Name	Open-end TNA (RMB Bln)	Open-end Share (RMB Bln)	Share Ranking
1	Tianhong Asset Mgt.	832.09	831.29	1
2	ICBC Credit Suisse Asset Mgt.	561.13	557.25	2
3	China Asset Mgt.	530.07	491.22	3
4	E Fund Mgt.	432.06	409.95	4
5	China Southern Fund Mgt.	383.71	360.49	5
6	GF Fund Mgt.	356.64	338.38	6
7	China Universal Asset Mgt.	303.60	283.11	7
8	Harvest Fund Mgt.	295.24	281.60	9
9	CCB Principal Asset Mgt.	287.27	278.28	10
10	Bank of China Investment Mgt.	286.77	282.70	8
11	Bosera Fund Mgt.	286.62	277.61	11
12	China Merchants Fund Mgt.	271.69	247.69	12
13	Penghua Fund Mgt.	238.93	220.57	13
14	Fullgoal Fund Mgt.	215.57	173.37	14
15	Yinhua Fund Mgt.	179.62	152.36	15
16	HuaAn Fund Mgt.	164.39	142.31	16
17	Fortune SG Fund Mgt.	154.10	142.25	17
18	Aegon-Industrial Fund Mgt.	140.08	120.54	18
19	Lion Fund Mgt.	111.22	105.27	20
20	CIB Fund Mgt.	110.91	107.13	19
21	China International Fund Mgt.	102.48	102.47	21
22	Rongtong Fund Mgt.	98.32	96.88	22
23	Dacheng Fund Mgt.	96.29	96.03	23
24	Invesco Great Wall Fund Mgt.	94.76	91.46	24
25	Guotai Asset Mgt.	85.96	78.25	26
26	Huatai-Pinebridge Fund Mgt.	84.40	70.51	29
27	Zhong Ou Asset Mgt.	84.12	76.00	27
28	Great Wall Fund Mgt.	83.62	80.62	25
29	Minsheng Royal Fund Mgt.	79.71	75.04	28
30	Bank of Communications Schroder Fund Mgt.	71.52	66.66	30
31	ABC-CA Fund Mgt.	68.06	63.85	32
32	UBS SDIC Fund Mgt.	67.64	65.70	31
33	China Post Fund Mgt.	65.25	55.69	36
34	Chang Xin Asset Mgt.	63.20	54.01	37
35	Xingyin Fund Mgt.	61.48	60.96	33

China Mutual Funds 2017

TNC Ranking	Company Name	Open-end TNA (RMB Bln)	Open-end Share (RMB Bln)	Share Ranking
36	Huashang Fund Mgt.	58.27	45.66	41
37	China Life AMP Asset Mgt.	58.26	57.93	34
38	Ping An Uob Fund Mgt.	57.10	57.37	35
39	Citic-Prudential Fund Mgt.	52.57	48.04	40
40	BOSC Asset Mgt.	52.52	52.16	38
41	Changsheng Fund Mgt.	52.13	49.03	39
42	First Seafront Fund Mgt.	51.01	40.82	46
43	Baoying Fund Mgt.	47.93	45.52	42
44	Everbright Pramerica Fund Mgt.	46.63	41.87	44
45	AXA SPDB Investment Managers	45.26	43.46	43
46	MANULIFE TEDA Fund Mgt.	42.07	40.52	48
47	Bank of Beijing Scotiabank Asset Mgt.	41.99	41.32	45
48	SWS MU Fund Mgt.	41.35	26.90	56
49	HFT Investment Mgt.	40.65	35.45	50
50	Zhonghai Fund Mgt.	38.50	40.71	47
51	Zhongrong Fund Mgt.	37.85	33.79	51
52	GTJA Allianz Fund Mgt.	37.69	36.05	49
53	New China Fund Mgt.	32.92	29.14	54
54	Galaxy Asset Mgt.	32.71	29.87	53
55	Wanjia Asset Mgt.	31.65	28.23	55
56	Morgan Stanley Huaxin Fund Mgt.	31.23	24.33	59
57	Essence Fund Mgt.	31.18	30.33	52
58	Orient Fund Mgt.	28.55	25.68	58
59	Orient Securities Asset Mgt.	28.20	25.70	57
60	Franklin Templeton Sealand Fund Mgt.	25.75	24.16	60
61	Tebon Fund Mgt.	24.16	24.10	61
62	Xinyuan Asset Mgt.	23.65	22.17	64
63	Founder Fubon Fund Mgt.	23.22	23.09	62
64	Gfund Mgt.	22.84	22.60	63
65	Golden Eagle Asset Mgt.	22.55	22.00	65
66	Hongde Fund Mgt.	17.93	16.79	66
67	HSBC Jintrust Fund Mgt.	14.84	11.18	73
68	Harfor Fund Mgt.	14.17	13.22	68
69	Caitong Securities Asset Mgt.	13.83	13.80	67
70	First State Cinda Fund Mgt.	12.92	12.67	69
71	Truvalue Asset Mgt.	12.71	12.38	71
72	Soochow Asset Mgt.	12.37	12.60	70
73	Taiping Fund Mgt.	11.92	11.92	72
74	Qianhai Alliance Asset Mgt.	10.76	10.76	74
75	JYAH Asset Mgt.	9.47	9.47	75
76	Goldstate Capital Fund Mgt.	9.02	8.43	79
77	China Fund Mgt.	9.02	8.91	76
78	Zheshang Fund Mgt.	8.69	7.92	82

TNC Ranking	Company Name	Open-end TNA (RMB Bln)	Open-end Share (RMB Bln)	Share Ranking
79	JT Asset Mgt.	8.59	8.88	77
80	Dongxing Securities	8.56	8.62	78
81	Golden Trust Sinopac Fund Mgt.	8.38	7.90	83
82	Caitong Fund Mgt.	8.36	8.01	81
83	Maxwealth Fund Mgt.	8.17	8.17	80
84	Taikang Asset Mgt.	7.43	7.31	85
85	Western Leadbank Fund Mgt.	7.37	7.33	84
86	First-trust Fund Mgt.	5.90	6.42	86
87	Beixin Ruifeng Fund Mgt.	5.56	5.47	87
88	BOC International (China) Limited	5.41	5.37	88
89	China Great Asset Mgt.	4.31	4.31	89
90	Changan Fund Mgt.	4.29	4.21	90
91	Shanxi Securities	4.10	4.07	91
92	Nuode Asset Mgt.	3.97	3.41	92
93	CR Yuanta Fund Mgt.	3.17	2.89	94
94	China Nature Asset Mgt.	3.04	3.41	93
95	Jiangxin Fund Mgt.	3.02	2.87	95
96	Fuanda Fund Mgt.	2.91	2.02	98
97	CICC Fund Mgt.	2.83	2.84	96
98	Yimin Asset Mgt.	2.02	2.75	97
99	Hongta Hotland Mgt.	2.01	1.82	100
100	Yingda Asset Mgt.	1.91	1.86	99
101	CDBS Cathay Asset Mgt.	1.79	1.69	102
102	CS Richland Fund Mgt.	1.78	1.78	101
103	Sinvo Fund	1.32	1.32	104
104	Zheshang Securities Asset Mgt.	1.15	1.41	103
105	Huarong Securities	0.58	0.61	105
106	JX Asset Mgt.	0.31	0.30	106
107	Donghai Fund Mgt.	0.21	0.25	107
108	Hotland Innovation Asset Mgt.	0.18	0.19	108
109	Guodu Securities	0.16	0.16	109
110	Mirae Asset Mgt.	0.02	0.02	110

Source: China Knowledge Mutual Funds Database

In the first three quarters of 2016, Tianhong Asset Mgt., ICBC Credit Suisse Asset Mgt. and China Asset Mgt. are the top 3 companies in terms of total assets under management of open-end funds, with amount of RMB 832.09 billion (US$ 124.76 Bln), RMB 561.13 billion (US$ 84.13 Bln) and RMB 530.07 billion (US$ 79.47 Bln) respectively. A total of 21 fund companies saw their AUM of open-end funds above RMB 100 billion, while that of 36 fund companies were under RMB 10 billion (US$ 1.5 Bln). Meanwhile, AUM of open-end funds from the top 10 companies reached RMB 4.27 trillion (US$ 640.21 Bln), accounting for 48.59% of the total amount in the industry.

Table 2.5 Ranking of Equity Funds (Q1-Q3, 2016)

TNC Ranking	Company Name	Equity TNC (RMB Bln)	Equity Share (RMB Bln)	Share Ranking
1	Fullgoal Fund Mgt.	77.83	78.68	1
2	China Asset Mgt.	54.61	37.12	6
3	Harvest Fund Mgt.	49.10	53.30	2
4	China Universal Asset Mgt.	42.82	37.69	5
5	Penghua Fund Mgt.	41.23	49.46	3
6	China Southern Fund Mgt.	35.72	25.05	10
7	ICBC Credit Suisse Asset Mgt.	35.06	45.01	4
8	E Fund Mgt.	32.91	31.94	8
9	HuaAn Fund Mgt.	28.99	21.59	12
10	China Merchants Fund Mgt.	26.23	33.45	7
11	SWS MU Fund Mgt.	23.49	25.75	9
12	Guotai Asset Mgt.	21.86	23.03	11
13	Huatai-Pinebridge Fund Mgt.	20.85	7.83	20
14	First Seafront Fund Mgt.	15.65	16.14	13
15	Yinhua Fund Mgt.	12.22	13.31	14
16	Bosera Fund Mgt.	11.22	12.17	16
17	CCB Principal Asset Mgt.	10.20	11.33	17
18	GF Fund Mgt.	9.92	12.92	15
19	Invesco Great Wall Fund Mgt.	9.30	9.99	18
20	Rongtong Fund Mgt.	7.42	6.34	23
21	China International Fund Mgt.	7.27	8.08	19
22	ABC-CA Fund Mgt.	6.24	6.68	22
23	Bank of China Investment Mgt.	5.98	7.37	21
24	Everbright Pramerica Fund Mgt.	4.85	4.06	27
25	Citic-Prudential Fund Mgt.	4.53	4.56	26
26	HSBC Jintrust Fund Mgt.	4.26	2.26	36
27	Zhongrong Fund Mgt.	4.23	5.46	24
28	Lion Fund Mgt.	4.12	4.78	25
29	Fortune SG Fund Mgt.	3.86	2.87	33
30	Aegon-Industrial Fund Mgt.	3.72	2.19	37
31	Dacheng Fund Mgt.	3.62	3.25	29
32	Tianhong Asset Mgt.	2.93	3.14	31
33	Morgan Stanley Huaxin Fund Mgt.	2.79	2.30	35
34	Great Wall Fund Mgt.	2.79	2.50	34
35	UBS SDIC Fund Mgt.	2.66	3.27	28
36	Changsheng Fund Mgt.	2.64	3.10	32
37	Bank of Communications Schroder Fund Mgt.	2.37	3.20	30

TNC Ranking	Company Name	Equity TNC (RMB Bln)	Equity Share (RMB Bln)	Share Ranking
38	Chang Xin Asset Mgt.	2.32	2.15	38
39	Galaxy Asset Mgt.	1.69	1.16	45
40	Wanjia Asset Mgt.	1.63	2.10	39
41	China Life AMP Asset Mgt.	1.58	1.84	40
42	New China Fund Mgt.	1.56	1.56	42
43	Essence Fund Mgt.	1.50	1.60	41
44	MANULIFE TEDA Fund Mgt.	1.30	1.15	46
45	Golden Eagle Asset Mgt.	0.92	1.31	43
46	Franklin Templeton Sealand Fund Mgt.	0.89	0.61	50
47	Hongde Fund Mgt.	0.88	0.78	48
48	First State Cinda Fund Mgt.	0.80	1.19	44
49	GTJA Allianz Fund Mgt.	0.78	0.82	47
50	Zhong Ou Asset Mgt.	0.67	0.65	49
51	Baoying Fund Mgt.	0.62	0.61	51
52	Golden Trust Sinopac Fund Mgt.	0.55	0.44	52
53	CICC Fund Mgt.	0.39	0.44	53
54	Minsheng Royal Fund Mgt.	0.39	0.41	54
55	Truvalue Asset Mgt.	'0.28	0.24	56
56	Zhonghai Fund Mgt.	0.25	0.24	57
57	HFT Investment Mgt.	0.25	0.24	55
58	CR Yuanta Fund Mgt.	0.24	0.20	59
59	Founder Fubon Fund Mgt.	0.23	0.22	58
60	Western Leadbank Fund Mgt.	0.20	0.20	60
61	Soochow Asset Mgt.	0.14	0.13	62
62	AXA SPDB Investment Managers	0.13	0.10	64
63	Donghai Fund Mgt.	0.12	0.15	61
64	China Post Fund Mgt.	0.12	0.07	65
65	First-trust Fund Mgt.	0.09	0.11	63
66	Changan Fund Mgt.	0.07	0.06	66
67	Ping An Uob Fund Mgt.	0.06	0.04	70
68	Zheshang Fund Mgt.	0.05	0.05	68
69	Gfund Mgt.	0.05	0.06	67
70	Caitong Fund Mgt.	0.05	0.03	71
71	Harfor Fund Mgt.	0.04	0.04	69
72	Nuode Asset Mgt.	0.02	0.01	72

Source: China Knowledge Mutual Funds Database

In the first three quarters of 2016, Fullgoal Fund Mgt., China Asset Mgt. and Harvest Fund Mgt. are the top 3 companies in terms of total assets under management of equity funds, with amount of RMB 77.83 billion (US$ 11.67 Bln), RMB 54.61 billion (US$ 8.19 Bln) and RMB 49.1 billion (US$ 7.36 Bln) respectively. 17 fund companies saw their AUM of equity funds above RMB 10 billion (US$ 1.5 Bln), while that of 28 fund companies were under RMB 1 billion (US$ 149.93 Mln). Total amount of equity funds from the top 10 companies reached RMB 424.51 billion (US$ 63.65 Bln), accounting for 64.68% of the total amount in the industry.

Table 2.6 Ranking of Money Market Funds (Q1-Q3, 2016)

TNC Ranking	Company Name	Money Market TNC (RMB Bln)	Money Market Share (RMB Bln)	Share Ranking
1	Tianhong Asset Mgt.	804.20	804.20	1
2	ICBC Credit Suisse Asset Mgt.	329.32	329.32	2
3	China Asset Mgt.	322.17	322.16	3
4	GF Fund Mgt.	227.28	227.28	4
5	CCB Principal Asset Mgt.	206.12	204.63	5
6	E Fund Mgt.	193.53	192.75	6
7	China Southern Fund Mgt.	187.15	185.15	7
8	China Universal Asset Mgt.	173.07	171.74	8
9	Bank of China Investment Mgt.	149.41	149.41	9
10	Fortune SG Fund Mgt.	118.58	110.39	13
11	Bosera Fund Mgt.	118.21	118.85	10
12	Harvest Fund Mgt.	115.63	114.87	11
13	China Merchants Fund Mgt.	113.88	114.02	12
14	Yinhua Fund Mgt.	105.03	100.89	14
15	Penghua Fund Mgt.	97.86	94.80	15
16	Aegon-Industrial Fund Mgt.	78.42	78.42	16
17	China International Fund Mgt.	62.68	62.68	17
18	CIB Fund Mgt.	59.22	59.21	18
19	Fullgoal Fund Mgt.	59.10	55.77	19
20	Invesco Great Wall Fund Mgt.	48.78	48.57	20
21	Dacheng Fund Mgt.	48.07	48.41	21
22	ABC-CA Fund Mgt.	47.40	47.40	22
23	Minsheng Royal Fund Mgt.	47.14	47.14	23
24	Rongtong Fund Mgt.	47.02	45.64	27
25	Lion Fund Mgt.	46.74	46.74	24
26	China Life AMP Asset Mgt.	46.50	46.43	25
27	Ping An Uob Fund Mgt.	46.06	46.07	26
28	Xingyin Fund Mgt.	44.38	44.38	28
29	BOSC Asset Mgt.	44.07	44.07	29
30	HuaAn Fund Mgt.	39.62	39.60	30
31	Huatai-Pinebridge Fund Mgt.	39.52	39.52	31
32	Bank of Beijing Scotiabank Asset Mgt.	32.47	32.47	32
33	Citic-Prudential Fund Mgt.	30.92	30.92	33
34	Bank of Communications Schroder Fund Mgt.	27.86	27.85	34
35	Great Wall Fund Mgt.	27.66	27.66	35
36	Zhongrong Fund Mgt.	27.07	26.81	36
37	Guotai Asset Mgt.	22.52	22.52	37
38	Founder Fubon Fund Mgt.	22.52	22.52	38
39	Gfund Mgt.	22.13	22.13	39
40	Zhong Ou Asset Mgt.	22.06	22.06	40

TNC Ranking	Company Name	Money Market TNC (RMB Bln)	Money Market Share (RMB Bln)	Share Ranking
41	UBS SDIC Fund Mgt.	21.77	21.77	41
42	MANULIFE TEDA Fund Mgt.	21.17	21.17	42
43	AXA SPDB Investment Managers	20.08	20.08	43
44	Baoying Fund Mgt.	17.60	17.60	45
45	Essence Fund Mgt.	17.54	18.64	44
46	Everbright Pramerica Fund Mgt.	16.23	16.23	46
47	Tebon Fund Mgt.	15.65	15.65	47
48	Changsheng Fund Mgt.	15.04	15.04	48
49	HFT Investment Mgt.	14.74	14.74	49
50	Wanjia Asset Mgt.	13.12	13.12	50
51	First Seafront Fund Mgt.	12.74	12.74	51
52	Caitong Securities Asset Mgt.	12.47	12.46	52
53	Franklin Templeton Sealand Fund Mgt.	12.45	12.45	53
54	Taiping Fund Mgt.	11.91	11.91	54
55	SWS MU Fund Mgt.	11.71	11.71	55
56	Xinyuan Asset Mgt.	11.59	11.59	56
57	GTJA Allianz Fund Mgt.	11.07	11.07	57
58	Qianhai Alliance Asset Mgt.	10.56	10.56	58
59	Golden Eagle Asset Mgt.	10.09	10.09	59
60	JYAH Asset Mgt.	9.45	9.45	60
61	New China Fund Mgt.	8.54	8.54	61
62	Chang Xin Asset Mgt.	8.08	8.08	62
63	Dongxing Securities	8.06	8.06	63
64	First State Cinda Fund Mgt.	7.94	7.94	64
65	Orient Fund Mgt.	6.41	6.41	65
66	Soochow Asset Mgt.	6.29	6.29	66
67	Caitong Fund Mgt.	6.21	6.21	67
68	Goldstate Capital Fund Mgt.	5.19	5.19	68
69	Zhonghai Fund Mgt.	5.16	5.16	69
70	Hongde Fund Mgt.	4.37	4.37	70
71	Galaxy Asset Mgt.	3.98	3.98	71
72	China Fund Mgt.	3.98	3.98	72
73	Western Leadbank Fund Mgt.	3.86	3.86	73
74	Harfor Fund Mgt.	3.68	3.68	74
75	Changan Fund Mgt.	3.65	3.65	75
76	Maxwealth Fund Mgt.	3.59	3.59	76
77	HSBC Jintrust Fund Mgt.	3.51	3.51	77
78	Taikang Asset Mgt.	3.01	3.01	78
79	China Post Fund Mgt.	2.91	2.91	79
80	China Great Asset Mgt.	2.81	2.81	80
81	Shanxi Securities	2.74	2.74	81
82	CR Yuanta Fund Mgt.	1.98	1.98	82
83	CICC Fund Mgt.	1.94	1.94	83

TNC Ranking	Company Name	Money Market TNC (RMB Bln)	Money Market Share (RMB Bln)	Share Ranking
84	Beixin Ruifeng Fund Mgt.	1.75	1.75	84
85	First-trust Fund Mgt.	1.71	1.71	85
86	CS Richland Fund Mgt.	1.56	1.56	86
87	Zheshang Fund Mgt.	1.37	1.37	87
88	Nuode Asset Mgt.	1.34	1.34	88
89	Sinvo Fund	1.12	1.12	89
90	China Nature Asset Mgt.	1.10	1.10	90
91	Huashang Fund Mgt.	0.87	0.87	91
92	CDBS Cathay Asset Mgt.	0.79	0.79	92
93	Yingda Asset Mgt.	0.64	0.64	93
94	JT Asset Mgt.	0.58	0.58	94
95	Fuanda Fund Mgt.	0.33	0.33	95
96	Huarong Securities	0.32	0.32	96
97	Hongta Hotland Mgt.	0.18	0.18	97
98	Truvalue Asset Mgt.	0.15	0.15	98
99	Yimin Asset Mgt.	0.11	0.11	99

In the first three quarters of 2016, Tianhong Asset Mgt., ICBC Credit Suisse Asset Mgt. and China Asset Mgt. are the top 3 companies in terms of total assets under management of money market funds, with amount of RMB 804.2 billion (US$ 120.58 Bln), RMB 329.32 billion (US$ 49.38 Bln) and RMB 322.17 billion (US$ 48.3 Bln) respectively. 14 fund companies saw their AUM of money market funds above RMB 100 billion (US$ 14.99 Bln), while that of 9 fund companies were under RMB 1 billion (US$ 149.93 Mln). Total amount of money market funds from the top 10 companis reached RMB 2.71 trillion (US$ 406.32 Bln), accounting for 57.55% of the total industry.

Table 2.7 Ranking of Bond Funds (Q1-Q3, 2016)

TNC Ranking	Company Name	Bond TNC (RMB Bln)	Bond Share (RMB Bln)	Share Ranking
1	ICBC Credit Suisse Asset Mgt.	162.03	140.45	1
2	Bank of China Investment Mgt.	96.35	89.40	2
3	Bosera Fund Mgt.	96.23	88.58	3
4	E Fund Mgt.	61.92	50.20	4
5	Gf Fund Mgt.	46.63	36.25	7
6	CIB Fund Mgt.	44.66	41.46	5
7	Penghua Fund Mgt.	40.05	41.06	6
8	China Southern Fund Mgt.	39.07	36.01	8
9	China Merchants Fund Mgt.	32.68	30.97	9
10	Chang Xin Asset Mgt.	32.14	26.22	12
11	Harvest Fund Mgt.	31.79	28.72	11
12	Fullgoal Fund Mgt.	30.70	28.84	10
13	China Asset Mgt.	27.44	24.14	13
14	CCB Principal Asset Mgt.	25.67	20.95	17
15	Minsheng Royal Fund Mgt.	25.43	21.74	16

16	Yinhua Fund Mgt.	24.49	22.50	15
17	Zhonghai Fund Mgt.	23.49	22.91	14
18	Zhong Ou Asset Mgt.	21.31	19.63	18
19	Aegon-Industrial Fund Mgt.	19.39	16.30	20
20	Morgan Stanley Huaxin Fund Mgt.	18.76	16.37	19
21	Xingyin Fund Mgt.	16.58	16.04	21
22	Huashang Fund Mgt.	16.07	12.66	25
23	HuaAn Fund Mgt.	15.83	14.09	24
24	Rongtong Fund Mgt.	15.65	14.91	22
25	AXA SPDB Investment Managers	15.26	14.45	23
26	Invesco Great Wall Fund Mgt.	14.28	12.30	26
27	China Post Fund Mgt.	13.89	12.00	27
28	HFT Investment Mgt.	13.85	6.06	44
29	China Universal Asset Mgt.	12.75	11.19	28
30	Everbright Pramerica Fund Mgt.	12.17	10.83	29
31	Bank of Communications Schroder Fund Mgt.	10.89	10.10	30
32	Great Wall Fund Mgt.	10.76	9.07	32
33	Xinyuan Asset Mgt.	10.55	9.38	31
34	Dacheng Fund Mgt.	10.13	8.73	33
35	Wanjia Asset Mgt.	9.62	6.25	42
36	Tianhong Asset Mgt.	9.35	8.43	35
37	UBS SDIC Fund Mgt.	9.08	8.35	36
38	Citic-Prudential Fund Mgt.	9.07	8.44	34
39	Orient Securities Asset Mgt.	8.39	8.16	37
40	BOSC Asset Mgt.	8.23	7.92	38
41	Lion Fund Mgt.	8.15	7.21	39
42	Changsheng Fund Mgt.	7.54	7.05	40
43	New China Fund Mgt.	6.85	6.04	45
44	Bank of Beijing Scotiabank Asset Mgt.	6.57	5.96	46
45	Truvalue Asset Mgt.	6.46	6.27	41
46	Golden Trust Sinopac Fund Mgt.	6.33	6.14	43
47	Tebon Fund Mgt.	5.72	5.57	47
48	Orient Fund Mgt.	5.49	4.89	48
49	Huatai-Pinebridge Fund Mgt.	5.36	4.42	51
50	China International Fund Mgt.	5.22	4.63	49
51	MANULIFE TEDA Fund Mgt.	5.14	4.57	50
52	Maxwealth Fund Mgt.	4.40	4.37	52
53	Zheshang Fund Mgt.	4.34	4.27	53
54	Guotai Asset Mgt.	3.94	2.84	58
55	First Seafront Fund Mgt.	3.64	3.63	54

56	ABC-CA Fund Mgt.	3.62	3.44	55
57	Essence Fund Mgt.	3.58	3.34	56
58	Galaxy Asset Mgt.	3.38	2.41	62
59	GTJA Allianz Fund Mgt.	3.21	2.54	60
60	Goldstate Capital Fund Mgt.	3.19	2.63	59
61	Ping An Uob Fund Mgt.	2.96	2.93	57
62	Harfor Fund Mgt.	2.69	1.89	66
63	Franklin Templeton Sealand Fund Mgt.	2.68	2.25	65
64	Jiangxin Fund Mgt.	2.68	2.54	61
65	China Life AMP Asset Mgt.	2.61	2.35	63
66	Hongde Fund Mgt.	2.38	2.31	64
67	Beixin Ruifeng Fund Mgt.	2.01	1.88	67
68	First State Cinda Fund Mgt.	1.90	1.67	68
69	Taikang Asset Mgt.	1.67	1.66	69
70	Soochow Asset Mgt.	1.55	1.49	71
71	China Great Asset Mgt.	1.50	1.50	70
72	Zhongrong Fund Mgt.	1.37	1.32	73
73	Caitong Securities Asset Mgt.	1.37	1.34	72
74	Fortune SG Fund Mgt.	1.22	1.03	74
75	Baoying Fund Mgt.	1.21	0.89	79
76	China Fund Mgt.	1.01	0.95	76
77	Nuode Asset Mgt.	1.01	0.95	75
78	CDBS Cathay Asset Mgt.	1.00	0.90	78
79	China Nature Asset Mgt.	0.98	0.62	82
80	Western Leadbank Fund Mgt.	0.98	0.93	77
81	HSBC Jintrust Fund Mgt.	0.88	0.80	80
82	Golden Eagle Asset Mgt.	0.76	0.70	81
83	SWS MU Fund Mgt.	0.67	0.55	83
84	Yingda Asset Mgt.	0.52	0.46	84
85	First-trust Fund Mgt.	0.44	0.41	85
86	CICC Fund Mgt.	0.37	0.34	87
87	CR Yuanta Fund Mgt.	0.37	0.36	86
88	Caitong Fund Mgt.	0.35	0.33	88
89	Hongta Hotland Mgt.	0.26	0.26	89
90	Zheshang Securities Asset Mgt.	0.21	0.21	90
91	Shanxi Securities	0.20	0.20	92
92	Qianhai Alliance Asset Mgt.	0.20	0.20	91
93	Donghai Fund Mgt.	0.07	0.07	93
94	Fuanda Fund Mgt.	0.06	0.05	94
95	Mirae Asset Mgt.	0.02	0.02	96
96	Yimin Asset Mgt.	0.02	0.02	95
97	Founder Fubon Fund Mgt.	0.01	0.01	97

Source: China Knowledge Mutual Funds Database

In the first three quarters of 2016, ICBC Credit Suisse Asset Mgt. toped the fund companies in terms of AUM of bond funds with a total amount of RMB 162.03 billion (US$ 24.29 Bln), RMB 65.68 billion (US$ 9.85 Bln) more than the second ranking. Bank of China Investment Mgt. and Bosera Fund Mgt. ranked second and third, with AUM of RMB 96.35 billion (US$ 14.45 Bln) and RMB 96.23 billion (US$ 14.43 Bln) respectively. The top 10 fund companies in terms of bond funds totaled RMB 651.76 billion (US$ 97.72 Bln), accounting for 50.72% of the total amount in the industry. A total of 7 companies saw their AUM of bond funds above RMB 40 billion (US$ 6 Bln), while 19 companies saw their bond funds AUM under RMB 1 billion (US$ 149.93 Mln).

Table 2.8 Ranking of Alternative Investment Funds (Q1-Q3, 2016)

TNC Ranking	Company Name	Alternative Investment TNA (RMB Mln)	Alternative Investment Share (RMB Mln)	Share Ranking
1	HuaAn Fund Mgt.	6,303.88	3,440.12	1
2	Penghua Fund Mgt.	3,277.81	30.00	19
3	Bosera Fund Mgt.	3,010.94	1,172.59	4
4	ICBC Credit Suisse Asset Mgt.	1,911.63	1,771.57	2
5	E Fund Mgt.	1,856.25	1,694.66	3
6	China Southern Fund Mgt.	1,036.84	982.66	5
7	HFT Investment Mgt.	964.21	795.38	6
8	China Post Fund Mgt.	734.33	776.61	7
9	Fortune SG Fund Mgt.	718.14	609.88	8
10	GF Fund Mgt.	683.88	597.39	9
11	Guotai Asset Mgt.	673.06	352.45	11
12	Harvest Fund Mgt.	553.75	505.28	10
13	UBS SDIC Fund Mgt.	353.53	331.48	12
14	Huatai-Pinebridge Fund Mgt.	324.61	319.74	13
15	MANULIFE TEDA Fund Mgt.	300.95	302.52	14
16	Fullgoal Fund Mgt.	188.94	186.99	15
17	CICC Fund Mgt.	131.10	127.27	16
18	Maxwealth Fund Mgt.	101.60	122.04	17
19	Dacheng Fund Mgt.	45.62	46.35	18

Source: China Knowledge Mutual Funds Database

HuaAn Fund Mgt. retained its top spot with total AUM of RMB 6.3 billion (US$ 944.58 Mln), which is larger than the combined AUM of RMB 6.29 billion (US$ 943.08 Mln) of the second and third-ranking companies. A total of 6 companies saw their AUM of alternative investment funds over RMB 1 billion (US$ 149.93 Mln), taking up 75.08% of the total.

Table 2.9 Ranking of Hybrid Funds (Q1-Q3, 2016)

TNC Ranking	Company Name	Hybrid TNC (RMB Mln)	Hybrid Share (RMB Mln)	Share Ranking
1	E Fund Mgt.	133,854.69	125,517.68	1
2	China Asset Mgt.	114,594.44	94,639.50	4
3	China Southern Fund Mgt.	112,016.87	103,988.49	2
4	Harvest Fund Mgt.	105,335.77	87,059.33	5
5	China Merchants Fund Mgt.	99,814.91	95,386.95	3
6	China Universal Asset Mgt.	73,114.53	62,006.95	6
7	GF Fund Mgt.	69,473.54	59,264.75	8
8	HuaAn Fund Mgt.	68,954.20	61,627.03	7
9	Bosera Fund Mgt.	58,966.30	58,225.90	9
10	Penghua Fund Mgt.	58,278.66	56,464.98	10
11	Lion Fund Mgt.	51,012.02	45,263.67	11
12	China Post Fund Mgt.	47,590.51	39,927.17	16
13	CCB Principal Asset Mgt.	45,817.75	43,105.72	13
14	Fullgoal Fund Mgt.	45,768.70	41,322.24	14
15	Great Wall Fund Mgt.	44,545.07	43,397.14	12
16	Huashang Fund Mgt.	41,338.50	32,136.43	22
17	Zhong Ou Asset Mgt.	40,077.59	33,678.34	21
18	Aegon-Industrial Fund Mgt.	38,550.07	23,767.37	30
19	UBS SDIC Fund Mgt.	36,455.21	36,219.64	18
20	Guotai Asset Mgt.	36,325.96	33,782.62	20
21	Dacheng Fund Mgt.	35,319.59	37,042.13	17
22	Bank of China Investment Mgt.	33,845.82	35,357.83	19
23	Yinhua Fund Mgt.	33,458.09	25,579.02	27
24	ICBC Credit Suisse Asset Mgt.	32,044.15	40,772.22	15
25	Bank of Communications Schroder Fund Mgt.	31,762.22	27,554.36	26
26	Orient Securities Asset Mgt.	31,126.11	28,236.27	25
27	Baoying Fund Mgt.	30,749.11	28,421.29	24
28	Rongtong Fund Mgt.	28,201.90	30,599.42	23
29	Galaxy Asset Mgt.	27,009.87	25,321.29	28
30	Changsheng Fund Mgt.	26,835.62	24,466.51	29
31	Fortune SG Fund Mgt.	26,117.14	22,703.92	31
32	GTJA Allianz Fund Mgt.	22,629.82	21,794.26	32
33	Invesco Great Wall Fund Mgt.	22,190.40	20,433.49	33
34	China International Fund Mgt.	22,159.25	18,962.75	34
35	Chang Xin Asset Mgt.	20,387.39	17,302.29	37
36	First Seafront Fund Mgt.	18,979.28	18,135.72	36
37	Huatai-Pinebridge Fund Mgt.	18,307.39	18,389.81	35
38	Orient Fund Mgt.	16,645.95	14,382.28	39
39	New China Fund Mgt.	15,975.99	13,405.41	40
40	Tianhong Asset Mgt.	15,617.86	15,822.21	38

TNC Ranking	Company Name	Hybrid TNC (RMB Mln)	Hybrid Share (RMB Mln)	Share Ranking
41	Caitong Fund Mgt.	13,899.50	13,293.46	42
42	MANULIFE TEDA Fund Mgt.	13,467.96	12,629.10	43
43	Everbright Pramerica Fund Mgt.	13,385.35	10,762.43	45
44	ABC-CA Fund Mgt.	10,801.23	6,331.52	58
45	Golden Eagle Asset Mgt.	10,775.98	9,887.52	47
46	Citic-Prudential Fund Mgt.	10,710.32	10,169.11	46
47	HFT Investment Mgt.	10,593.25	13,395.81	41
48	Hongde Fund Mgt.	10,297.76	9,333.08	49
49	AXA SPDB Investment Managers	9,785.45	8,834.78	50
50	Morgan Stanley Huaxin Fund Mgt.	9,671.28	5,663.94	62
51	Zhonghai Fund Mgt.	9,607.90	12,419.27	44
52	Ping An Uob Fund Mgt.	9,339.51	9,645.70	48
53	Franklin Templeton Sealand Fund Mgt.	9,310.76	8,518.88	51
54	Essence Fund Mgt.	8,560.03	7,920.79	53
55	JT Asset Mgt.	8,007.61	8,296.52	52
56	Harfor Fund Mgt.	7,766.24	7,620.54	54
57	China Life AMP Asset Mgt.	7,564.40	7,365.88	55
58	Wanjia Asset Mgt.	7,280.75	6,788.64	56
59	CIB Fund Mgt.	7,033.47	6,464.38	57
60	Minsheng Royal Fund Mgt.	6,743.96	5,744.04	60
61	HSBC Jintrust Fund Mgt.	6,195.26	4,607.85	66
62	Truvalue Asset Mgt.	5,812.36	5,715.00	61
63	SWS MU Fund Mgt.	5,483.47	6,293.16	59
64	BOC International (China) Limited	5,405.82	5,374.32	63
65	Zhongrong Fund Mgt.	5,176.92	5,115.76	64
66	Soochow Asset Mgt.	4,384.35	4,799.29	65
67	China Fund Mgt.	4,036.03	3,981.72	68
68	First-trust Fund Mgt.	3,644.16	4,209.00	67
69	Bank of Beijing Scotiabank Asset Mgt.	3,204.26	3,068.62	69
70	Zheshang Fund Mgt.	2,925.33	2,243.99	74
71	Tebon Fund Mgt.	2,797.96	2,887.35	70
72	Taikang Asset Mgt.	2,754.29	2,648.96	71
73	Fuanda Fund Mgt.	2,517.77	1,641.66	78
74	Western Leadbank Fund Mgt.	2,330.16	2,347.48	73
75	First State Cinda Fund Mgt.	2,280.13	1,875.80	75
76	Yimin Asset Mgt.	1,885.69	2,620.00	72
77	Beixin Ruifeng Fund Mgt.	1,792.12	1,838.54	76
78	Nuode Asset Mgt.	1,603.76	1,114.52	84
79	Hongta Hotland Mgt.	1,578.77	1,387.65	80
80	Golden Trust Sinopac Fund Mgt.	1,506.11	1,321.29	81
81	Xinyuan Asset Mgt.	1,502.86	1,475.98	79
82	Shanxi Securities	1,161.50	1,131.82	83
83	China Nature Asset Mgt.	960.55	1,687.03	77
84	Zheshang Securities Asset Mgt.	937.79	1,202.01	82

TNC Ranking	Company Name	Hybrid TNC (RMB Mln)	Hybrid Share (RMB Mln)	Share Ranking
85	Yingda Asset Mgt.	756.91	759.19	85
86	Gfund Mgt.	653.30	431.30	91
87	Goldstate Capital Fund Mgt.	639.41	610.39	86
88	CR Yuanta Fund Mgt.	578.67	342.74	92
89	Changan Fund Mgt.	560.69	503.49	90
90	Xingyin Fund Mgt.	518.78	542.54	88
91	Dongxing Securities	499.81	559.93	87
92	Founder Fubon Fund Mgt.	461.36	529.89	89
93	Jiangxin Fund Mgt.	344.16	335.55	93
94	JX Asset Mgt.	313.72	302.76	94
95	Huarong Securities	269.02	291.22	95
96	BOSC Asset Mgt.	219.19	171.02	99
97	CS Richland Fund Mgt.	213.82	213.73	96
98	Sinvo Fund	201.83	201.83	97
99	Hotland Innovation Asset Mgt.	176.26	192.29	98
100	Guodu Securities	163.63	155.10	100
101	Maxwealth Fund Mgt.	78.85	80.81	101
102	Donghai Fund Mgt.	25.47	25.44	102
103	JYAH Asset Mgt.	20.40	18.59	103
104	Taiping Fund Mgt.	9.64	13.46	104

Source: China Knowledge Mutual Funds Database

In the first three quarters of 2016, E Fund Mgt., China Asset Mgt. and China Southern Fund Mgt. are the top 3 companies in terms of total assets under management of hybrid funds, with amount of RMB 133.86 billion (US$ 20.07 Bln), RMB 114.59 billion (US$ 21.68 Bln) and RMB 112.02 billion (US$ 16.8 Bln) respectively. In Jan-Sep, a total of 4 fund companies saw their AUM of hybrid funds above RMB 100 billion (US$ 14.99 Bln), while that of 22 fund companies were under RMB 1 billion (US$ 149.93 Mln). Total amount of hybrid funds from the top 10 companies reached RMB 894.4 billion (US$ 134.1 Bln), accounting for 42.33% of the total amount in the industry.

Table 2.10 Ranking of QDII Funds (Q1-Q3, 2016)

TNC Ranking	Company Name	QDII TNA (RMB Bln)	QDII Share (RMB Bln)	Share Ranking
1	China Asset Mgt.	11.27	13.15	2
2	E Fund Mgt.	10.68	12.84	3
3	Harvest Fund Mgt.	10.54	13.49	1
4	China Southern Fund Mgt.	8.71	9.85	4
5	Yinhua Fund Mgt.	7.16	9.40	5
6	HuaAn Fund Mgt.	6.01	5.73	7
7	China International Fund Mgt.	5.15	8.12	6

TNC Ranking	Company Name	QDII TNA (RMB Bln)	QDII Share (RMB Bln)	Share Ranking
8	Fortune SG Fund Mgt.	3.60	4.93	8
9	GF Fund Mgt.	2.66	2.11	10
10	Bosera Fund Mgt.	2.65	2.36	9
11	Penghua Fund Mgt.	2.30	1.93	11
12	Fullgoal Fund Mgt.	1.98	1.14	16
13	China Universal Asset Mgt.	1.85	1.92	12
14	Guotai Asset Mgt.	1.74	1.75	13
15	Lion Fund Mgt.	1.20	1.28	14
16	Bank of China Investment Mgt.	1.18	1.17	15
17	ICBC Credit Suisse Asset Mgt.	0.76	0.64	18
18	MANULIFE TEDA Fund Mgt.	0.70	0.70	17
19	Bank of Communications Schroder Fund Mgt.	0.65	0.58	19
20	Franklin Templeton Sealand Fund Mgt.	0.42	0.48	20
21	UBS SDIC Fund Mgt.	0.33	0.31	21
22	China Merchants Fund Mgt.	0.30	0.31	22
23	Chang Xin Asset Mgt.	0.28	0.26	23
24	HFT Investment Mgt.	0.25	0.21	24
25	Invesco Great Wall Fund Mgt.	0.22	0.17	25
26	Dacheng Fund Mgt.	0.11	0.08	28
27	CCB Principal Asset Mgt.	0.11	0.14	26
28	Changsheng Fund Mgt.	0.08	0.07	29
29	Citic-Prudential Fund Mgt.	0.07	0.13	27
30	Rongtong Fund Mgt.	0.03	0.03	30
31	Huatai-Pinebridge Fund Mgt.	0.03	0.03	31

Source: China Knowledge Mutual Funds Database

China Asset Mgt., E Fund Mgt. and Harvest Fund Mgt. saw their asset under management of QDII funds total RMB 11.27 billion (US$ 1.69 Bln), RMB 10.68 billion (US$ 1.6 Bln) and RMB 10.54 billion (US$ 1.58 Bln) respectively, making up 39% of the total industry. 7 companies saw their AUM of QDII funds above RMB 5 billion (US$ 0.75 Bln), while 4 companies saw their AUM of QDII funds under RMB 100 million (US$ 15 Mln). In Jan-Sep, the top 10 QDII funds reached RMB 68.43 billion (US$ 10.26 Bln), accounting for 82.44% of the total industry.

Table 2.11 Ranking of Profits (Mid-2016)

Name of Fund Company	Total Profit (RMB Mln)	Name of Fund Company	Total Profit (RMB Mln)
Tianhong Asset Mgt.	8,856.42	JT Asset Mgt.	-248.71
CIB Fund Mgt.	952.37	Zhongrong Fund Mgt.	-259.99
Xingyin Fund Mgt.	767.22	Minsheng Royal Fund Mgt.	-272.25
BOSC Asset Mgt.	584.64	Caitong Fund Mgt.	-344.12
Bank of Beijing Scotiabank Asset Mgt.	434.76	China Nature Asset Mgt.	-349.29
Gfund Mgt.	354.99	Wanjia Asset Mgt.	-380.16
Hongde Fund Mgt.	326.62	CCB Principal Asset Mgt.	-383.82
China Life AMP Asset Mgt.	298.58	Yimin Asset Mgt.	-404.30
JYAH Asset Mgt.	208.51	Golden Eagle Asset Mgt.	-489.46
Tebon Fund Mgt.	171.59	Soochow Asset Mgt.	-515.46
Zheshang Fund Mgt.	170.05	Aegon-Industrial Fund Mgt.	-531.72
Founder Fubon Fund Mgt.	166.53	Fuanda Fund Mgt.	-534.72
Xinyuan Asset Mgt.	136.63	Harfor Fund Mgt.	-570.49
Golden Trust Sinopac Fund Mgt.	123.98	Franklin Templeton Sealand Fund Mgt.	-584.34
Taikang Asset Mgt.	62.15	HFT Investment Mgt.	-630.04
Truvalue Asset Mgt.	47.93	First State Cinda Fund Mgt.	-683.19
Qianhai Alliance Asset Mgt.	45.16	First Seafront Fund Mgt.	-706.01
China Fund Mgt.	39.38	HSBC Jintrust Fund Mgt.	-786.40
Yingda Asset Mgt.	32.83	Zhonghai Fund Mgt.	-846.30
Jiangxin Fund Mgt.	30.20	Orient Fund Mgt.	-848.80
Changan Fund Mgt.	23.49	GTJA Allianz Fund Mgt.	-957.40
Shanxi Securities	20.58	Morgan Stanley Huaxin Fund Mgt.	-1,082.14
CDBS Cathay Asset Mgt.	17.51	Chang Xin Asset Mgt.	-1,084.08
Guodu Securities	9.11	First-trust Fund Mgt.	-1,115.33
BOC International (China) Limited	7.79	Citic-Prudential Fund Mgt.	-1,121.31
Sinvo Fund	7.34	Lion Fund Mgt.	-1,171.68
Essence Fund Mgt.	5.15	UBS SDIC Fund Mgt.	-1,233.77
Goldstate Capital Fund Mgt.	4.61	ABC-CA Fund Mgt.	-1,598.13
JX Asset Mgt.	1.08	MANULIFE TEDA Fund Mgt.	-1,673.20
Mirae Asset Mgt.	0.10	Everbright Pramerica Fund Mgt.	-1,827.90
Western Leadbank Fund Mgt.	-0.52	AXA SPDB Investment Managers	-2,030.70
Taiping Fund Mgt.	-0.98	Great Wall Fund Mgt.	-2,240.61
Hongta Hotland Mgt.	-1.45	New China Fund Mgt.	-2,285.80
Huarong Securities	-20.95	Bank of China Investment Mgt.	-2,335.51
CR Yuanta Fund Mgt.	-22.63	Yinhua Fund Mgt.	-2,764.48
Hotland Innovation Asset Mgt.	-24.49	Bank of Communications Schroder Fund Mgt.	-2,865.43
Donghai Fund Mgt.	-50.75	China Merchants Fund Mgt.	-3,056.78
CICC Fund Mgt.	-54.07	Fortune SG Fund Mgt.	-3,131.22
Dongxing Securities	-74.69	Guotai Asset Mgt.	-3,138.28
Maxwealth Fund Mgt.	-113.75	Changsheng Fund Mgt.	-3,152.80
Ping An Uob Fund Mgt.	-115.88	Zhong Ou Asset Mgt.	-3,607.38
Beixin Ruifeng Fund Mgt.	-131.19	Galaxy Asset Mgt.	-3,632.24
Nuode Asset Mgt.	-161.48	Invesco Great Wall Fund Mgt.	-3,652.78
Zheshang Securities Asset Mgt.	-242.41		

Name of Fund Company	Total Profit (RMB Mln)
Dacheng Fund Mgt.	-3,735.83
SWS MU Fund Mgt.	-4,174.36
Bosera Fund Mgt.	-4,487.40
China International Fund Mgt.	-5,069.96
Huatai-Pinebridge Fund Mgt.	-5,192.35
GF Fund Mgt.	-5,842.48
HuaAn Fund Mgt.	-6,010.08
Huashang Fund Mgt.	-6,810.64
Penghua Fund Mgt.	-6,890.70

Name of Fund Company	Total Profit (RMB Mln)
Baoying Fund Mgt.	-6,900.82
Rongtong Fund Mgt.	-6,944.83
China Post Fund Mgt.	-7,757.13
ICBC Credit Suisse Asset Mgt.	-8,042.82
China Southern Fund Mgt.	-10,284.41
China Universal Asset Mgt.	-12,404.74
Harvest Fund Mgt.	-15,560.13
China Asset Mgt.	-18,816.97
E Fund Mgt.	-22,235.69
Fullgoal Fund Mgt.	-26,303.94

Source: China Knowledge Mutual Funds Database

In the first half of 2016, 30 fund companies were profitable while 76 companies suffered losses. Tianhong Asset Mgt. led the ranking of fund companies in Q3 profits, with a total amount of RMB 8.86 billion (US$ 1.33 Bln), RMB 7.9 billion (US$ 1.18 Bln) more than CIB Fund Mgt. which was in second place. The former is the sole partner of online giant Alibaba in the sale of its popular online money market fund, Yu'E Bao, on the company's e-commerce platform.

2.2 FUND MANAGEMENT COMPANY PROFILES

Our research team collected each fund management companies data as of end Nov 2016. The ranking is according to the total net asset value under by the fund management company. The top five big players were Tianhong Asset Management Co., Ltd., ICBC Credit Suisse Asset Management Co., Ltd., China Asset Management Co., Ltd., E Fund Management Co., Ltd. and China Southern Fund Management Co., Ltd..

1. Tianhong Asset Management Co., Ltd.

Company Profile:
Tianhong Asset Management Co., Ltd. was established on November 8, 2004 upon the approval of China Securities Regulatory Commission (CSRC). With RMB 514.3 million in registered capital, it is one of China's mutual fund management companies. In 2013, in collaboration with Alipay, the company launched the first ever Internet fund "Yu'ebao", charting a course for the future of Internet finance.

As of end Nov 2016, there were 50 funds (49 open-end funds and 1 closed-end funds) with total assets of RMB 832.49 billion under the management of Tianhong Asset Management Co., Ltd., which is ranked first in China in terms of total NAV. Tianhong is committed to building itself into a well-rounded asset management company characterized by a large customer base and prudent Internet-based operations across the board. It strives to lead the trend of scenario-based finance and create value for clients, helping them fulfill aspirations for a better future. It never ceases to introduce innovations to effect changes in the industry while growing together with all stakeholders.

Majority Shareholder:
Ant Financial Services Group is the largest shareholder with 51% shares in Tianhong Asset Management. In fact, Ant Financial Services Group ("Ant Financial"), was officially founded in October 2014 and originated from Alipay which is the world's leading third-party payment platform founded in 2004. With its vision of "bringing small and beautiful changes to the world," Ant Financial is dedicated to create an open ecosystem, enabling financial institutions and partners to make rapid progress towards "Internet+" goals through its "Internet Booster Plan," and providing inclusive financial services to small and micro enterprises and individual consumers.

Ant Financial runs Alipay, Ant Fortune, Ant Financial Cloud and other financial services. Ant Financial's invested companies and affiliates also work with these businesses units and support Ant Financial's ecosystem. The services provided by Ant Financial and its affiliates cover payment, wealth management, credit reporting, private bank and cloud computing.

Relationship with Alibaba Group:
Tianhong Asset Management Co., Ltd. manages Yu'ebao, China's first ever Internet fund specially designed for Alipay. As of June 30 2016, Yu'ebao has more than 260 million subscribers. As a part of Alibaba Group, Ant Financial has a controlling 51% stake in the company.

2. ICBC Credit Suisse Asset Management Co., Ltd.

Company Profile:
ICBC Credit Suisse Asset Management Co., Ltd. was established in June 2005 as a joint venture between ICBC and Credit Suisse First Boston. At present, the company is the second largest fund management company and has branches in Beijing, Shanghai, Shenzhen.

As of end Nov 2016, there were 96 funds (90 open-end funds and 6 closed-end funds) with a total NAV of RMB 562.33 billion under its managed. After ten years of development, ICBC Credit Suisse has become an all-round asset management company with various business qualifications such as fund raising, special account management, enterprise annuity, entrusted investment of insurance fund inside and outside the country, insurance fund entrusted investment, enterprise annuity product, QDII, QFII, RQFII.

Majority Shareholder:
Industrial and Commercial Bank of China is the largest shareholder with 80% stake in ICBC Credit Suisse Asset AMC. With continuous effort and steady development, ICBC has entered the ranks of the world's leading banks, with a high-quality customer base, diversified business structure, strong innovation capacity and market competitiveness. The Bank has provided a wide range of financial products and services to 5.32 million corporate customers and 496 million individual customers. Under the lead of ICBC, ICBC Credit Suisse Asset AMC achieved success both in stocks and bonds in its recent 10 years. The fund's total revenue is RMB 54.9 billion, and the cumulative dividend is 18 billion.

Relationship with Credit Suisse First Boston:
Credit Suisse First Boston is the second shareholder of ICBC Credit Suisse AMC. As a leading global private bank and wealth manager with distinctive investment banking capabilities, ICBC Credit Suisse Asset AMC usually has close relationship with Credit Suisse First Boston. Founded in 1856, Credit Suisse First Boston today have a global reach with operations in over 50 countries and 48,200 employees from over 150 different nations. The broad footprint helps Credit Suisse First Boston to generate a geographically balanced stream of revenues and net new assets that allows them to capture growth opportunities around the world.

3. China Asset Management Co., Ltd.

Company Profile:
As one of the first five fund management companies, China AMC has been the leading fund management company in China. On December 30, 2004, China 50 ETF, the first Exchange-traded Fund in China was established by China AMC. Moreover, China AMC launched one of China's first QDII funds in 2007. And China AMC became one of the first investment managers of RQFII funds in 2011.

By the end of Nov 2016, there were 84 open-end funds with a total NAV of RMB 530.93 billion under the management of China Asset Management Co., Ltd., which ranked third in China in terms of total NAV. China AMC is also one of the first six fund management companies designed as investment managers for the social funds.

Majority Shareholder:
China AMC 's largest shareholder is CITIC Securities, which owns 62.20% shares. CITIC Securities (CITICS) was incorporated in Beijing on October 25, 1995.Upon approval of Chinese Securities Regulatory Commission (CSRC) on December 13, 2002, CITICS undertook an initial public offering (IPO) of 400 million common A shares. On January 6, 2003, CITICS (Ticker: 600030) was listed on the Shanghai Stock Exchange. On October 6, 2011, CITICS (Ticker: 6030) was listed on the Hong Kong Exchange.

In 2015, the Company recorded a revenue of RMB 56 billion (according to China GAAP), net profits of RMB19.8 billion, both striking new record high, and maintaining the leading position among domestic securities companies. The major businesses of the Company continue to rank in the forefront in the market.

Relationship with China Securities:
No direct relationship but China Securities was acquired by CITIC Securities.

4. E Fund Management Co., Ltd.

Company Profile:
E Fund was registered in Zhuhai, but currently, the main operating force is all in Guangzhou. Although it is not the traditional "old 10 FMC", E Fund has made rapid expansion in recent years. Since its establishment, the Company was the first in the industry to develop the "outlines for internal control" which helped standardize the Company's governance structure and rules for internal control. Based on these, the Company has developed rules and regulations and formed a set of proprietary risk management systems, which ensure the compliance and efficient operation of the Company, which are highly appraised by national authorities and assessment agencies.

By the end of Nov 2016, there were 110 funds (101 open-end funds and 9 closed-end funds) with a total NAV of RMB 434.79 billion under the management of E Fund Management Co., Ltd. which is ranked fourth in China in terms of total NAV.

Majority Shareholder:
Currently Infore Holding Group, GF Securities and Guangdong Finance Trust are the three major shareholders with 25% shares each. Infore Group owns Infore Capital, an integrated asset management company ranked one of the

Top 10 in the industry. Infore Capital is not only one of the two biggest shareholders of E Fund Management, but also the biggest stake-holder of SDEBANK and Kaiyuan Securities. Guangdong Finance Trust Co., Ltd. is the only trust company remaining in Guangdong after the reshuffle of trust sector in early 2000s. As for GF Securities, besides holding 25% interest in E Fund, GF Securities is the major shareholder of GF FMC, which has 51.13% shares.

5. China Southern Fund Management Co., Ltd.

Company Profile:
As one of the first five regularized fund management companies established after the release of the Provisional Measures for Managing Securities Investment Funds, China Southern Fund Management Co., Ltd. was the pioneer of China's fund management industry.

As of end Nov 2016, there were 117 funds (113 open-end funds and 4 closed-end funds) with a total NAV of RMB 388.64 billion under the management of China Southern Fund Management Co., Ltd., which ranked fifth in China in terms of total NAV. China Southern Fund Management is the first batch of fund managers for social security funds. The size of social security funds under its management was estimated around RMB 20 billion at the end of November 2016.

Majority Shareholder:
Huatai Securities Co., Ltd. formerly known as Jiangsu Securities is the single biggest shareholder of China Southern Fund Management Co., Ltd., which holds 45% Shares. Huatai Securities is very active in China mutual fund industry.

Relationship with China Southern Securities:
Although China Southern Securities Co., Ltd. was one of the promoters of China Southern FMC, it had transferred all its interest in China Southern Fund Management Co., Ltd. to other Shareholders in September 2003. Currently, there is no direct relationship between China Southern Fund Management Co., Ltd. and China Southern Securities Co., Ltd.

6. CCB Principal Asset Management Corporation Limited

Company Profile:
CCB Principal Asset Management Corporation Limited manages a family of equity and fixed-income mutual funds for its clients. The firm primarily invests in growth, value, and core stocks of companies. CCB Principal Asset

Management Corporation Limited operates as a subsidiary of China Construction Bank Corporation.

As of end Nov 2016, there were 84 funds (80 open-end funds and 4 closed-end funds) with total assets of RMB 368.82 billion under the management of CCB Principal Asset Management Corporation, which ranked sixth in China in terms of total assets.

Major Shareholders (2016 Nov):

Share Holder Name	Share Holding
China Construction Bank	65%
Principal Financial Service Company	25%
China Huadian Corporation	10%

7. GF Fund Management Co., Ltd.

Company Profile:
GF Fund Management Co., Ltd., headquartered in Guangzhou, was established in August 2003 upon approval of CSRC with registered capital of RMB 126.88 million. GF Fund has been granted with requisite licenses to provide comprehensive services in asset management containing mutual funds, specific customers' assets management, securities investment advisory, Qualified Domestic Institutional Investor (QDII) programs, insurance funds entrusted management and social security funds in China.

As of end Nov 2016, there were 122 funds (120 open-end funds and 2 closed-end funds) with total assets of RMB 359.68 billion under the management of GF Fund Mgt Co., Ltd. which ranked seventh in China in terms of total assets.

Major Shareholders (2016 Nov):

Share Holder Name	Share Holding
GF Securities Co., Ltd.	51.14%
FiberHome Technologies Group	15.76%
Shenzhen Qianhai Heungkong Holding Group Co., Ltd.	15.76%
Kangmei Pharmaceutical Co., Ltd.	9.46%
Canton Venture Capital Co., Ltd.	7.88%

8. Harvest Fund Management Co., Ltd.

Company Profile:

Harvest Fund Management Co., Ltd. is a leading asset management company and one of the industry leaders in China with 10 offices throughout China serving more than 30 million clients. Since its establishment in 1999, HFM has grown to be one of the largest asset managers in China. The firm provides its services to pension and profit sharing plans, insurance companies, and enterprises. It also provides retirement planning services to its clients. As of end Nov 2016, there were 107 funds (103 open-end funds and 4 closed-end funds) with total assets of RMB 318.9 billion under the management of Harvest Fund Mgt Co., Ltd. which ranked eighth in China in terms of total assets.

Major Shareholders (2016 Nov):

Share Holder Name	Share Holding
China Credit Trust Co., Ltd.	40%
Deutsche Asset Management Co., Ltd.	30%
Lixin Investment Co., Ltd.	30%

9. Bank of China Investment Management Co., Ltd.

Company Profile:
Bank of China Investment Management Co., Ltd. is a privately-owned investment manager. It provides services to investment companies. The firm launches and manages equity, fixed income funds and balanced mutual funds for its clients. It invests in the public equity and fixed income markets across the globe. As of end Nov 2016, there were 72 open-end funds with total assets of RMB 306.17 billion under the management of Bank of China Investment Management Co., Ltd., which ranked ninth in China in terms of total assets.

Major Shareholders (2016 Nov):

Share Holder Name	Share Holding
Bank of China	83.5%
BlackRock Investment Management (UK) Co., Ltd.	16.5%

10. China Universal Asset Management Co., Ltd.

Company Profile:
China Universal Asset Management Co., Ltd. is a privately-owned investment manager. It provides services for individuals and institutions. The firm launches and manages equity funds, fixed income funds, and balanced mutual

funds for its clients. As of end Nov 2016, there were 69 funds (including 68 open-end funds and 1 closed-end fund) with total assets of RMB 303.29 billion under the management of China Universal Asset Management Co., Ltd., which ranked tenth in China in terms of total assets.

Major Shareholders (2016 Nov):

Share Holder Name	Share Holding
Orient Securities Co., Ltd.	39.96%
CES Capital Co., Ltd.	22.53%
Shanghai Shangbao Asset Management Co., Ltd.	22.53%
Shanghai Jing Jujin Investment Management Partnership	14.98%

11. Bosera Asset Management Co., Ltd.

Company Profile:
Bosera Asset Management Co., Ltd. is a privately-owned investment manager. It is one of the largest fund houses in China, with its pension fund assets under management ranked in top tier. Authorized by the National Council of Social Security Fund, Bosera manages part of the National Social Security Fund portfolios. As of end Nov 2016, there were 156 funds (151 open-end funds and 5 closed-end funds) with total assets of RMB 295.22 billion under the management of Bosera Asset Mgt Co., Ltd. which ranked eleventh in China in terms of total assets.

Major Shareholders (2016 Nov):

Share Holder Name	Share Holding
China Merchant Securities Co., Ltd.	49%
China Great Wall Asset Management Co., Ltd.	25%
Shanghai Huihua Industry Co., Ltd.	12%
Shanghai Shengye Equity Investment Fund Co., Ltd.	6%
Tianjin Port Group Co., Ltd.	6%
Guangsha Construction Group Co., Ltd.	2%

12. China Merchants Fund Management Co., Ltd.

Company Profile:
China Merchants Fund Management Co., Ltd. is a privately-owned investment manager. The firm manages separate client focused portfolios. It also launches and manages equity funds, fixed income funds, and balanced mutual funds for its clients. The firm invests in the public equity and fixed income

markets of China. As of end Nov 2016, there were 113 funds (103 open-end funds and 10 closed-end funds) with total assets of RMB 273.96 billion under the management of China Merchants Fund Mgt Co., Ltd. which ranked twelfth in China in terms of total assets.

Major Shareholders (2016 Nov):

Share Holder Name	Share Holding
China Merchants Bank	55%
China Merchants Securities Co., Ltd.	45%

13. Penghua Fund Management Co., Ltd.

Company Profile:
Penghua Fund Management Co., Ltd. is a China-based,independent investment manager. Its sole business is the management of third party asset, principally through equities and fixed income, including retail fund, Social Security Fund (SSF), Qualified Domestic Institutional Investor (QDII) and Separately Managed Account. As of end Nov 2016, there were 141 funds (122 open-end funds and 19 closed-end funds) with total assets of RMB 249.21 billion under the management of Penghua Fund Mgt Co., Ltd. which ranked thirteenth in China in terms of total assets.

Major Shareholders (2016 Nov):

Share Holder Name	Share Holding
Guosen Securities Holdings Co., Ltd	50%
Eurizon Capital SGR S.p.A.	49%
Shenzhen Beirong Credit Investment Co., Ltd.	1%

14. Fullgoal Fund Management Co., Ltd.

Company Profile:
Fullgoal Fund Management Co., Ltd. is one of China's most trusted names in investment management. It provides investment management solutions to clients in Beijing, Guangzhou, and Chengdu. The company offers both close-end and open-end mutual funds that include Han Sheng, Han Xing, Han Ding, Han Bo, and Fullgoal Dynamic Balancing Funds. As of end Nov 2016, there were 87 funds (77 open-end funds and 10 closed-end funds) with total assets of RMB 226.75 billion under the management of Fullgoal Fund Mgt Co., Ltd. which ranked fourteenth in China in terms of total assets.

Major Shareholders (2016 Nov):

Share Holder Name	Share Holding
Haitong Securities Co., Ltd.	27.775%
Bank of Montreal	27.775%
Shenyin & Wanguo Securities Co., Ltd.	27.775%
Shandong International Trust Co., Ltd.	16.675%

15. Yinhua Fund Management Co., Ltd.

Company Profile:

Yinhua Fund Management Co., Ltd. is a privately-owned investment manager. The firm provides services to individuals and pension plans. It manages separate client-focused equity portfolios. As of end Nov 2016, there were 76 funds (65 open-end funds and 11 closed-end funds) with total assets of RMB 185.71 billion under the management of Yinhua Fund Mgt Co., Ltd. which ranked fifteenth in China in terms of total assets.

Major Shareholders (2016 Nov):

Share Holder Name	Share Holding
Southwest Securities Co., Ltd.	49%
First Capital Co., Ltd.	29%
Northeast Securities Co., Ltd.	21%
Shanxi Haixin Industrial Co., Ltd.	1%

16. HuaAn Fund Management Co., Ltd.

Company Profile:

HuaAn Fund Management Co., Ltd. is a privately owned investment manager. The firm manages separate client-focused equity, fixed income funds, and balanced portfolios. It launches and manages mutual funds and exchange traded funds for its clients. The firm invests in the public equity and fixed income markets. As of end Nov 2016, there were 89 funds (84 open-end funds and 5 closed-end funds) with total assets of RMB 167.06 billion under the management of Hua An Fund Management Co., Ltd., which ranked sixteenth in China in terms of total assets.

Major Shareholders (2016 Nov):

Share Holder Name	Share Holding
Guotai Junan Investment Management Co., Ltd.	20%
Shanghai Electric (Group) Corp.	20%
Shanghai Industrial Investment Group Co., Ltd.	20%
Shanghai International Trust Co., Ltd.	20%
Shanghai Jin Jiang International Holdings Co., Ltd.	20%

17. Fortune SG Fund Management Co., Ltd.

Company Profile:
Fortune SG Fund Management Co., Ltd. is a privately-owned investment manager. It started its business on February 12, 2003. It is one of the first joint venture fund management companies in China, as well as the one established by a domestic trust company and a foreign asset management company. With powerful shareholders the company benefits from its simple and stable equity structure. As of end Nov 2016, there were 49 funds (47 open-end funds and 2 closed-end funds) with total assets of RMB 154.08 billion under the management of Fortune SG Fund Management Co., Ltd., which ranked seventeenth in China in terms of total assets.

Major Shareholders (2016 Nov):

Share Holder Name	Share Holding
Hwabao Trust Co., Ltd.	51%
Lyxor Asset Management Co., Ltd.	49%

18. Aegon-Industrial Fund Management Co., Ltd.

Company Profile:
Aegon-Industrial Fund Management Co., Ltd. was established on September 30th, 2003 in Shanghai. The firm provides client focused portfolios. It also launches and manages equity, fixed income, and balanced mutual funds for its clients. The firm invests in public equity and fixed income markets across the globe. It also does socially responsible investing. As of end Nov 2016, there were 18 funds (17 open-end funds and 1 closed-end funds) with total assets of RMB 140.22 billion under the management of Aegon-Industrial Fund Management Co., Ltd., which ranked eighteenth in China in terms of total assets.

Major Shareholders (2016 Nov):

Share Holder Name	Share Holding
Industrial Securities Co., Ltd.	51%
AEGON International N.V	49%

19. CIB Fund Management Co., Ltd.

Company Profile:
CIB Fund Management Co., Ltd was established on April 17, 2013 in Fuzhou. The head quarter of the firm is in Shanghai. Its business scope includes fund raising, fund sales, asset management, specific customer asset management and other business under the permission of CSRC. As of end Nov 2016, there were 34 open-end funds with total assets of RMB 110.8 billion under the management of CIB Fund Management Co., Ltd., which ranked nineteenth in China in terms of total assets.

Major Shareholders (2016 Nov):

Share Holder Name	Share Holding
Industrial Bank Co., Ltd.	90%
China Shipping Investment Co., Ltd.	10%

20. Lion Fund Management Co., Ltd.

Company Profile:
Lion Fund Management Co., Ltd. is a privately-owned investment manager. The firm manages mutual funds for its clients. It invests in public equity and fixed income markets. Lion Fund Management Co., Ltd. was founded in 2003 and is based in Shenzhen, China. As of end Nov 2016, there were 53 funds (52 open-end funds and 1 closed-end fund) with total assets of RMB 108.92 billion under the management of Lion Fund Management Co., Ltd., which ranked twentieth in China in terms of total assets.

Major Shareholders (2016 Nov):

Share Holder Name	Share Holding
Shenzhen Jielong Investment Co., Ltd.	40%
China Foreign Economic and Trade Trust Co., Ltd.	40%
Daheng New Era Technology Co., Ltd.	20%

21. China International Fund Management Co. Ltd.

Company Profile:
China International Fund Management Co., Ltd. ("CIFM"), based in Shanghai, is one of the leading Sino-Foreign joint ventures in China's asset management industry. It invests in the public equity and fixed income markets. As of end Nov 2016, there were 51 open-end funds with total assets of RMB 102.73 billion under the management of China International Fund Management Co., Ltd., which ranked twenty-first in China in terms of total assets.

Major Shareholders (2016 Nov):

Share Holder Name	Share Holding
Shanghai International Trust & Investment Co., Ltd.	51%
J.P. Morgan Asset Management (UK) Limited	49%

22. Rongtong Fund Management Co., Ltd.

Company Profile:
Rongtong Fund Management (RFM) is a Sino-Foreign joint venture fund management company between New Times Securities and Nikko Asset Management and is established in 2001 in Shenzhen. The Company maintains assets for individual and institutional investors in equity and fixed income funds. As of end Nov 2016, there were 62 funds (including 59 open-end funds and 3 close ended funds) with total assets of RMB 99.36 billion under the management of Rongtong Fund Management Co., Ltd., which ranked twenty-second in China in terms of total assets.

Major Shareholders (2016 Nov):

Share Holder Name	Share Holding
New Times Securities Co., Ltd.	60%
Nikko Asset Management Co., Lltd.	40%

23. Dacheng Fund Management Co., Ltd.

Company Profile:
Dacheng Fund Management Co., Ltd. is a privately-owned investment manager. The firm manages mutual funds for its clients. It invests in the

public equity and fixed income markets. It employs quantitative analysis stock picking approach to make its investments. As of end Nov 2016, there were 78 funds (including 76 open-end funds and 2 close ended funds) with total assets of RMB 97.91 billion under the management of Dacheng Fund Management Co., Ltd., which ranked twenty-third in China in terms of total assets.

Major Shareholders (2016 Nov):

Share Holder Name	Share Holding
Zhongtai Trust Co., Ltd.	50%
Everbright Securities Co., Ltd.	25%
China Galaxy Investment Management Co., Ltd.	25%

24. Invesco Great Wall Fund Management Co., Ltd.

Company Profile:
Invesco Great Wall Fund Management Co., Ltd is a privately-owned investment manager. The firm launches and manages equity, fixed income and balanced mutual funds for its clients. It also launches and manages exchange traded funds for its clients. As of end Nov 2016, there were 60 open-end funds with total assets of RMB 96.76 billion under the management of Invesco Great Wall Fund Management Co., Ltd., which ranked twenty fourth in China in terms of total assets.

Major Shareholders (2016 Nov):

Share Holder Name	Share Holding
Inversco Asset Management Limited	49%
Great Wall Securities Co., Ltd.	49%
Dalian Shide Group Co., Ltd.	1%
Kailuan Group Co., Ltd.	1%

25. Zhong Ou Asset Management Co., Ltd

Company Profile:
Zhong Ou Asset Management is an active manager which utilizes in-house, bottom-up proprietary research to screen stocks. Their equity analysts perform grass roots research, including company meetings and company interviews focused on business strategy and management motivation. As of end Nov 2016, there were 50 funds (including 49 open-end funds and 1 close-end fund) with total assets of RMB 88.04 billion under the management of

Zhong Ou Asset Management Co., Ltd., which ranked twenty-fifth in China in terms of total assets.

Major Shareholders (2016 Nov):

Share Holder Name	Share Holding
UBI Banca	35%
Beijing Baijun Investment Co., Ltd.	20%
Guodu Securities Co., Ltd.	20%
Shanghai Muyi Investment Management Partner	20%
Xiamen Winner Key Group Co., Ltd.	5%

26. Guotai Fund Management Co., Ltd.

Company Profile:
Guotai Asset Management Co., Ltd. is a privately-owned investment manager. The firm launches and manages equity, fixed income funds and balanced mutual funds for its clients. It invests in the public equity and fixed income markets of China. As of end Nov 2016, there were 74 funds (including 68 open-end funds and 6 close-end funds) with total assets of RMB 87.31 billion under the management of Guotai Asset Management Co., Ltd., which ranked twenty-sixth in China in terms of total assets.

Major Shareholders (2016 Nov):

Share Holder Name	Share Holding
China Jianyin Investment Ltd.	60%
Generali Group	30%
China Power Finance Co., Ltd.	10%

27. Great Wall Fund Management Co., Ltd.

Company Profile:
Great Wall Fund Management Co., Ltd. is a privately-owned investment manager. The firm manages mutual funds for its clients. It invests in the public equity and fixed income markets of China. As of end Nov 2016, there were 40 funds (including 38 open-end funds and 2 close-end funds) with total assets of RMB 86.14 billion under the management of Great Wall Fund Management Co., Ltd., which ranked twenty-seventh in China in terms of total assets.

Major Shareholders (2016 Nov):

Share Holder Name	Share Holding
China Great Wall Securities Co., Ltd.	47.06%
Northern International Trust Co., Ltd.	17.65%
Orient Securities Co., Ltd.	17.65%
Zhongyuan Trust Co., Ltd.	17.65%

28. Huatai-Pinebridge Fund Management Co., Ltd.

Company Profile:

Huatai-Pinebridge Fund Management Co., Ltd. is a privately-owned investment manager. The firm manages mutual funds for its clients. It invests in the public equity markets and fixed income markets. Huatai-Pinebridge Fund Management Co., Ltd. was founded in 2004 and is based in Shanghai, China. As of end Nov 2016, there were 42 open-end funds with total assets of RMB 84.87 billion under the management of Huatai-Pinebridge Fund Management Co., Ltd., which ranked twenty-eighth in China in terms of total assets.

Major Shareholders (2016 Nov):

Share Holder Name	Share Holding
PineBridge Investments LLC.	49%
Huatai Securities Co., Ltd.	49%
Suzhou New District Hi-Tech Industrial Co., Ltd.	2%

29. Minsheng Royal Fund Management Co., Ltd.

Company Profile:

Minsheng Royal Asset Management Co., Ltd. operates as a subsidiary of China Minsheng Banking. The company is the first joint venture company in China who has both domestic bank and foreign bank as major shareholders. As of end Nov 2016, there were 35 open-end funds with total assets of RMB 79.94 billion under the management of Minsheng Royal Asset Management Co., Ltd., which ranked twenty-ninth in China in terms of total assets.

Major Shareholders (2016 Nov):

Share Holder Name	Share Holding
China Minsheng Bank	63.33%
Royal Bank of Canada	30%
Three Gorges Finance Co., Ltd.	6.67%

30. Bank of Communications Schroder Fund Management Co., Ltd.

Company Profile:
Bank of Communications Schroder Fund Management Co., Ltd. is a privately-owned investment manager. The firm provides services to individuals, retail investors, and institutional investors. It manages separate client-focused equity and fixed income mutual funds for its clients. As of end Nov 2016, there were 67 funds (65 open-end funds and 2 closed-end funds) with total assets of RMB 74.78 billion under the management of Bank of Communications Schroder Fund Management Co., Ltd., which ranked thirtieth in China in terms of total assets.

Major Shareholders (2016 Nov):

Share Holder Name	Share Holding
Bank of Communications	65%
Schroder Investment Management Limited	30%
China International Marine Containers (Group) Ltd.	5%

31. UBS SDIC Fund Management Co., Ltd.

Company Profile:
UBS SDIC Fund Management Co., Ltd. is a privately-owned investment manager. Its business scope covers mutual fund, discretionary portfolio management, capital management and international business. Currently UBS SDIC has obtained the QDII, RQFII, QFII, and QDIE business qualifications. As of end Nov 2016, there were 65 funds (62 open-end funds and 3 closed-end funds) with total assets of RMB 70.65 billion under the management of UBS SDIC Fund Management Co., Ltd., which ranked thirty-first in China in terms of total assets.

Major Shareholders (2016 Nov):

Share Holder Name	Share Holding
SDIC TAIKANG Trust Co., Ltd.	51%
UBS AG	49%

32. ABC-CA Fund Management Co., Ltd.

Company Profile:
ABC-CA Fund Management Co., Ltd. was established on March 18, 2008 in Shanghai. The firm adhere to build a Leading asset management brand in China. The business scope of ABC-CA includes fund raising, fund sales, asset management, specific customer asset management and other business under the permission of CSRC.As of end Nov 2016, there were 35 open-end funds with total assets of RMB 68.25 billion under the management of ABC-CA Fund Management Co., Ltd., which ranked thirty-second in China in terms of total assets.

Major Shareholders (2016 Nov):

Share Holder Name	Share Holding
Agricultural Bank of China	51.67%
Amundi Asset Management Co., Ltd.	33.33%
Chinalco Capital Holdings Co., Ltd.	15%

33. China Post & Capital Fund Management Co., Ltd.

Company Profile:
China Post & Capital Fund Management Co., Ltd. engages in fund raising, fund sales, asset management, and other business under the permission of CSRC. The Company offers various funds and investment opportunities to its clients in China. As of end Nov 2016, there were 28 funds with total assets of RMB 65.16 billion under the management of China Post & Capital Fund Management Co., Ltd., which ranked thirty-third in China in terms of total assets.

Major Shareholders (2016 Nov):

Share Holder Name	Share Holding
Capital Securities Co., Ltd.	47%
China Post Group Corporation	29%
Sumitomo Mitsui Banking Corporation	24%

34. Chang Xin Asset Management Co., Ltd.

Company Profile:
Chang Xin Asset Management Co., Ltd. was incorporated in Shanghai, whose shares are jointly holded by Changjiang Securities Co., Ltd., Shanghai Haixin Group Co., Ltd. and Wuhan Iron and Steel Co. Ltd. The Company's line of

business includes providing investment information and advice to companies and individuals. The Company offers various funds and investment opportunities to its clients in China. As of end Nov 2016, there were 45 funds with total assets of RMB 63.32 billion under the management of Chang Xin Asset Management Co., Ltd., which ranked thirty-fourth in China in terms of total assets.

Major Shareholders (2016 Nov):

Share Holder Name	Share Holding
Changjiang Securities Co., Ltd.	49%
Shanghai Haixin Group Co., Ltd.	34.33%
Wuhan Iron and Steel Group Corporation	16.67%

35. Xingyin Fund Management Co., Ltd.

Company Profile:
Xingyin Fund Management Co., Ltd. operates in the real estate sector. The company engages in fund raising, fund sales, asset management, and other business under the permission of CSRC.As of end Nov 2016, there were 12 funds with total assets of RMB 61.72 billion under the management of Xingyin Fund Management Co., Ltd., which ranked thirty-fifth in China in terms of total assets.

Major Shareholders (2016 Nov):

Share Holder Name	Share Holding
Huafu Securities Co., Ltd.	76%
Guomai Technologies, Inc.	24%

36. Ping An Uob Fund Management Co., Ltd.

Company Profile:
Headquartered in Shenzhen, Ping An UOB FMC undertakes fund management activities in China, offering retail investors in China, the opportunity to invest into China's domestic markets. Their geographic focus is in China. As of end Nov 2016, there were 27 funds with total assets of RMB 58.91 billion under the management of Ping An UOB FMC, which ranked thirty-sixth in China in terms of total assets.

Major Shareholders (2016 Nov):

Share Holder Name	Share Holding
Ping An Trust Co., Ltd.	60.7%
UOB Asset Management Ltd.	25%
Sanya Yingwan Tourism Co., Ltd.	14.3%

37. China Life AMP Asset Management Co., Ltd.

Company Profile:
China Life AMP Asset Management Co., Ltd. is a joint venture asset management entity formed between China Life Insurance Asset Management and Australia-based AMP Capital. The company is one of earliest insurance asset management companies established in China. As of end Nov 2016, there were 25 funds with total assets of RMB 58.28 billion under the management of China Life AMP Asset Management Co., Ltd., which ranked thirty-seventh in China in terms of total assets.

Major Shareholders (2016 Nov):

Share Holder Name	Share Holding
China Life Asset Management Co., Ltd.	85.03%
AMP Capital	14.97%

38. Huashang Fund Management Co., Ltd.

Company Profile:
Huashang Fund Management Co., Ltd. is a privately-owned investment manager. The firm provides services to individuals and pension plans. It manages separate client-focused equity portfolios. The firm also launches and manages equity, fixed income, and balanced mutual funds for its clients. It invests in the public equity and fixed income markets. As of end Nov 2016, there were 36 open-end funds with total assets of RMB 58.28 billion under the management of Huashang Fund Management Co., Ltd., which ranked thirty-eighth in China in terms of total assets.

Major Shareholders (2016 Nov):

Share Holder Name	Share Holding
China Dragon Securities Co., Ltd.	46%
China Huadian Finance Co., Ltd.	34%
SD Steel Co., Ltd.	20%

39. Citic-Prudential Fund Management Co., Ltd.

Company Profile:
CITIC-Prudential Fund Management Co., Ltd. operates as an investment advisory firm. The Company maintains assets for individuals and institutional investors in equity and fixed income portfolios. CITIC-Prudential Fund Management Company serves clients throughout China. As of end Nov 2016, there were 61 funds (including 51 open-end funds and 10 closed-end funds) with total assets of RMB 55.46 billion under the management of CITIC-Prudential Fund Management Company Ltd., which ranked thirty-ninth in China in terms of total assets.

Major Shareholders (2016 Nov):

Share Holder Name	Share Holding
Prudential plc	49%
CITIC Trust Co., Ltd.	49%
China-Singapore Suzhou Industrial Park Ventures Co., Ltd.	2%

40. Changsheng Fund Management Co., Ltd.

Company Profile:
Changsheng Fund Management Co., Ltd. is a privately-owned investment manager. The firm launches and manages equity, fixed income funds and balanced mutual funds for its clients. It also manages separate client focused portfolios. The firm invests in the public equity and fixed income markets of China. As of end Nov 2016, there were 62 funds (including 56 open-end funds and 6 closed-end funds) with total assets of RMB 53.43 billion under the management of Changsheng Fund Management Co., Ltd., which ranked fortieth in China in terms of total assets.

Major Shareholders (2016 Nov):

Share Holder Name	Share Holding
Guoyuan Securities Co., Ltd.	41%
DBS Bank	33%
Anhui Investment Group Co., Ltd.	13%
Anhui Credit Guaranty Group Co., Ltd.	13%

41. BOSC Asset Management Co., Ltd.

Company Profile:
BOSCAMC is an active, risk-aware, long-term manager which aims to provide stable returns and liquidity reserves for investors by investing through their equity and money market funds in a range of instruments including equities, fixed-income securities, cash, short-term bonds, bank deposits, certificates of deposit, asset-backed securities, medium-term notes, central bank notes and other money market instruments with good liquidity. As of end Nov 2016, there were 4 open-end funds with total assets of RMB 52.52 billion under the management of BOSC Asset Management Co., Ltd., which ranked forty-first in China in terms of total assets.

Major Shareholders (2016 Nov):

Share Holder Name	Share Holding
Bank of Shanghai	90%
China National Machinery Industry Corporation	10%

42. First Seafront Fund Management Co., Ltd.

Company Profile:
First Seafront Fund Management Co., Ltd.'s business scope includes fund raising, fund sales, asset management and others . The company is based in Qianhai Shenzhen-Hong Kong Modern Service Industry Cooperation Zone. As of end Nov 2016, there were 45 funds (including 43 open-end funds and 2 closed-end funds) with total assets of RMB 51.73 billion under the management of First Seafront Fund Co., Ltd., which ranked forty-second in China in terms of total assets.

Major Shareholders (2016 Nov):

Share Holder Name	Share Holding
Beijing Zhongsheng Jinqi Investment Management Co., Ltd.	25%
Ever Union Asset Management Ltd.	25%
Kaiyuan Securities Co., Ltd.	25%
Shenzhen Hehe Investment Asset Management Partnership	25%

43. Baoying Fund Management Co., Ltd.

Company Profile:
Baoying Fund Management Co., Ltd. is a privately-owned investment manager. The firm manages separate client focused portfolios. It also launches and manages equity, fixed income funds and balanced mutual funds for its clients. As of end Nov 2016, there were 22 funds (including 21 open-end funds and 1 closed-end fund) with total assets of RMB 50.15 billion under the management of Baoying Fund Management Co., Ltd., which ranked forty-third in China in terms of total assets.

Major Shareholders (2016 Nov):

Share Holder Name	Share Holding
China Railway Trust Co., Ltd.	75%
China Foreign Economy and Trade Trust Co., Ltd.	25%

44. AXA SPDB Investment Managers Co., Ltd.

Company Profile:
AXA SPDB Investment Managers Co., Ltd. operates as a subsidiary of Shanghai Pudong Development Bank Co., Ltd. The company is a Sino-French joint venture fund management company approved by the CSRD. As of end Nov 2016, there were 27 open-end funds with total assets of RMB 49.19 billion under the management of AXA SPDB Investment Managers, which ranked forty-fourth in China in terms of total assets.

Major Shareholders (2016 Nov):

Share Holder Name	Share Holding
Shanghai Pudong Development Bank Co., Ltd.	51%
AXA Investment Managers Co., Ltd.	39%
Shanghai Guosheng Assets Co., Ltd.	10%

45. Everbright Pramerica Fund Management Co., Ltd.

Company Profile:

Everbright Pramerica Fund Management Co., Ltd. was founded in April 2004 and is based in Shanghai,China. Everbright Pramerica Fund Management Co., Ltd. operates as a subsidiary of Everbright Securities Co., Ltd. As of end Nov 2016, there were 29 open-end funds with total assets of RMB 46.62 billion under the management of Everbright Pramerica Fund Management, which ranked forty-fifth in China in terms of total assets.

Major Shareholders (2016 Nov):

Share Holder Name	Share Holding
Everbright Securities Co., Ltd.	55%
Pramerica Investment Management Co., Ltd.	45%

46. MANULIFE TEDA Fund Management Co., Ltd.

Company Profile:

MANULIFE TEDA Fund Management Co., Ltd. operates as an investment management firm. The Company provides portfolio management and consulting services to its clients. The company was formerly a subsidiary of Xiangcai Securities Limited. As of end Nov 2016, there were 45 funds (including 44 open-end funds and 1 closed-end fund) with total assets of RMB 43.8 billion under the management of MANULIFE TEDA Fund Management, which ranked forty-sixth in China in terms of total assets.

Major Shareholders (2016 Nov):

Share Holder Name	Share Holding
Northern International Trust Co., Ltd.	51%
Manulife Asset Management (Hong Kong) Co., Ltd.	49%

47. Bank of Beijng Scotiabank Asset Management Co., Ltd.

Company Profile:
Bank of Beijing Scotiabank Asset Management Co., Ltd. operates as a subsidiary of Bank of Beijing Co., Ltd. The company was among the first fund companies approved the CSRC in the third bank pilots. As of end Nov 2016, there were 13 funds (including 12 open-end funds and 1 closed-end fund) with total assets of RMB 43.58 billion under the management of Bank of Beijing Scotiabank Asset Management, which ranked forty-seventh in China in terms of total assets.

Major Shareholders (2016 Nov):

Share Holder Name	Share Holding
Bank of Beijing	62%
Scotiabank	33%
General Research Institute for Nonferrous Metals	5%

48. SWS MU Fund Management Co., Ltd.

Company Profile:
SWS MU Fund Management Co., Ltd. is a privately-owned investment manager. The firm manages equity, fixed income Funds and balanced mutual funds. It invests in the public equity and fixed income markets of China. As of end Nov 2016, there were 35 funds (including 27 open-end funds and 8 closed-end funds) with total assets of RMB 41.86 billion under the management of SWS MU Fund Management Co., Ltd., which ranked forty-eighth in China in terms of total assets.

Major Shareholders (2016 Nov):

Share Holder Name	Share Holding
Shenwan Hongyuan Securities Co., Ltd.	67%
Mitsubishi UFJ Trust and Banking Corporation	33%

49. HFT Investment Management Co., Ltd.

Company Profile:
HFT Investment Management Co., Ltd. was officially established in April, 2003 as one of the first joint venture fund management companies granted approval from China Securities Regulatory Commission (CSRC). As of end Nov 2016, there were 42 open ended funds with total assets of RMB 40.95 billion

under the management of HFT Investment Management Co., Ltd., which ranked forty-ninth in China in terms of total assets.

Major Shareholders (2016 Nov):

Share Holder Name	Share Holding
Haitong Securities Co., Ltd.	51%
BNPP IP BE Holding	49%

50. Shanghai Orient Securities Asset Management Co., Ltd.

Company Profile:
Shanghai Orient Securities Asset Management Co., Ltd. operates as a securities company in China. The company offers securities, futures, asset management, wealth management, investment banking and securities research services. As of end Nov 2016, there were 26 funds (including 21 open-end funds and 5 closed-end funds) with total assets of RMB 40.35 billion under the management of Shanghai Orient Securities Asset Management Co., Ltd., which ranked fiftieth in China in terms of total assets.

Major Shareholders (2016 Nov):

Share Holder Name	Share Holding
Orient Securities Co., Ltd.	100%

51. Zhongrong Fund Management Co., Ltd.

Company Profile:
Zhongrong Fund Management Co., Ltd. offers fund management services. The Company provides fund investment in capital, finance, real estate, and venture fields. The company's business scope includes fund raising, fund sales, asset management and other businesses approved by the CSRC. As of end Nov 2016, there were 26 funds (including 22 open-end funds and 4 closed-end funds) with total assets of RMB 40.05 billion under the management of Zhongrong Fund Management Co., Ltd., which ranked fifty-first in China in terms of total assets.

Major Shareholders (2016 Nov):

Share Holder Name	Share Holding
Zhongrong International Trust Co., Ltd.	51%
Shanghai Rongsheng Investment Co., Ltd.	49%

52. Zhonghai Fund Management Co., Ltd.

Company Profile:
Zhonghai Fund Management Co., Ltd., formerly known as Guo Lian Fund Management Co., Ltd., is a private investment firm specializing in public equity and mutual fund investments. Zhonghai Fund currently owns dozens of mutual fund products. As of end Nov 2016, there were 34 funds (including 33 open-end funds and 1 closed-end fund) with total assets of RMB 38.5 billion under the management of Zhonghai Fund Management Co., Ltd., which ranked fifty-second in China in terms of total assets.

Major Shareholders (2016 Nov):

Share Holder Name	Share Holding
Zhonghai Trust Co., Ltd.	41.59%
Guolian Securities Co., Ltd.	33.41%
La Compagnie Financière Edmondde Rothschild Banque	25%

53. GTJA Allianz Fund Management Co., Ltd.

Company Profile:
GTJA Allianz Fund Management Co. Ltd. offers four open-end investment funds - De-sheng Stable Fund, De-sheng Small Cap Selective Fund, De-sheng Reliable Growth Securities Investment Fund, and De-sheng Selective Equity Fund - to its Chinese customers. As of end Nov 2016, there were 36 funds (including 35 open-end funds and 1 closed-end fund) with total assets of RMB 38.09 billion under the management of GTJA Allianz Fund Management Co., Ltd., which ranked fifty-third in China in terms of total assets.

Major Shareholders (2016 Nov):

Share Holder Name	Share Holding
Guotai Junan Securities Co., Ltd.	51%
Allianz Group	49%

54. Galaxy Asset Management Co., Ltd.

Company Profile:
Galaxy Asset Management Co., Ltd. is a privately-owned investment manager. It invests in the public equity and fixed income markets of China. The firm employs combination of fundamental and quantitative analysis along with bottom-up and top-down stock picking approaches to create its portfolios. As of end Nov 2016, there were 37 funds (including 35 open-end funds and 2 closed-end funds) with total assets of RMB 36.45 billion under the management of Galaxy Asset Management Co., Ltd., which ranked fifty-fourth in China in terms of total assets.

Major Shareholders (2016 Nov):

Share Holder Name	Share Holding
China Galaxy Financial Holding Co., Ltd.	50%
Beijing Capital International Airport Co., Ltd.	12.5%
Hunan TV & Broadcast Intermediary Co., Ltd.	12.5%
Shanghai Municipal Investment Group Corporation	12.5%
China National Petroleum Corporation	12.5%

55. Wanjia Asset Management Co., Ltd.

Company Profile:
Wanjia Asset Management Co., Ltd. operates as an investment management firm. The Company offers investment advisory and portfolio management services. As of end Nov 2016, there were 40 funds (including 39 open-end funds and 1 closed-end fund) with total assets of RMB 34.26 billion under the management of Wanjia Asset Management Co., Ltd., which ranked fifty-fifth in China in terms of total assets.

Major Shareholders (2016 Nov):

Share Holder Name	Share Holding
Qilu Securities Co., Ltd.	49%
Xinjiang International Industry Co., Ltd.	40%
Shandong State-owned Assets Investment Holdings Co., Ltd	11%

56. New China Fund Management Co., Ltd.

Company Profile:
New China Fund Management Co., Ltd. is an active manager which provides a range of funds investing in a variety of strategies including preferred stock, generic resources, growth stocks, mixed, cycle rotation, small and medium-sized preferred stocks and theme stocks. As of end Nov 2016, there were 42 funds (including 40 open-end funds and 2 closed-end funds) with total assets of RMB 33.11 billion under the management of New China Fund Management Co., Ltd., which ranked fifty-sixth in China in terms of total assets.

Major Shareholders (2016 Nov):

Share Holder Name	Share Holding
HengTai Securities Co., Ltd.	58.62%
New China Trust Co., Ltd.	35.31%
Hangzhou Yongyuan Network Co., Ltd.	6.07%

57. Morgan Stanley Huaxin Fund Management Co., Ltd.

Company Profile:
Morgan Stanley Huaxin Funds provides diversified and excellent management services to investors, including actively managed products, indexing investment products, quantitative investment products, fixed income products and separately-managed account (SMA) products. As of end Nov 2016, there were 24 open-end funds with total assets of RMB 31.17 billion under the management of Morgan Stanley Huaxin Funds Co., Ltd., which ranked fifty-seventh in China in terms of total assets.

Major Shareholders (2016 Nov):

Share Holder Name	Share Holding
China Fortune Securities Co., Ltd.	39.56%
Morgan Stanley International Holding Co., Ltd.	37.36%
Shenzhen Merchants Finance Investment Holdings Co., Ltd.	10.99%
Hantang Securities Co., Ltd.	6.59%
Shenzhen Zhongji Entity Group Co., Ltd.	5.50%

58. Essence Fund Management Co., Ltd.

Company Profile:
Essence Fund Management Co., Ltd is a privately-owned investment manager. The firm launches and manages mutual fund for its clients. The company is one of the biggest securities companies in China. As of end Nov 2016, there were 29 funds (including 28 open-end funds and 1 closed-end fund) with total assets of RMB 31.17 billion under the management of Essence Fund Management Co., Ltd., which ranked fifty-eighth in China in terms of total assets.

Major Shareholders (2016 Nov):

Share Holder Name	Share Holding
Minmetals Capital Holdings Ltd.	38.72%
Essence Securities Co., Ltd.	33%
Foshan Shunde Xinbi Trade Co., Ltd.	19.71%
CGN Financial Co., Ltd.	8.57%

59. Orient Fund Management Co., Ltd.

Company Profile:
Orient Fund Management Co. Ltd. is a privately-owned investment manager. The firm manages mutual funds for its clients. It invests in the public equity and fixed income markets. As of end Nov 2016, there were 39 open-end funds with total assets of RMB 28.74 billion under the management of Orient Fund Management Co., Ltd., which ranked fifty-ninth in China in terms of total assets.

Major Shareholders (2016 Nov):

Share Holder Name	Share Holding
Northeast Securities Co., Ltd.	64%
Hebei State-Owned Assets Holding & Operation Co., Ltd.	27%
Bohai International Trust Co., Ltd.	9%

60. Tebon Fund Management Co., Ltd.

Company Profile:
Tebon Fund Management Co., Ltd.'s business scope includes fund raising, fund sales, asset management and others. The firm conducts fundamental

analysis and practices strict risk control, seeking to identify market trends. As of end Nov 2016, there were 20 funds (include 19 open-end funds and 1 closed-end fund) with total assets of RMB 26.65 billion under the management of Tebon Fund Management Co., Ltd., which ranked sixtieth in China in terms of total assets.

Major Shareholders (2016 Nov):

Share Holder Name	Share Holding
Tebon Securities Co., Ltd.	70%
Zhejiang Native Produce & Animal By-Products I/E Group Co., Ltd.	20%
XIZI United Holding Corporation	10%

61. Franklin Templeton Sealand Fund Management Co., Ltd.

Company Profile:

Franklin Templeton Sealand Fund Management Co., Ltd. is a privately-owned investment manager. The firm invests in the public equity and fixed income markets across the globe. It operates as a subsidiary of Sealand Securities Co. Ltd. As of end Nov 2016, there were 29 funds (include 27 open-end funds and 2 closed-end funds) with total assets of RMB 25.74 billion under the management of Franklin Templeton Sealand Fund Management Co., Ltd., which ranked sixty-first in China in terms of total assets.

Major Shareholders (2016 Nov):

Share Holder Name	Share Holding
Sealand Securities Co., Ltd.	51%
Franklin Templeton Investments Co., Ltd.	49%

62. Xinyuan Asset Management Co., Ltd.

Company Profile:

Xinyuan Asset Management Co., Ltd. is headquartered in China. The Company's line of business includes holding or owning securities of companies other than banks. The firm was founded in 2013. As of end Nov 2016, there were 17 funds (include 15 open-end funds and 2 closed-end fund) with total assets of RMB 23.63 billion under the management of Xinyuan Asset Management Co., Ltd., which ranked sixty-second in China in terms of total assets.

Major Shareholders (2016 Nov):

Share Holder Name	Share Holding
Bank of Nanjing	80%
Nanjing High-Tech Co., Ltd.	20%

63. Caitong Fund Management Co., Ltd.

Company Profile:
Caitong Fund Management Co., Ltd. is based in Shanghai, China. The firm was established on June 21,2011. The firm has managed more than 1600 products including fixed income funds and balanced mutual funds. As of end Nov 2016, there were 12 funds (include 9 open-end funds and 3 closed-end funds) with total assets of RMB 23.56 billion under the management of Caitong Fund Management Co., Ltd., which ranked sixty-third in China in terms of total assets.

Major Shareholders (2016 Nov):

Share Holder Name	Share Holding
Caitong Securities Co., Ltd.	40%
Hangzhou Industrial Asset Operation Investment Group Co., Ltd.	30%
Zhejiang Shenghua Biok Biology Co., Ltd.	30%

64. Founder Fubon Fund Management Co., Ltd.

Company Profile:
Founder Fubon Fund Management Co., Ltd. is the first mainland-Taiwan joint venture fund management company. It operates as a subsidiary of Founder Securities Co., Ltd. and Fubon Securities Investment Trust Co., Ltd. As of end Nov 2016, there were 8 funds (include 7 open-end funds and 1 closed-end fund) with total assets of RMB 23.22 billion under the management of Founder Fubon Fund Management Co., Ltd., which ranked sixty-fourth in China in terms of total assets.

Major Shareholders (2016 Nov):

Share Holder Name	Share Holding
Founder Securities Co., Ltd.	66.7%
Fubon Financial Holdings Co., Ltd.	33.3%

65. Golden Eagle Fund Management Co., Ltd.

Company Profile:
Golden Eagle Fund Management Co., Ltd. is an open-end equity mutual fund company launched in 2002. The company operates as a financial firm offering

investment management services. The company provides portfolio and fund management services as well as provides research and other financial services. As of end Nov 2016, there were 29 open-end funds with total assets of RMB 23.02 billion under the management of Golden Eagle Fund Management Co., Ltd., which ranked sixty-fifth in China in terms of total assets.

Major Shareholders (2016 Nov):

Share Holder Name	Share Holding
Guangzhou Securities Co., Ltd.	49%
Guangdong Midea Electric Appliances Co., Ltd.	20%
Guangzhou Phar. Holdings Co., Ltd.	20%
BEA Union Investment Management Ltd.	11%

66. Gfund Management Co., Ltd.

Company Profile:

Gfund Management Co., Ltd.'s business scope includes fund raising, fund sales and asset management. The company's shareholders have jointly contributed RMB 280 million. As of end Nov 2016, there were 11 funds (include 9 open-end funds and 2 closed-end funds) with total assets of RMB 22.84 billion under the management of Gfund Management Co., Ltd., which ranked sixty-sixth in China in terms of total assets.

Major Shareholders (2016 Nov):

Share Holder Name	Share Holding
Sinolink Securities Co., Ltd.	49%
Guangdong Baolihua New Energy Stock Co., Ltd.	19.5%
Suzhou Industrial Park Trirun Holding Group Co., Ltd.	19.5%
Yongjin Investment Holding Co., Ltd.	12%

67. Hongde Fund Management Co., Ltd.

Company Profile:

Hongde Fund Management Co., Ltd.'s business scope includes fund raising, fund sales, asset management and other businesses approved by the CSRC. The company is the first mutual fund management company established by professionals with official approval. As of end Nov 2016, there were 14 open-end funds with total assets of RMB 19.07 billion under the management of

Hongde Fund Management Co., Ltd., which ranked sixty-seventh in China in terms of total assets.

Major Shareholders (2016 Nov):

Share Holder Name	Share Holding
Wang Dexiao	26%
Sunshine Insurance Group Co., Ltd.	25%
Zhuhai Fund Changqing Equity Investment Limited Partnership	16.67%
Jiangsu Daocun Entity Development Co., Ltd.	13.88%
Nanjing Minsheng Leasing Co., Ltd.	13.88%
Shanghai Jieshuo Information Tech Co., Ltd.	4.58%

68. HSBC Jintrust Fund Management Co., Ltd.

Company Profile:

HSBC Jintrust Fund Management Co., Ltd. is a joint venture between Shanxi Trust Co., Ltd. and HSBC Global Asset Management (UK) Limited. The company's business scope includes manage the sales, subscription, redemption and registration of funds. As of end Nov 2016, there were 17 open-end funds with total assets of RMB 16.08 billion under the management of HSBC Jintrust Fund Management Co., Ltd., which ranked sixty-eighth in China in terms of total assets.

Major Shareholders (2016 Nov):

Share Holder Name	Share Holding
Shanxi Trust Co., Ltd.	51%
HSBC Global Asset Management (UK) Limited	49%

69. Harfor Fund Management Co., Ltd.

Company Profile:

Harfor Fund Management Co., Ltd. is a fund management company established in accordance with marketization mechanism. The company's business scope includes fund raising, fund sales, asset management and other businesses approved by the CSRC. As of end Nov 2016, there were 29 open-end funds with total assets of RMB 14.78 billion under the management of Harfor Fund Management Co., Ltd., which ranked sixty-ninth in China in terms of total assets.

Major Shareholders (2016 Nov):

Share Holder Name	Share Holding
Huaan Securities Co., Ltd.	49%
Anhui Credit Guaranty Group Co., Ltd.	27%
Hefei Xingtai Financial Holding Group Co., Ltd.	24%

70. Caitong Securities Asset Management Co., Ltd.

Company Profile:
Caitong Securities Assets Management Co., Ltd. provides financial advisory and investment management services. The company's financial products cover property investment and financing, financing of governments' infrastructure projects, securities investment and others. As of end Nov 2016, there were 2 open-end funds with total assets of RMB 13.83 billion under the management of Caitong Securities Assets Management Co., Ltd., which ranked seventieth in China in terms of total assets.

Major Shareholders (2016 Nov):

Share Holder Name	Share Holding
Caitong Securities Co., Ltd.	100%

71. First State Cinda Fund Management Co., Ltd.

Company Profile:
First State Cinda Fund Management Co., Ltd. is a privately-owned investment manager. The firm launches and manages equity, fixed income funds and balanced mutual funds for its clients. The company is the first fund company held by a state-owned asset management company as well as the first fund company with a shareholder from Australia. As of end Nov 2016, there were 16 open-end funds with total assets of RMB 13.12 billion under the management of First State Cinda Fund Management Co., Ltd., which ranked seventy-first in China in terms of total assets.

Major Shareholders (2016 Nov):

Share Holder Name	Share Holding
Cinda Securities Co., Ltd.	54%
Colonial First State Group Ltd.	46%

72. Truvalue Asset Management Co., Ltd.

Company Profile:
Truvalue Asset Management Co., Ltd. operates as a private equity firm. The Company serves customers in China. As of end Nov 2016, there were 22 open-end funds with total assets of RMB 12.74 billion under the management of Truvalue Asset Management Co., Ltd., which ranked seventy-second in China in terms of total assets.

Major Shareholders (2016 Nov):

Share Holder Name	Share Holding
First Capital Securities Co., Ltd.	70%
Shenzhen Jin Hexin Investment Parnership	30%

73. Soochow Asset Management Co., Ltd.

Company Profile:
Soochow Asset Management Co., Ltd. is a privately-owned investment manager. The firm manages equity, fixed-income funds and balanced mutual funds for its clients. The company's scope includes fund management, fund issuance and other businesses approved by the CSRC. As of end Nov 2016, there were 26 funds (including 25 open-end funds and 1 closed-end fund) with total assets of RMB 12.64 billion under the management of Soochow Asset Management Co., Ltd., which ranked seventy-third in China in terms of total assets.

Major Shareholders (2016 Nov):

Share Holder Name	Share Holding
Soochow Securities Co., Ltd.	70%
Shanghai Lansheng Corporation	30%

74. Taiping Fund Management Co., Ltd.

Company Profile:
Taiping Fund Management Co., Ltd.'s business scope includes fund raising, fund sales, asset management and others. The company was established in Shanghai with total registered capital of more than RMB 200 million. As of end Nov 2016, there were 2 open-end funds with total assets of RMB 11.92

billion under the management of Taiping Fund Management Co., Ltd., which ranked seventy-fourth in China in terms of total assets.

Major Shareholders (2016 Nov):

Share Holder Name	Share Holding
Taiping Asset Management Co., Ltd.	70.04%
Ashmore Investment Management Ltd.	14.98%
Central China Securities Co., Ltd.	14.98%

75. Qianhai Alliance Asset Management Co., Ltd.

Company Profile:
Qianhai Alliance Asset Management Co., Ltd.'s business scope includes fund raising, fund sales, asset management and others. The company is the 99th fund management company received approval from the CSRC. As of end Nov 2016, there were 6 open-end funds with total assets of RMB 11.73 billion under the management of Qianhai Alliance Asset Management Co., Ltd., which ranked seventy-fifth in China in terms of total assets.

Major Shareholders (2016 Nov):

Share Holder Name	Share Holding
Shenzhen Ju Shenghua Co., Ltd.	30%
Shenzhen Shenyue Holding Co., Ltd.	25%
Shenzhen Yueshang Logistics Co., Ltd	25%
Shenzhen Kaicheng Hengxin warehouse Co.,Ltd	20%

76. JT Asset Management Co., Ltd.

Company Profile:
JT Asset Management Co., Ltd. is the first public placement fund management company established by a PE investment management institution in China. The company's business scope includes fund raising, fund sales, asset management and other businesses approved by the CSRC. As of end Nov 2016, there were 11 open-end funds with total assets of RMB 11.6 billion under the management of JT Asset Management Co., Ltd., which ranked seventy-sixth in China in terms of total assets.

Major Shareholders (2016 Nov):

Share Holder Name	Share Holding
Kunwu Jiuding Capital Holdings Co., Ltd.	26%
Beijing Tongchuang Jiuding Management Co., Ltd.	25%
Lhasa Kunwu Jiuding Industry Investment Management Co., Ltd.	25%
Jiuzhou Securities Co., Ltd.	24%

77. China Fund Management Co., Ltd.

Company Profile:

China Fund Management Co., Ltd.'s business scope includes fund raising, fund sales, asset management and other businesses approved by the CSRC. As of end Nov 2016, there were 11 open-end funds with total assets of RMB 10.06 billion under the management of China Fund Management Co., Ltd., which ranked seventy-seventh in China in terms of total assets.

Major Shareholders (2016 Nov):

Share Holder Name	Share Holding
China Securities Co., Ltd.	55%
Aerospace Science & Technology Finance Co., Ltd.	25%
Jiangsu TV & Broadcast Intermediary Co., Ltd.	20%

78. JYAH Asset Management Co., Ltd.

Company Profile:

JYAH Asset Management Co., Ltd.'s business scope includes fund raising, fund sales, asset management and other businesses approved by the CSRC. As of end Nov 2016, there were 2 open-end funds with total assets of RMB 9.47 billion under the management of JYAH Asset Management Co., Ltd., which ranked seventy-eighth in China in terms of total assets.

Major Shareholders (2016 Nov):

Share Holder Name	Share Holding
AVIC Trust Co., Ltd.	30%
Guangdong Vanward New Electric Co., Ltd.	25%
Shanghai Huihong International Trade Co., Ltd.	25%
Fujian Shengnong Entity Co., Ltd.	20%

79. Zheshang Fund Management Co., Ltd.

Company Profile:

Zheshang Fund Management Co., Ltd. is a principal investment firm. The company's business scope includes fund raising, fund sales, asset management and other businesses approved by the CSRC. As of end Nov 2016, there were 15 funds (including 14 open-end funds and 1 closed-end fund) with total assets of RMB 9.29 billion under the management of Zheshang Fund Management Co., Ltd., which ranked seventy-ninth in China in terms of total assets.

Major Shareholders (2016 Nov):

Share Holder Name	Share Holding
Tonglian Capital Management Co., Ltd.	25%
Yang Shengtang Co., Ltd.	25%
Insigma Technology Co., Ltd.	25%
Zheshang Securities Co., Ltd.	25%

80. Goldstate Capital Fund Management Co., Ltd.

Company Profile:

Goldstate Capital Fund Management Co., Ltd.'s business scope includes fund raising, fund management and other businesses approved by the CSRC. The company was established in 13 Nov with registration in Free Trade Zone Supervision Administration Bureau. As of end Nov 2016, there were 11 open-end funds with total assets of RMB 9.02 billion under the management of Goldstate Capital Fund Management Co., Ltd., which ranked eightieth in China in terms of total assets.

Major Shareholders (2016 Nov):

Share Holder Name	Share Holding
Goldstate Securities Co., Ltd.	51%
Shanghai Quanyi Financial Information Service Co., Ltd.	49%

81. Dongxing Securities Co., Ltd.

Company Profile:

Dongxing Securities Co., Ltd. provides securities underwriting and sponsorship, trading, brokerage, and financing services. The company owns 72 branches and securities sales departments throughout the country. As of end Nov 2016, there were 5 open-end funds with total assets of RMB 8.56 billion under the management of Dongxing Securities Co., Ltd., which ranked eighty-first in China in terms of total assets.

Major Shareholders (2016 Nov):

Share Holder Name	Share Holding
China Orient Asset Management Co., Ltd.	52.74%
Shandong Hi-Speed Group Co., Ltd.	4.35%
Shanghai Guosheng Group Asset Co., Ltd.	3.52%
Fujian Tianbao Mining Group Co., Ltd.	3.36%
Tahoe Group Co., Ltd.	1.96%
Beijing Yongxin International Investment Group Co., Ltd.	1.83%
National Council for Social Security Fund	1.76%
Fujian New Lionful Investment Co., Ltd.	1.54%
China Chengtong Holding Group Ltd.	1.47%
Fujian Tahoe Investment Co., Ltd.	1.05%

82. Golden Trust Sinopac Fund Management Co., Ltd.

Company Profile:
Golden Trust Sinopac Fund Management Co., Ltd. provides securities underwriting and sponsorship, trading, brokerage, and financing services. The company is the first securities investment fund management company in Xiamen. As of end Nov 2016, there were 6 open-end funds with total assets of RMB 8.38 billion under the management of Golden Trust Sinopac Fund Management Co., Ltd., which ranked eighty-second in China in terms of total assets.

Major Shareholders (2016 Nov):

Share Holder Name	Share Holding
Xiamen International Trust Co., Ltd.	51%
Taiwan Yongfeng Securities Investment Trust Co., Ltd.	49 %

83. Maxwealth Fund Management Co., Ltd.

Company Profile:
Maxwealth Fund Management Co., Ltd. provides securities underwriting and sponsorship, trading, brokerage, and financing services. The company is among the third batch of pilot fund companies linked to banks. As of end Nov 2016, there were 5 open-end funds with total assets of RMB 8.17 billion

under the management of Maxwealth Fund Management Co., Ltd., which ranked eighty-third in China in terms of total assets.

Major Shareholders (2016 Nov):

Share Holder Name	Share Holding
Bank of Ningbo	67.5%
Lian Asset Management Co., Ltd.	10%
Song Yinong	4.995%
Zhao Nan	3.005%
Tian Zhongjia	2.775%
Zhao Peng	2.75%
Xu Manqing	1.85%
Li Jun	1.65%
Mao Hui	1.5%
Others	3.975%

84. Taikang Asset Management Co., Ltd.

Company Profile:
Taikang Asset Management Co., Ltd. is an asset management company. The company's investment scope includes fixed income investment, equity investment, foreign investment, infrastructure and real estate investment and others. As of end Nov 2016, there were 11 open-end funds with total assets of RMB 7.78 billion under the management of Taikang Asset Management Co., Ltd., which ranked eighty-fourth in China in terms of total assets.

Major Shareholders (2016 Nov):

Share Holder Name	Share Holding
Taikang Life Insurance Co., Ltd.	99.41%
China Credit Trust Co., Ltd.	0.59%

85. Western Leadbank Fund Management Co., Ltd.

Company Profile:
Western Leadbank Fund Management Co., Ltd. operates as a subsidiary of Western Securities Co., Ltd. The company's business scope includes fund raising, fund sales, asset management and other businesses approved by the CSRC. As of end Nov 2016, there were 16 funds (including 15 open-end funds and 1 closed-end fund) with total assets of RMB 7.78 billion under the management of Western Leadbank Fund Management Co., Ltd., which ranked eighty-fifth in China in terms of total assets.

Major Shareholders (2016 Nov):

Share Holder Name	Share Holding
Western Securities Co., Ltd.	51%
Shanghai Leadbank Fortune Asset Management Co., Ltd.	49%

86. First-trust Fund Management Co., Ltd.

Company Profile:
First-Trust Fund Management Co., Ltd. investment priorities are energy, transportation, raw materials. It has high reputation, stable reputation and excellent performance in the capital market. As of end Nov 2016, there were 19 funds (including 18 open-end funds and 1 closed-end fund) with total assets of RMB 5.90 billion under the management of First-Trust Fund Management Co., Ltd., which ranked eighty-sixth in China in terms of total assets.

Major Shareholders (2016 Nov):

Share Holder Name	Share Holding
Shandong International Trust Co., Ltd.	45%
Jiangsu Province Investment Management Co., Ltd.	30%
Qingdao Guosen Industrial Company	25%

87. Beixin Ruifeng Fund Management Co., Ltd.

Company Profile:
Beixin Ruifeng Fund Management Co., Ltd. is a small organization with approximately 20 full-time employees. It is focused on the open-end funds and provides professional service. As of end Nov 2016, there were 11 open-end funds with total assets of RMB 5.56 billion under the management of Beixin Ruifeng Fund Management Co., Ltd., which ranked eighty-seventh in China in terms of total assets.

Major Shareholders (2016 Nov):

Share Holder Name	Share Holding
Beijing International Trust Co., Ltd.	60%
Laizhou Ruihai Investment Co., Ltd.	40%

88. BOC International (China) Limited

Company Profile:
BOCI's mainland subsidiary, BOC International (China) Limited, was incorporated in Shanghai in February 2002, becoming the first Sino-foreign joint venture with a comprehensive securities dealer's license covering the primary and secondary A-share markets. To date, BOC International (China) Limited provides underwriting and broking of RMB-denominated stocks, government bonds, corporate bonds and B-share brokerage services. As of end Nov 2016, there were 2 open-end funds with total assets of RMB 5.41 billion under the management of BOC International (China) Limited, which ranked eighty-eighth in China in terms of total assets.

Major Shareholders (2016 Nov):

Share Holder Name	Share Holding
BOC International Holdings Limited	37.14%
China National Petroleum Corporation	15.92%
Shanghai Financial Industry Investment Fund	10.53%
Yunnan Investment Holding Group	9.09%
Jiangxi Copper Company Limited	5.26%

89. Changan Fund Management Co., Ltd.

Company Profile:
Changan Fund Management Co., Ltd. offers investment management services. The Company creates, markets, and manages funds, as well as provides management and counseling services for institutional investors and individuals. Changan Fund Management also offers telephone, mailing, e-mail, online, and short message services. As of end Nov 2016, there were 7 open-end funds with total assets of RMB 4.49 billion under the management of Changan Fund Management Co., Ltd., which ranked eighty-ninth in China in terms of total assets.

Major Shareholders (2016 Nov):

Share Holder Name	Share Holding
Changan International Trust Co.,Ltd.	29.63%
Shanghai Greenwoods Investment Development Co., Ltd.	25.93%
Shanhai Hengjia Meilian Development Co., Ltd.	24.44%
Fivestar Holdings Group Co., Ltd.	13.33%
China South Industries Group Finance Co., Ltd.	6.67%

90. Changjiang Securities (Shanghai) Asset Management Co., Ltd.

Company Profile:
Changjiang Securities (Shanghai) Asset Management Co., Ltd. provides financial asset management services. It offers acquires, manages, and disposes non-performing assets in state-owned commercial banks. It also provides debt collection, asset exchange and leasing, asset assignment and sale, debt restructure and enterprises reorganization, debt-equity swap, and asset securitization services. The company caters to real estate, textile, and pharmaceuticals sectors. Changjiang Securities (Shanghai) Asset Management was founded in 1999 and is based in Beijing, China. As of end Nov 2016, there were 2 open-end funds with total assets of RMB 4.3 billion under the management of Changjiang Securities (Shanghai) Asset Management Co., Ltd, which ranked ninetieth in China in terms of total assets.

Major Shareholders (2016 Nov):

Share Holder Name	Share Holding
Changjiang Securities Co., Ltd.	100%

91. Shanxi Securities Co., Ltd.

Company Profile:
Shanxi Securities Co., Ltd. operates as a security company in China. It engages in security broking, security proprietary, security asset management, security investment consulting, security investment advising, security investment fund agent distribution, and others. The company is also involved in the underwriting of stocks and bonds, as well as futures broking business. Shanxi Securities Co., Ltd. was founded in 1988 and is based in Taiyuan, China. As of end Nov 2016, there were 3 open-end funds with total assets of RMB 4.1 billion under the management of Shanxi Securities Co., Ltd., which ranked ninety-first in China in terms of total assets.

Major Shareholders (2016 Nov):

Share Holder Name	Share Holding
Shanxi Financial Investment Holding Group Co., Ltd.	30.42%
Taiyuan Iron & Steel (Group) Co., Ltd.	9.99%
Shanxi International Electricity Group Limited Company	7.52%

92. Nuode Asset Management Co., Ltd.

Company Profile:
Nuode Asset Management Co., Ltd. has the advanced investment experience and advanced theory to catch the market trend. It also provides debt collection, asset exchange and leasing, asset assignment and sale, debt restructure and enterprises reorganization, debt-equity swap, and asset securitization services. As of end Nov 2016, there were 12 funds (including 11 open-end funds and 1 closed-end fund) with total assets of RMB 3.97 billion under the management of Nuode Asset Management Co., Ltd., which ranked ninety-second in China in terms of total assets.

Major Shareholders (2016 Nov):

Share Holder Name	Share Holding
Tsinghua Holdings Co., Ltd.	51%
Creditease Huimin Investment Management (Beijing) Co., Ltd.	49%

93. CR Yuanta Fund Management Co., Ltd.

Company Profile:
CR Yuanta Fund Management Co., Ltd. is a joint venture company. CR Yuanta has launched different types of funds include money market funds, mixed type funds, index funds and bond funds to meet the demand of investors. As of end Nov 2016, there were 10 open-end funds with total assets of RMB 3.17 billion under the management of CR Yuanta Fund Management Co., Ltd., which ranked ninety-third in China in terms of total assets.

Major Shareholders (2016 Nov):

Share Holder Name	Share Holding
China Resources Szitic Trust Co., Ltd.	51%
Taiwan Yuanta Securities Investment Trust Co., Ltd.	49%

94. Jiangxin Fund Management Co., Ltd.

Company Profile:
Jiangxin Fund Management Co., Ltd. was approved by China securities regulatory commission (CSRC) and was established on January 28, 2013. Jiangxin Fund Management's business scope including fund raising, fund sales, specific customer asset management, asset management and other business licensed by the CSRC. As of end Nov 2016, there were 5 open-end funds with total assets of RMB 3.12 billion under the management of Jiangxin Fund Management Co., Ltd., which ranked ninety-fourth in China in terms of total assets.

Major Shareholders (2016 Nov):

Share Holder Name	Share Holding
Golden Sun Securities Co., Ltd.	30%
Hengsheng Sunshine Group	17.5%
Jiangxi Golden Unicorn Investment Co., Ltd.	17.5%
Yingtan Red stone Investment Management Co., Ltd.	17.5%
Yingtan Jufu Investment Management Co., Ltd.	17.5%

95. China Nature Asset Management Co., Ltd.

Company Profile:
China Nature Asset Management Co., Ltd. is a privately owned investment manager. It launches and manages equity, fixed income, and balanced mutual funds for its clients. The firm invests in the public equity and fixed income markets. China Nature AMC, which was founded in 2003 and is based in Shanghai, China. As of end Nov 2016, there were 10 open-end funds with total assets of RMB 3.04 billion under the management of China Nature Asset Management Co., Ltd., which ranked ninety-fifth in China in terms of total assets.

Major Shareholders (2016 Nov):

Share Holder Name	Share Holding
Jinlin Province Trust Co., Ltd.	61.25%
China Jilin Forest Industry Group	38.75%

96. CICC Fund Management Co., Ltd.

Company Profile:
CICC Fund Management Co., Ltd. (refers to as "CICC Fund") was founded in February 2014, wholly owned by CICC. CICC Fund is the ninetieth mutual fund management company approved by China Securities Regulatory Commission (CSRC). Meanwhile, it is the first mutual fund management company established by a single shareholder under China's regulation rules.

Supported by the advantages of CICC's franchise, business network and collective creativity, CICC Fund is aiming to be a leading fund management company with characteristic branding in the market, providing a fully-fledged, trustable and quality asset management service to investors. As of end Nov 2016, there were 7 open-end funds with total assets of RMB 3.03 billion under the management of CICC Fund Management Co., Ltd., which ranked ninety-sixth in China in terms of total assets.

Major Shareholders (2016 Nov):

Share Holder Name	Share Holding
China International Capital Corporation Limited	100%

97. Fuanda Fund Management Co., Ltd.

Company Profile:
Fuanda Fund Management Co., Ltd operates as an investment company. The company offers investment advisory, asset management services. As of end Nov 2016, there were 7 open-end funds with total assets of RMB 2.9 billion under the management of Fuanda Fund Management Co., Ltd., which ranked ninety-seventh in China in terms of total assets.

Major Shareholders (2016 Nov):

Share Holder Name	Share Holding
Nanjing Securities Co., Ltd.	49%
Jiangsu Communications Holding Co., Ltd.	26%
Nanjing Hexi New Town Assets Management Co., Ltd.	25%

98. Yingda Asset Management Co., Ltd.

Company Profile:
Since the establishment of the Yingda Asset Management Co., Ltd. has the integrity, responsibility and established "honesty, responsibility, professional and innovative" as the core of enterprise culture. Yingda Asset Management adheres to the interest of the fund holders as the operating principles. As of end Nov 2016, there were 7 open-end funds with total assets of RMB 2.20 billion under the management of Yingda Asset Management Co., Ltd., which ranked ninety-eighth in China in terms of total assets

Major Shareholders (2016 Nov):

Share Holder Name	Share Holding
Yingda International Trust Co., Ltd.	49%
China Communications Construction Co., Ltd.	36%
Aerospace Science and Engineering Finance Co., Ltd.	15%

99. Yimin Asset Management Co., Ltd.

Company Profile:
Yimin Asset Management Co., Ltd. operates as an investment advisor. The Company offers investment advisory and portfolio management services. It manages separate client-focused equity portfolios. As of end Nov 2016, there were 7 open-end funds with total assets of RMB 2.02 billion under the management of Yimin Asset Management Co., Ltd., which ranked ninety-ninth in China in terms of total assets.

Major Shareholders (2016 Nov):

Share Holder Name	Share Holding
Chongqing International Trust Co., Ltd.	49%
China New Era Co., Ltd.	31%
Zhongshan Securities Co., Ltd.	20%

100. Hongta Hotland Asset Management Co., Ltd.

Company Profile:
Hongta Hotland Asset Management Co., Ltd. is a professional investment services institution to provide asset management and adhere to the value investment idea and holder's interests first in order to achieve the fund holder asset appreciation. As of end Nov 2016, there were 6 open-end funds with total assets of RMB 1.82 billion under the management of Hongta Hotland Management Co., Ltd.

Major Shareholders (2016 Nov):

Share Holder Name	Share Holding
Hongta Securities Co., Ltd.	49%
Shenzhen Capital Group Co., Ltd.	26%
Beijing Huayuan Group Co., Ltd.	25%

101. CS Richland Asset Management Co., Ltd.

Company Profile:

CS Richland Asset Management Co., Ltd. was officially opened on September 6, 2015, which is the 101th mutual fund management companies and be with strong background of private equity fund. CS Richland Asset Management always implement the "holder interests first" top management guidelines and adhere to the operating principle of good faith. They provide professional, high-quality products, the innovation of finance and investment services, create growth value and the wealth for the investors. As of end Nov 2016, there were 2 open-end funds with total assets of RMB 1.78 billion under the management of CS Richland Asset Management Co., Ltd.

Major Shareholders (2016 Nov):

Share Holder Name	Share Holding
China Science&Merchants Capital Management Co., Ltd.	51%
Technology Financial Group	20%
Zhuhai Hengqin Wofu Investment Co., Ltd.	4.9%
Zhuhai Hengqin Wohai Investment Co., Ltd.	4.9%
Zhuhai Hengqin Wotu Innovation Investment Co., Ltd.	4.9%
Zhuhai Hengqin Woze Investment Co., Ltd.	4.9%
Zhuhai Hengqin Wozhi Investment Co., Ltd.	4.9%
Guangdong Zhongguang Investment Mangagement Co., Ltd.	4.5%

102. CDBS Cathay Asset Management Co., Ltd.

Company Profile:

CDBS Cathay Asset Management Co., Ltd. is a joint venture between Cathay securities Investment Trust and CDB Securities, the largest corporate bond underwriter in China, an affiliate of China Development Bank. As of end Nov 2016, there were 2 open-end funds with total assets of RMB 1.74 billion under the management of CDBS Cathay Asset Management Co., Ltd.

Major Shareholders (2016 Nov):

Share Holder Name	Share Holding
China Development Bank Securities	66.7%
Cathay Securities Investment Trust Co., Ltd	33.3%

103. Sinvo Fund Co., Ltd.

Company Profile:
Sinvo Fund Co., Ltd. is established with the approval of CSRC, to provide customers with professional fund management services for national fund management companies. Sinvo Fund use "professional to create opportunities, cooperation to achieve" value for the company development philosophy and adhere to the "people-oriented" development strategy. Meanwhile, Sinvo Fund is trying to build a great brand into the general investors. As of end Nov 2016, there were 2 open-end funds with total assets of RMB 1.32 billion under the management of Sinvo Fund Co., Ltd.

Major Shareholders (2016 Nov):

Share Holder Name	Share Holding
Sinvo Capital Holding Group	70%
Sinvo United Asset Management Co., Ltd.	30%

104. Zheshang Securities Asset Management Co., Ltd.

Company Profile:
Zheshang Securities Co., Ltd. engages in asset management, investment banking, securities brokerage, and futures brokerage business activities in China. As of end Nov 2016, there were 4 open-end funds with total assets of RMB 1.15 billion under the management of Zheshang Securities Asset Management Co., Ltd.

Major Shareholders (2016 Nov):

Share Holder Name	Share Holding
Zheshang Securities Co., Ltd.	100%

105. Huarong Securities Co., Ltd.

Company Profile:
Huarong Securities Co., Ltd., together with its subsidiaries, provides securities brokerage and trading services. The company offers investment banking, asset management and customer service. As of end Nov 2016, there were 3 open-end funds with total assets of RMB 585 million under the management of Huarong Securities Co., Ltd.

Major Shareholders (2016 Nov):

Share Holder Name	Share Holding
China Huarong Asset Management Co., Ltd.	81.56%
China Gezhouba (Group) Corporation	4.61%
Shenzhen Keming Industrial Co., Ltd	2.27%
Beijing Niusente investment Co., Ltd.	2.24%
Jiujiang Hehui Import and Export Co., Ltd.	1.69%

106. V-FUND Co., Ltd.

Company Profile:
V-FUND Co., Ltd. was jointly sponsored by well-known listed companies, PE organization and securities. V-FUND faces the prospect, open inclusive, fierce competition in the market for big capital tube, aims to build a fund management company with Internet financial strategy and internationalization strategy. As of end Nov 2016, there were 2 open-end funds with total assets of RMB 389 million under the management of V-FUND Co., Ltd.

Major Shareholders (2016 Nov):

Share Holder Name	Share Holding
United Venture Guarantee Group	38%
Dalian UCF Capital	37%
Beijing Pengkang Investment Co., Ltd.	25%

107. JX Asset Management Co., Ltd.

Company Profile:
JX Asset Management Co., Ltd. was established in Shenzhen with the approval of CSRC. Its business scope includes fund raising, fund sales, asset management, specific customer asset management and other business under the permission of CSRC. As of end Nov 2016, there were 4 open-end funds with total assets of RMB 314 million under the management of JX Asset Management Co., Ltd.

Major Shareholders (2016 Nov):

Share Holder Name	Share Holding
Shenzhen Excellence Investment Co., Ltd.	34%
Anhui Guoyuan Trust Co., Ltd.	31%
Shenzhen Giant Wealth Investment Co., Ltd.	28.5%
Yin Kesheng	6.5%

108. Donghai Fund Management Co., Ltd.

Company Profile:

Donghai Fund Management Co., Ltd. is an organization in the open-end investment management companies in China. On February 25 2013, Donghai Fund Management is formally established by Donghai securities Co., Ltd., Ever-Rising Group and Suzhou Xiangcheng District Jiangnan Chemical Fiber Group Co., Ltd. As of end Nov 2016, there were 3 open-end funds with total assets of RMB 207 million under the management of Donghai Fund Management Co., Ltd.

Major Shareholders (2016 Nov):

Share Holder Name	Share Holding
Donghai Securities Co., Ltd.	45%
Ever-Rising Group	30%
Suzhou Xiangcheng District Jiangnan Chemical Fiber Group Co., Ltd.	25%

109. Horizon Asset Management Co., Ltd.

Company Profile:

Horizon Asset Management Co., Ltd was founded in 2016, which is an investment firm focusing on fixed-income and equity investment in China. It provides customers with professional fund management services for national fund management companies. As of end Nov 2016, there were 1 open-end funds with total assets of RMB 200 million under the management of Horizon Asset Management Co., Ltd. which ranked one hundred and ninth in China in terms of total assets.

Major Shareholders (2016 Nov):

Share Holder Name	Share Holding
He Bin	35.7%
Qin Jun	35.5%
Dai Xinhua	4.9%
Guo Xiaofeng	4.9%
Zhao Yi	4.9%
Guo Zhaoqiang	4.5%
Liu Qiang	4.5%
Yin Xijie	3.3%
Wang Fude	1.8%

110. Hotland Innovation Asset Management Co., Ltd.

Company Profile:
Hotland Innovation Asset Management Co., Ltd. engages as a fund company that specializes in VC/PE investment management which is based in China. As of end Nov 2016, there were 2 open-end funds with total assets of RMB 176 million under the management of Hotland Innovation Asset Management Co., Ltd.

Major Shareholders (2016 Nov):

Share Holder Name	Share Holding
Shenzhen Capital Group Co., Ltd.	100%

111. Guodu Securities Co., Ltd.

Company Profile:
GuoDu Securities Co., Ltd., together with its subsidiaries, provides securities brokerage services in China. The company operates through brokerage, trading, credit transaction, entrusted asset management, investment banking, and other business segments. It also offers securities investment consultation services; financial consultation services related to securities trading and investment activities; securities underwriting and sponsorship services; securities dealing services; asset management services; consignment services related to securities investment funds and financial products business; and securities lending and borrowing services. As of end Nov 2016, there were 1 open-end fund with total assets of RMB 163 million under the management of Guodu Securities Co., Ltd.

Major Shareholders (2016 Nov):

Share Holder Name	Share Holding
China Credit Trust Co., Ltd.	13.3264%
Beijing International Trust Co., Ltd.	8.5926%
Guohua Energy Investment Co., Ltd.	7.6933%
Oriental Venture Capital Management Co., Ltd.	5.1288%
Shandong Ocean Investment Co., Ltd.	5.1288%
Tianjin Chongxin Asset Management Co., Ltd.	4.717%
Chongqing International Trust Co., Ltd	4.717%
Waranty Asset Management Co., Ltd.	3.7736%
Shenzhen Yuanwei Investment Co., Ltd.	3.3089%
Shanghai Lihua investment and Development Co. Ltd.	3.1435%

112. Mirae Asset Management Co., Ltd.

Company Profile:
Mirae Asset Management primarily provides its services to institutional and private investors. It provides investment advisory services. The firm launches and manages equity, fixed income, and balanced mutual funds for its clients. It invests in the public equity and fixed income markets of Asia. As of end Nov 2016, there were 1 open-end fund with total assets of RMB 18 million under the management of Mirae Asset Management Co., Ltd.

Major Shareholders (2016 Nov):

Share Holder Name	Share Holding
Huachen Trust Co., Ltd.	40%
Buchang Pharma Co., Ltd.	35%
Mirae Asset Management Co., Ltd.	25%

HSBC Jintrust has a comprehensive onshore fund product line of 17 products, which include fund types such as Equities, Bonds, Mixed, Money Market etc., while also serving as the investment adviser for many offshore products (QFII/RQFII/CIBM). HSBC Jintrust is innovative and oversaw the issuance of the first domestic life cycle fund – HSBC Jintrust 2016 Lifecycle Fund, the first low carbon themed fund – Carbon Awareness Equity Fund and its first strategy themed fund Dual Core Strategy Fund, with the newest fund being the HSBC Jintrust All China Equity Fund.

Do the right thing for our clients

As CEO Wang Dong recounted the company's journey over the past 10 years, the core principle he always adhered to was "drawing a clear line between the 'dos and don'ts' when making business decisions".

"We always put the interests of our customers first and use it as a barometer as to what we will or will not do. For example, we do not offer any structured products nor do we provide leverage for our retail customers because we ultimately believe that retail products should be simple and transparent.

We emphasize on the core product principle of "true to label", and every fund product has a distinct investment theme. We are able to guarantee our customers that we will stick with our stated investment theme. As long as we do not deviate from the theme, we will be able to produce a more consistent risk/return profile within the target investment scope over a longer horizon of five years or more when compared with other similar funds."

— CEO Wang Dong

HSBC Jintrust Large Cap Equity Fund and Technology Equity Fund invest mainly in large-cap blue chip stocks and TMT growth stocks respectively, and are 2 very different types of funds. However, in the past 5 years (as of 31 Oct 2016), the Large Cap Equity Fund had an annual return of 19%, placing it 2nd amongst 140 equity funds on Morningstar. The Technology Equity Fund had an annual return of 18%, pacing it 4th on the list.

Performance can be better explained, predicted and repeated

According to HSBC Jintrust CIO Cao Qing (Quentin), the reasons behind good performance is down to three key components: Explainable, Predictable and Repeatable. Explainable performance means we understand the sources of our excess returns from taking various risk exposures; Predictable performance means clients are able to expect similar returns in the future with our products taking similar risk exposures; and finally Repeatable performance means our excess returns are down to investment strategies and processes, not through pure luck, hence can be repeated in the future. As a result, investors can select our products that match their own needs to achieve their investment objectives, which is what we value as "true to label" investment.

Our investment strategies include stock selection strategies, sector allocation strategies, asset allocation strategies and are used in the construction and adjustments of portfolios. At the same time, there are risk measures to help fund managers control portfolio risks ex-ante and there are periodic performance attribution reports to analyze the effectiveness of investment strategies ex-post, thereby helping to further improve portfolio construction. Through establishment and implementation of a disciplined approach, it allows HSBC Jintrust to achieve an "explainable, predictable and repeatable" investment process.

Foreign FMCs in China

Since the first deal inked between China Merchants and ING in 2003, more foreign managers are opting to set up joint ventures in China.

Foreign fund managers are attracted by the positive performance of joint venture fund management companies (JV FMCs), the Chinese government's willingness to open up the sector and the surging growth the industry. As of today, 45 mutual fund companies in China are joint ventures.

There are a few ways to enter China's fund management industry, but the preferred method of most foreign institutions is to cooperate with a Chinese partner to set up a new JV FMC rather than to buy shares from an existing FMC. Currently, foreign players have partnerships with Chinese brokerage houses, trust and investment companies, financial holdings and banks.

Since December 2004, the Chinese government has been relaxing the limit on foreign ownership in JV FMCs. According to WTO agreements, foreign partners in a JV FMC now can go up to beyond 33 per cent to 49 per cent. 2005 will prove to be the year of foreign FMC. It will witness existing foreign institutions in JV FMC increasing their stake to 49%.

Compared to the local FMCs, JV FMCs, though still in a weak position as they are relatively new in the industry, have expanded very quickly. Only three JV FMCs are ranked in the top 10 FMCs in terms of NAV in China.

Table 2.12 List of Joint-Venture Fund Management Companies (as of end Oct 2016)

Fund Management Company	Name of Foreign Parnter	Foreign Parnter Nationality	Shares Held By Foreign %
Guotai Asset Management Co., Ltd.	Assicurazioni Generali S.P.A	Italy	30
China Asset Management Co., Ltd.	Power Corporation of Canada	Canada	10
Penghua Fund Management Co., Ltd.	Eurizon Capital SGR S.p.A.	Italy	49
Harvest Fund Management Co., Ltd.	Deutsche Assets Management (Asia) Limited	Singapore	30
Changsheng Fund Management Co., Ltd.	DBS Bank Ltd.	Singapore	33
Fullgoal Fund Management Co., Ltd.	Bank of Montreal	Canada	27.78
Rongtong Fund Management Co., Ltd.	Nikko Asset Management Co., Ltd.	Japan	40
UBS SDIC Fund Management Co., Ltd.	Union Bank of Switzerland	Switzerland	49
Manulife Teda Fund Management Co., Ltd.	Manulife Asset anagement (Hongkong) Limited	China Hong Kong	49
Golden Eagle Asset Management Co., Ltd.	BEA Union Investment Management Ltd.	China Hong Kong	11
Fortune Sg Fund Management Co., Ltd.	Lyxor Asset Management S.A.	France	49
Morgan Stanley Huaxin Fund Management Co., Ltd.	Morgan Stanley International Holdings Inc.	United States	37
GTJA Allianz Fund Management Limited Company	Allianz Group	Germany	49
HFT Investment Management Co., Ltd.	BNPP IP BE Holding	Belgium	49
Invesco Great Wall Fund Management Co., Ltd.	INVESCO Asset Management Limited	United Kingdom	49
Aegon-Industrial Fund Management Co., Ltd.	AEGON International B.V.	Netherlands	49
SWS MU Fund Management Co., Ltd.	SWS MU Fund Management Co., Ltd.	Japan	33
Zhong Hai Fund Management Co., Ltd.	Lacompagnie Financiere Edmond De Rothschild Banque	France	25
China International Fund Management Co., Ltd.	J.P. Morgan Asset Management (U.K.) Limited	United Kingdom	49
Everbright Pramerica Fund Management Co., Ltd.	Pramerical Investment Management Co., Ltd.	United States	45

Fund Management Company	Name of Foreign Parnter	Foreign Parnter Nationality	Shares Held By Foreign %
Bank of China Investment Management Co., Ltd.	(Blackrock Investment Management (UK) Ltd.	United Kingdom	16.5
Franklin Templeton Sealand Fund Management Co., Ltd.	Templeton International Inc.	United States	49
Huatai-Pinebridge Fund Management Co., Ltd.	PineBridge Investments LLC	United States	49
ICBC Credit Suisse Asset Management Co., Ltd.	Credit Suisse AG	Switzerland	20
Bank of Communications Schroder Fund Management Co., Ltd.	Schroder Investment Management Limited	United Kingdom	30
Citic-prudential Fund Management Co., Ltd.	Prudential Group	United Kingdom	49
CCB Principal Asset Management Co., Ltd.	Principal Financial Services, Inc.	United States	25
HSBC Jintrust Fund Management Co., Ltd.	HSBC Investments (UK) Limited	United Kingdom	49
China Post Fund Management Co., Ltd.	Sumitomo Mitsui Banking Corporation	Japan	24
First State Cinda Fund Management Co., Ltd.	Colonial First State Group Ltd.	Australia	46
Zhong Ou Asset Management Co., Ltd.	Unione di Banche Italiane S.c.p.a	Italy	35
Everbright Pramerica Fund Management Co., Ltd.	Pramerical Investment Management Co., Ltd.	United States	45
Goldstate Capital Fund Management Co., Ltd.	Value Parters HongKong Limited	China Hong Kong	49
Axa Spdb Investment Managers Co., Ltd.	AXA Investment Managers	France	39
ABC-CA Fund Management Co., Ltd.	Credit Agricole Asset Management	France	33
Minsheng Royal Fund Management Co., Ltd.	Royal Bank of Canada	Canada	30
Ping An Uob Fund Management Co., Ltd.	UOB Asset Management Ltd.	Singapore	25
Founder Fubon Fund Management Co., Ltd.	Fubon Asset Management Co.,Ltd.	China Taiwan	33
ZhongYuan Yingshi Stone Fund Management Co., Ltd.	Ashmore Investment Management Limited	United Kingdom	49
CR Yuanta Fund Management Co., Ltd.	Yuanta Securities Investment Trust Co., Ltd.	China Taiwan	49
Bank of Beijing Scotiabank Asset Management Co., Ltd.	Bank of Nova Scotia	Canada	33
CDBS Cathay Asset Management Co., Ltd.	Cathay Securities Investment Trust Co., Ltd.	China Taiwan	33
Maxwealth Fund Management Co., Ltd.	Lion Global Investors Limited	Singapore	10
China Life AMP Asset Management Co., Ltd.	AMP Capital Investors Limited	Australia	14.97
Golden Trust Sinopac Fund Management Co., Ltd.	SinoPac Securities Investment Trust Co., Ltd.	China Taiwan	49

Source: China Knowledge Mutual Funds Database

Foreign Mutual Funds Vying China's US$ 1.2 Trillion Market

As recent as 30 June 2016, the China Securities Regulatory Commission (CSRC) authorized the Asset Management Association of China (AMAC) to publish Q&As clarifying qualification requirements for foreign companies looking to set up private securities fund management entities. This will allow foreign companies to raise funds non-publicly from qualified investors within China and invest it in domestic capital markets.

This is a giant step forward by the Chinese government as they continue to open their financial markets. By allowing foreign fund management companies to raise capital locally to invest in domestic stocks, bonds, futures etc, it will serve as a proxy for foreigners to participate directly in China's financial markets. This is great news for foreign investors as China's financial instruments such as bonds and treasuries tend to offer higher coupons than other international countries. As China's mutual funds markets continue to mature, there will be greater growth; retail investors are turning to Fund of Funds as they look to financial professionals to invest their money.

Foreign fund management companies can look to establish themselves in China through either a Sino-Foreign Joint Venture Fund (JV) or as a Wholly Foreign-owned Enterprise (WFOE). A Sino-foreign JV would require a domestic and foreign shareholder who must have a minimum paid up capital of RMB 300 million in convertible currency, and are only entitled up to 49% stake in the JV. In contrast, a WFOE would allow a foreign company to own the company completely if the WFOE can help facilitate the development of China's economy while attaining significant economic results.

How to Set Up a Fund in China

There are several ways a foreign company can look to set up a fund management company in China. 2 of the most popular ways would be through a Sino-foreign joint venture (JV) with a local company or setting up a Wholly Foreign-owned Enterprise (WFOE).

Sino-foreign JV Fund

A Sino-foreign joint venture means starting a company in China with at least one foreign and one Chinese shareholder. The domestic shareholder with the highest shareholding stake will be the major shareholder, while foreign shareholders can only hold a maximum stake of 49%. As of today, 45 fund management companies in China are joint ventures.

Table 2.13 Sino-foreign JV Fund

Requirements	Domestic Shareholders > 5%	Domestic Major Shareholders, min > 25%	Foreign Shareholder
Registered Capital & Net Assets	>RMB 100 million	> RMB 300 million	> RMB 300 million in convertible currency
Axa Spdb Investment Managers Co., Ltd.	✓	✓	✓
ABC-CA Fund Management Co., Ltd.	✓	✓	✓
Minsheng Royal Fund Management Co., Ltd.	✓	✓	✓
Ping An Uob Fund Management Co., Ltd.	✓	✓	✓
Founder Fubon Fund Management Co., Ltd.	✓	✓	✓
ZhongYuan Yingshi Stone Fund Management Co., Ltd.	✓	✓	✓
CR Yuanta Fund Management Co., Ltd.	✓	✓	✓
Bank of Beijing Scotiabank Asset Management Co., Ltd.	✓	✓	✓
CDBS Cathay Asset Management Co., Ltd.	✓	✓	✓
Maxwealth Fund Management Co., Ltd.	✓	✓	✓
China Life AMP Asset Management Co., Ltd.	X	✓	✓
Golden Trust Sinopac Fund Management Co., Ltd.	X	X	✓

Source: *The Measures for the Administration of Securities Investment Fund Management Companies*

WFOE

A WFOE is a privately held limited liability company in China in which all shareholders are foreign.

The establishment of a WFOE must facilitate the development of China's economy and can achieve significant economic results.

Application Process

1. Apply for a corporate name from the Industrial and Commercial Bureau
2. Apply for a temporary foreign exchange account from the State Administration of Foreign Exchange
3. Apply for an approval certificate from the Municipal Commission of Commerce
4. Apply for the business license from the Industrial and Commercial Bureau within 30 days of securing an approval
5. Apply for company stamp and records from the Exit and Entry Administration Bureau

For more information, look into <Detailed Rules for the Implementation of the Law on Wholly Foreign-Owned Enterprises> on the PBoC website of Ministry of Commerce.

Entry ban lifted

As recent as 30 June 2016, the China Securities Regulatory Commission (CSRC) authorized the Asset Management Association of China (AMAC) to publish Q&As clarifying qualification requirements, registration and filing processes for WFOEs and JVs to apply for registration as private securities fund management entities. This will allow the registered entity to raise funds non-publicly from qualified investors in China and invest in domestic capital markets without involving cross-border capital flows. Moreover, investments that can be made with the assets of Privately-raised Investment Funds shall include trading stocks, equities, bonds, futures, options, fund units etc.

Qualified Investors

A qualified investor must have the appropriate capability of risk identification and risk tolerance, and invests at least RMB 1 million in a single Privately-raised Fund.

Moreover, the qualified should have net assets of no less than RMB 10 million or have financial assets of no less than RMB 3 million or average annual personal income of no less than RMB 500,000 in the past three years.

Application Process

1. Apply for registration to the AMAC and submit relevant documents.
2. Application results will be published via AMAC's website within 20 working days.
3. Record-filing procedure to be done via AMAC once fundraising is complete.

For more information, refer to <Interim Measures for the Supervision and Administration of Privately-Raised Investment Funds.

PART THREE:

FUND MANAGERS

There are more than 1,400 fund managers in China's mutual fund market. Each fund manager's investment strategy is almost identical.

In section 3.1, we reviewed statistics on different fund managers' performance. Then we filtered the data based on fund managers' experience. The tables included the performance of fund managers with 1-3 years of experience. In 2017, fund managers' medium- and long-term performance may be effected by an increased emphasis on fund of funds.

Section 3.2 lists information about 1,388 fund managers, including names, work experience, gender, and companies. More specific information can be found in our China Knowledge mutual fund database.

3.1 FUND MANAGERS' PERFORMANCE

Table 3.1 Top 10 QDII Fund Manager Performance

Ranking	Name	Experience (Yr)	Fund Mgt Company	Representative Fund	Recent 1Q Yields(%)
1	You Bainian	5	Penghua Fund Mgt.	Penghua Global High-Yield QDII Fund	43.65
2	Zhou Jing	3	Fortune SG Fund Mgt.	Fortune SG S&P Oil & Gas Exploration & Production QDII Fund	13.12
3	Zhang Jun	8	China International Fund Mgt.	China International Global Natural Resources QDII Fund	11.53
4	Chen Xuelin	3	Bank of China Investment Mgt.	BOC S&P Global Resources EW Index Fund (QDII)	11.29
5	Li Bohan	3	CCB Principal Asset Mgt.	CCB Principal Global Resources Hybrid QDII Fund	9.24
6	Zhao Yingkai	5	CCB Principal Asset Mgt.	CCB Principal Global Resources Hybrid QDII Fund	9.24
7	Li Yaozhu	1	GF Fund Mgt.	GF Global Agricultural Index Fund (QDII)	9.15
8	Wan Qiong	1	Bosera Fund Mgt.	Bosera S&P 500 ETF (QDII)	8.64
9	Ran Linghao	5	Dacheng Fund Mgt.	Dacheng S&P 500 QDII Fund	8.05
10	Xue Tian	5	Chang Xin Asset Mgt.	Changxin S&P 100 Index Fund(QDII)	7.16

Source: China Knowledge Mutual Funds Database

You Bainian who works in Penghua Fund Management Co., Ltd. remains 1St with 43.65% return in recent 1Q. His representative fund is Penghua Global High-Yield QDII Fund. Zhoujin came in second and manages Fortune SG S&P Oil & Gas Exploration & Production QDII Fund with 13.12% return in recent 1Q. Zhang Jun makes up top 3 with 11.53% return in recent 1Q. He is in charge of China International Global Natural Resources QDII Fund in the China International Fund Management Co., Ltd.

Table 3.2 Top 10 Guaranteed Fund Manager Performance

Ranking	Name	Experience (Yr)	Fund Mgt Company	Representative Fund	Recent 1Q Yields(%)
1	Wu Jianyi	2	China Southern Fund Mgt.	China Southern Hengyuan Principal Protected Hybrid Fund	3.56
2	Sun Lumin	6	China Southern Fund Mgt.	China Southern Guaranteed Fund	1.79
3	Zhang Yan	1	Bank of Communications Schroder Fund Mgt.	Bocom Schroders Enhanced Income Guaranteed Bond Fund	1.60
4	Zhao Nan	Less 1Yr	New China Fund Mgt.	New China Axin-1 Principal Guaranteed Hybrid Fund	0.88
5	Sun Hui	Less 1Yr	Yinhua Fund Mgt.	Yinhua Yongxiang Principal Guaranteed Hybrid Fund	0.49
6	Wang Yue	3	Zhongrong Fund Mgt.	Zhongrong Rong'an Principal Guaranteed Hybrid Fund	0.40
7	Zhu Hong	6	CCB Principal Asset Mgt.	CCB Principal Guaranteed III Hybrid Fund	0.30
8	Cai Bin	8	Changsheng Fund Mgt.	Changsheng Tongxiang Principal Guaranteed Hybrid Fund-A	0.10
9	Wu Lianggu	4	BOC International (China) Limited	BOC Securities Principal Guaranteed I Hybrid Fund	0
10	Bai Bingyang	Less 1Yr	BOC International (China) Limited	BOC Securities Principal Guaranteed I Hybrid Fund	0

Source: China Knowledge Mutual Funds Database

Wu jianyi in the China Southern Fund Management Co., Ltd. was top spot with 3.56% return in recent 1Q. His representative fund is China Southern Hengyuan Principal Protected Hybrid Fund. Sun Lumin took the second place and manages China Southern Guaranteed Fund with 1.79% return in recent 1Q, followed by Zhang Yan who works in Bank of Communications Schroder Fund Management Co., Ltd. She manages Bocom Schroders Enhanced Income Guaranteed Bond Fund with 1.6% return in recent 1Q.

Table 3.3 Top 10 Money Fund Manager Performance

Ranking	Name	Experience (Yr)	Fund Mgt Company	Representative Fund	Recent 1Q Yields(%)
1	Yu Qiming	4	JYAH Asset Mgt.	JYAH Money Market Fund-B	1.44
2	Ji Huijuan	1	JYAH Asset Mgt.	JYAH Money Market Fund-B	1.44
3	Wang Yuexi	3	JT Asset Mgt.	JT Ritianjin Money Market Fund-B	0.90
4	Sang Jingqiao	Less 1Yr	Huarong Securities	HUARONG Cash Income Money Market Fund-B	0.87
5	Yan Wenhao	2	UBS SDIC Fund Mgt.	UBS SDIC Value-Added Treasure Money Market Fund-A	0.87
6	Yao Hang	3	Orient Fund Mgt.	Orient Golden Account Book Money Market Fund-B	0.85
7	Liu Chaoyang	5	E Fund Mgt.	E Fund Wealth Express Money Market Fund-B	0.85
8	Lu Ying	Less 1Yr	Chang Xin Asset Mgt.	Changxin Interest Income Stock Fund-B	0.85
9	Liang Ying	2	E Fund Mgt.	E Fund Cash Income Money Market Fund-B	0.84
10	Shi Dayi	4	E Fund Mgt.	E Fund Cash Income Money Market Fund-B	0.84

Source: China Knowledge Mutual Funds Database

Yu Qiming and Ji Huijuan work in the JYAH Asset Management Co., Ltd. were 1st together with 1.44% return in recent 1Q. They both manage JYAH Money Market Fund-B. Wang Yuexi made up top 3 with 0.9% return in recent 1Q. She is in charge of JT Ritianjin Money Market Fund-B in the JT Asset Management Co., Ltd.

Table 3.4 Top 10 Structured Fund Manager Performance

Ranking	Name	Experience (Yr)	Fund Mgt Company	Representative Fund	Recent 1Q Yields(%)
1	Long Chuan	1	Essence Fund Mgt.	Anxin CSI One Belt One Road Theme Index Structured Fund	12.60
2	Liu Weilin	2	ICBC Credit Suisse Asset Mgt.	ICBCCS CSI High-Speed Railway Industry Index Structured Fund	12.36
3	Deng Hu	1	Chang Xin Asset Mgt.	Changxin CSI One Belt One Road Structured Fund	10.76
4	Chen Jianbo	Less 1Yr	China Merchants Fund Mgt.	China Merchants CSI Liquor Index Structured Fund	9.81
5	Li Jialiang	Less 1Yr	China Southern Fund Mgt.	China Southern Emerging Consumption Growth Structured Equity Fund	9.48
6	Jiang Qiujie	2	China Southern Fund Mgt.	China Southern Emerging Consumption Growth Structured Equity Fund	9.48
7	Sun Wei	1	China Southern Fund Mgt.	China Southern CSI State-Owned Enterprises Reform Index Structured Fund	9.01
8	Chen Long	1	Penghua Fund Mgt.	Penghua CNI FERROUS METALS Index Structured Fund	8.28
9	Yu Bin	2	Penghua Fund Mgt.	Penghua CSI Alcoholic Drink Index Structured Fund	8.18
10	Zhang Shengxian	1	Fullgoal Fund Mgt.	Fullgoal CSI State-Owned Enterprises Reform Index Structured Fund	7.08

Source: China Knowledge Mutual Funds Database

Long Chuan in the Essence Fund Management Co., Ltd. was top spot with 12.6% return in recent 1Q. His representative fund is Anxin CSI One Belt One Road Theme Index Structured Fund. Liu Weilin took the second place and manages ICBCCS CSI High-Speed Railway Industry Index Structured Fund with 12.36% return in recent 1Q, followed by Deng Hu who works in Chang Xin Asset Management Co., Ltd. He manages Changxin CSI One Belt One Road Structured Fund with 10.76% return in recent 1Q.

Table 3.5 Top 10 Equity Fund Manager Performance

Ranking	Name	Experience (Yr)	Fund Mgt Company	Representative Fund	Recent 1Q Yields(%)
1	Qiu Dongrong	2	HSBC Jintrust Fund Mgt.	HSBC Jintrust Large-Cap Fluctuate Selected Equity Fund-A	8.69
2	Yang Xinxin	3	HuaAn Fund Mgt.	Huaan New Silk Road Theme Equity Fund	7.92
3	Rao Yuhan	1	Guotai Asset Mgt.	Guotai Central Enterprises Reform Equity Fund	6.81
4	Zhou Yingbo	1	Zhong Ou Asset Mgt.	Lombarda China Times Pioneer Equity Initiating Fund	6.81
5	Han Dongyan	1	Lion Fund Mgt.	Lion Advanced Manufacturing Equity Fund	6.80
6	Xiao Nan	4	E Fund Mgt.	E Fund Consumption Sector Equity Fund	5.93
7	Dong Weiwei	1	Everbright Pramerica Fund Mgt.	E&P Mingxin Dynamic Allocation Equity Fund	5.62
8	Wei Xiaoxue	4	Everbright Pramerica Fund Mgt.	E&P Mingxin Dynamic Allocation Equity Fund	5.62
9	Zhang Yufan	Less 1Yr	ICBC Credit Suisse Asset Mgt.	ICBCCS Industry Logistic Equity Fund-A	4.97
10	Li Shuai	1	Harvest Fund Mgt.	Harvest Low Price Strategy Equity Fund	4.86

Source: China Knowledge Mutual Funds Database

Qiu Dongrong made up the top 1 with 8.69% return in recent 1Q. He works in the HSBC Jintrust Fund Management Co., Ltd. and his representative fund is HSBC Jintrust Large-Cap Fluctuate Selected Equity Fund-A, followed by Yan Xinxin is in the Hua An Fund Management Co., Ltd. with 7.92% return in recent 1Q. Rou Yuhan works in the Guotai Asset Management Co., Ltd. came in third and manages Guotai Central Enterprises Reform Equity Fund with 6.81% return in recent 1Q.

"First, we make a rankings table of listed stocks that possess low PB and high potential ROE. From there, we will pick out individual stocks and take corporate governance, asset quality and other factors that might affect ROE into consideration. Subsequently, we will take a bottom up approach in finding the most undervalued stocks and incorporate our product's investment objectives and risk controls requirements to construct a portfolio.

While making investments, the reason behind underperforming the market is a result of losses made during market adjustments rather than mediocre gains. The advantage of the "Profitability – Valuation" strategy is that it can provide a disciplined framework to compare and identify stocks with either limited downside, or stocks with sufficient upside. Leveraging on the asymmetry of investment risks and returns, the resulting portfolio construction can generate excess returns." Said Qiu Dongrong (Dolon), the fund manager of Dual Core Strategy Fund.

In 2015, China's A-shares market underwent volatile swings. The CSI 300 Index and ChiNext index suffered the largest declines of 45% and 55% from peak respectively. In comparison, Dual Core Strategy Fund's maximum drawdown was 24%, compared with an average of 44% maximum drawdown among funds in the same Morningstar category. As of December 9th, 2016, the HSBC Jintrust Dual Core Strategy Fund achieved 32.29% annualized return during the past two years, ranking in the top 10% among 531 similar type funds according to Morningstar China's rankings, and realizing its investment objectives of higher returns with lower risks.

According to fund manager Qiu, the crucial part of the investment process lies within disciplined risk controls and can help the fund manager to be more focused on factors that drives higher excess returns.

Table 3.6 Top 10 Bond Fund Manager Performance

Ranking	Name	Experience (Yr)	Fund Mgt Company	Representative Fund	Recent 1Q Yields(%)
1	Li Xianjun	Less 1Yr	New China Fund Mgt.	New China Credit Enhanced Gained Bond Fund-A	1.74
2	Yin Peijun	2	Harfor Fund Mgt.	Harfor Consolidate Return Bond Fund	1.50
3	Song Haijuan	3	Citic-Prudential Fund Mgt.	Citic-Prudential The Three Gains Bond Fund-A	1.24
4	Sun Chao	2	Bank of Communications Schroder Fund Mgt.	Bocom Schroders Regular Payment Yueyuefeng Bond Fund-A	1.10
5	Wang Wenhua	2	Soochow Asset Mgt.	Soochow Increase Income Bond Fund-A	1.04
6	Li Yiwen	6	UBS SDIC Fund Mgt.	UBS SDIC Optimization Enhanced Bond Fund-AB	1.03
7	Di Xiaojiao	1	UBS SDIC Fund Mgt.	UBS SDIC Optimization Enhanced Bond Fund-AB	1.03
8	Zhang Yongzhi	6	Huashang Fund Mgt.	Huashang Principal Sustaining Profit Bond-A	0.88
9	Zou Weina	3	Yinhua Fund Mgt.	Yinhua Credit Jijihong Bond Fund-A	0.79
10	Zhao Xiaodong	7	Franklin Templeton Sealand Fund Mgt.	Fts Hengrui Bond Fund-A	0.66

Source: China Knowledge Mutual Funds Database

Li Xianjun made up the top 1 with 1.74% return in recent 1Q. He works in New China Fund Management Co., Ltd. and his representative fund is New China Credit Enhanced Gained Bond Fund-A, followed by Yin Peijun is in the Harfor Fund Management Co., Ltd. with 1.5% return in recent 1Q. Song Haijuan works in Citic-prudential Fund Management Co., Ltd. came in third and manages Citic-Prudential The Three Gains Bond Fund-A with 1.24% return in recent 1Q.

Table 3.7 Top 10 Hybrid Fund Manager Performance

Ranking	Name	Experience (Yr)	Fund Mgt Company	Representative Fund	Recent 1Q Yields(%)
1	Chen Yuhui	4	Truvalue Asset Mgt.	Truvalue Hugangshen Research Selected Dynamic Allocation Hybrid Fund	13.55
2	Li Han	1	Truvalue Asset Mgt.	Truvalue Hugangshen Research Selected Dynamic Allocation Hybrid Fund	13.55
3	Luan Jiangwei	1	New China Fund Mgt.	New China Resource Opportunity Balanced Fund	13.53
4	Chen Ying	1	Golden Eagle Asset Mgt.	Golden Eagle Growth Hybrid Fund	11.49
5	Huang Yiming	3	Minsheng Royal Fund Mgt.	Minsheng Royal Urbanization Dynamic Allocation Hybrid Fund	9.95
6	Wu Jianfei	11	Minsheng Royal Fund Mgt.	Minsheng Royal Booming Sectors Hybrid Fund	9.69
7	Lu Wentao	1	New China Fund Mgt.	New China Industry Cyclical Rotation Hybrid Fund	9.57
8	Meng Yaqiang	Less 1Yr	JT Asset Mgt.	JT Jiusheng Quantitative Pioneer Dynamic Allocation Hybrid Fund	9.43
9	Zhao Shihong	Less 1Yr	Dacheng Fund Mgt.	Dacheng Jingli Hybrid Fund	8.67
10	Zhu Bei	5	Harfor Fund Mgt.	Harfor Quantum Vitality Hybrid Fund	8.54

Source: China Knowledge Mutual Funds Database

Chen Yuhui and Li Han work in the Truvalue Asset Management Co., Ltd. were 1st together with 13.55% return in recent 1Q. They both manage Truvalue Hugangshen Research Selected Dynamic Allocation Hybrid Fund. Luan Jiangwei made up top 3 with 13.53% return in recent 1Q. He manages New China Resource Opportunity Balanced Fund in the New China Fund Management Co., Ltd.

Table 3.8 Top 10 Index Fund Manager Performance

Ranking	Name	Experience (Yr)	Fund Mgt Company	Representative Fund	Recent 1Q Yields(%)
1	Zhou Hao	Less 1Yr	China Southern Fund Mgt.	China Security Southern Well-off Industry Index ETF Linked Fund	15.64
2	Fang Lei	4	HSBC Jintrust Fund Mgt.	HSBC Jintrust Hang Seng China A Industry Top Index Fund-A	8.95
3	Rong Ying	1	China Asset Mgt.	ChinaAMC Consumption Upgrade ETF Fund	7.82
4	Lu Zhiming	5	GF Fund Mgt.	GF CSI All Share Consumer Staples ETF Initiating Feeder Fund-A	6.89
5	Wang Xiang	Less 1Yr	Bosera Fund Mgt.	Bosera SSE 50 Index ETF Feeder Fund	6.77
6	Jin Fangyi	2	SWS MU Fund Mgt.	SWS MU CSI 300 Index Enhanced Fund	6.77
7	Guan Zefan	Less 1Yr	E Fund Mgt.	E Fund CSI 300 Quantitative Enhanced Fund	6.39
8	Shen Qing	6	Aegon-Industrial Fund Mgt.	Industrial CSI 300 Enhanced Index Fund (LOF)	6.35
9	Xue Xianzhi	1	Invesco Great Wall Fund Mgt.	Invesco Great Wall CSI 800 Food And Beverage ETF	6.19
10	Li Haiwei	3	Invesco Great Wall Fund Mgt.	Invesco Great Wall CSI 300 Index Enhanced Fund	6.06

Source: China Knowledge Mutual Funds Database

Zhou Hao who works China Southern Fund Management Co., Ltd. remains 1St with 15.64% return in recent 1Q. His representative fund is China Security Southern Well-off Industry Index ETF Linked Fund. Fang Lei came in second and manages HSBC Jintrust Hang Seng China A Industry Top Index Fund-A with 8.95% return in recent 1Q. Rong Ying made up top 3 with 7.82% return in recent 1Q. She is in charge of ChinaAMC Consumption Upgrade ETF Fund in the China Asset Management Co., Ltd.

Table 3.9 Top 10 1-Yr Experience Equity Fund Manager and Hybrid Fund Manager Performance

Ranking	Name	Fund Mgt Company	Representative Fund	2016 Yields(%)
1	La Bo	CIB Fund Mgt.	CIB Juli Dynamic Allocation Hybrid Fund	29.85
2	Hong Liu	Golden Trust Sinopac Fund Mgt.	Golden Trust Sinopac Youjia Life Equity Fund	17.96
3	Xiao Zhigang	Tianhong Asset Mgt.	Tianhong Yongding Value Growth Hybrid Fund	17.46
4	Li Huasong	Harvest Fund Mgt.	Harvest Environmental Protection Low Carbon Equity Fund	16.50
5	Cai Murong	Fortune SG Fund Mgt.	Fortune SG Resources Selected Hybrid Fund	16.34
6	Xie Yi	First Seafront Fund Mgt.	First Seafront Gold and Silver Jewelry Theme Selected Dynamic Allocation Hybrid Fund-A	15.86
7	Yuan Fang	ICBC Credit Suisse Asset Mgt.	ICBCCS Culture Sports Industry Equity Fund	15.72
8	Zhou Yingbo	Zhong Ou Asset Mgt.	Lombarda China Times Pioneer Equity Initiating Fund	15.03
9	Yang Dongdong	UBS SDIC Fund Mgt.	UBS SDIC Ruiying Dynamic Allocation Hybrid Fund (LOF)	14.13
10	Wang Chao	E Fund Mgt.	E Fund Resources Sector Hybrid Fund	13.63

Source: China Knowledge Mutual Funds Database

La Bo made up the top 1 with 29.85% return in 2016. He works in CIB Fund Management Co., Ltd. and his representative fund is CIB Juli Dynamic Allocation Hybrid Fund, followed by Hong Liu is in the Golden Trust Sinopac Fund Management Co., Ltd. with 17.96% return in 2016. Xiao Zhigang works in Tianhong Asset Management Co., Ltd. came in third and manages Tianhong Yongding Value Growth Hybrid Fund with 17.46% return in 2016.

Table 3.10 Top 10 3-Yr Experience Equity Fund Manager and Hybrid Fund Manager Performance

Ranking	Name	Fund Mgt Company	Representative Fund	Recent 3 Yrs Yields (%)
1	Xu Yanfang	Gfund Mgt.	Gfund Guoxin Dynamic Allocation Hybrid Initiating Fund	180.39
2	Xie Zhiyu	Aegon-Industrial Fund Mgt.	Industrial Herun Structured Fund	139.73
3	Ren Zesong	China Post Fund Mgt.	China Post Strategy Emerging Industries Hybrid Fund	137.98
4	Liu Xin	Manulife Teda Fund Mgt.	Manulife Teda Reverse Hybrid Fund	130.00
5	Yan Yao	ICBC Credit Suisse Asset Mgt.	ICBCCS Financial and Property Hybrid Fund	127.13
6	Wu Shengtao	Aegon-Industrial Fund Mgt.	Industrial Business Model Select Hybrid Fund (LOF)	126.16
7	Cui Jianbo	New China Fund Mgt.	New China Trend Navigation Hybrid Fund	123.57
8	Huang Yiming	Minsheng Royal Fund Mgt.	Minsheng Royal Urbanization Dynamic Allocation Hybrid Fund	123.55
9	Xiao Zhigang	Tianhong Asset Mgt.	Tianhong Yongding Value Growth Hybrid Fund	118.89
10	Chen Xiaoling	UBS SDIC Fund Mgt.	UBS SDIC Strategic Selection Dynamic Allocation Hybrid Fund	117.91

Source: China Knowledge Mutual Funds Database

Xu Yanfang made up the top 1 with 180.39% return in recent 3 years. She works in the Gfund Fund Management Co., Ltd. and her representative fund is Gfund Guoxin Dynamic Allocation Hybrid Initiating Fund, followed by Xie Zhiyu is in the Aegon-Industrial Fund Management Co., Ltd. with 139.73% return in recent 3 years. Ren Zesong works in the China Post Management Co., Ltd. came in third and manages China Post Strategy Emerging Industries Hybrid Fund with 137.98% return in recent 3 years.

Table 3.11 Top 10 1-Yr Experience Bond Fund Manager Performance

Ranking	Name	Fund Mgt Company	Representative Fund	2016 Yields(%)
1	Wu Pingping	Orient Fund Mgt.	Orient Value-Added Bond Fund	7.27
2	Zhong Ming	Aegon-Industrial Fund Mgt.	Industrial Stable Income Bond Fund	6.63
3	Chen Kaiyang	Bosera Fund Mgt.	Bosera Shuangyuexin Regular Payment Bond Fund	6.54
4	Xu Wenbo	Tebon Fund Mgt.	Tebon Xintianli Bond Fund-A	6.29
5	Wu Chen	Guotai Asset Mgt.	Guotai Dual Dividend Bond Fund-A	6.02
6	Liu Wanfeng	China Merchants Fund Mgt.	China Merchants Double-Bonds Enhanced Bond Fund (LOF)	6.00
7	Zhang Wei	Yingda Asset Mgt.	Yingda Pure Bond Fund-A	5.91
8	Liu Jianyan	Penghua Fund Mgt.	Penghua Credit Enhanced Bond Fund-A	4.94
9	Zhuang Yuan	Essence Fund Mgt.	Anxin Baoli	4.92
10	Song Bingshen	ICBC Credit Suisse Asset Mgt.	ICBCCS Dual Dividend Fund-A	4.87

Source: China Knowledge Mutual Funds Database

Wu Pingping who works in Orient Fund Management Co., Ltd. remains 1St with 7.27% return in 2016. Her representative fund is Orient Value-Added Bond Fund. Zhong Ming came in second and manages Industrial Stable Income Bond Fund with 6.63% return in 2016. Chen Kaiyang made up top 3 with 6.54% return in 2016. He is in charge of Bosera Shuangyuexin Regular Payment Bond Fund in the Bosera Fund Management Co., Ltd.

Table 3.12 Top 10 3-Yr Experience Bond Fund Manager Performance

Ranking	Name	Fund Mgt Company	Representative Fund	Recent 3 Yrs Yields (%)
1	Zhang Qinghua	E Fund Mgt.	E Fund Absolute Return Bond Fund-A	118.72
2	Guo Jun	Bosera Fund Mgt.	Bosera Credit Bond Fund-A	116.01
3	Zhang Qian	GF Fund Mgt.	GF Juxin Bond Fund-A	72.11
4	Du Haitao	ICBC Credit Suisse Asset Mgt.	ICBCCS Tianyi Bond Fund-A	63.98
5	Li Xiaoyu	Chang Xin Asset Mgt.	Changxin Lifeng Bond Fund	62.06
6	Hu Jian	E Fund Mgt.	E Fund Stable Income Bond Fund-B	61.11
7	Zhong Jingdi	CCB Principal Asset Mgt.	CCB Principal Dual Interest Dividend Bond Fund-A	59.65
8	Li Yi	Morgan Stanley Huaxin Fund Mgt.	Morgan Stanley Huaxin Diversification Income Bond Fund-A	57.66
9	Di Xiaojiao	UBS SDIC Fund Mgt.	UBS SDIC Optimization Enhanced Bond Fund-AB	56.03
10	Su Yuping	HuaAn Fund Mgt.	Huaan Strong Income BD FD-A	55.87

Source: China Knowledge Mutual Funds Database

Zhang Qinghua in the E Fund Management Co., Ltd. was top spot with 118.72% return in recent 3 years. His representative fund is E Fund Absolute Return Bond Fund-A. Guo Jun took the second place and manages Bosera Credit Bond Fund-A with 116.01% return in recent 3 years, followed by Zhang Qian who works in GF Fund Management Co., Ltd. She manages GF Juxin Bond Fund-A with 72.11% return in recent 3 years.

3.2 BASIC INFORMATION OF FUND MANAGERS

- For more information of fund managers, you can go visit **http://fund.chinaknowledge.com/Download/FM.pdf** and download the PDF.

Document open password is: **ck2017fm**

PART FOUR:

FUNDS CLASSIFICATION

4.1 MONEY MARKET FUNDS

4.1.1 DEFINITION OF MONEY MARKET FUNDS

Money market funds invest in short-term securities with an average maturity of 120 days, including treasury bonds, bank bills, commercial paper, certificates of deposit (CD) and corporate bonds with high credit ratings. Since the portfolio of money market funds is usually made up entirely of low-risk, low-return assets, they are regarded as safe havens for risk-averse investors. Not only they are assured that their principal is secure, they also receive higher interest rates than bank deposits. The characteristics of money market funds are as follows.

(1) Safety of Principal

Typically, money market fund contracts do not guarantee principal preservation. However, the securities included in money market funds' portfolios are low risk enough that it is highly unlikely that the principal will default. In general, money market funds are considered as safe as cash.

(2) High Liquidity

Money market funds are like demand deposits. Fund transactions are swift and convenient, highly liquid, and fund shares can usually be redeemed within 2-3 business days.

(3) High Yields

Most money market funds have yields similar to those of treasury bonds. Besides having access to a variety of investment tools, money market funds can also enter the interbank, central bank notes and repo markets. Their annual returns are comparable to those with annual fixed deposit interest payments. In recent years, they have outperformed bank deposits.

In addition, money market funds may avoid hidden losses. In times of high inflation, real interest rates tend to drop and may turn negative. However, these funds should adjust in a timely fashion based on inflationary and interest rate trends, with stable and relatively high returns.

(4) Low Capital

The sale of money market funds usually excludes additional costs like brokerage fees, redemption fees and subscription fees. This easy access to capital not only reduces the cost of capital, it also enables the liquidity of funds. The minimum share purchase order is RMB 1,000 (US$ 144), with increments of RMB 100 (US$ 14).

(5) Tax-free dividends

The majority of money market funds maintain a RMB 1 (US$ 0.14) dividend with interest compounded daily. This monthly dividend is then transferred as fund shares, resulting in tax-free dividends. This is more attractive than simple interest accrued in bank deposits.

In general, money market funds can be converted quickly and at a lower cost than other types of open-end funds that belong to the same fund management company. When stock markets are performing well, money market funds can be converted to equity funds. When bond markets are strong, they can be converted to bond funds. In times of market uncertainty, they serve as safe havens for capital. Money market funds' versatility thus allows investors to take advantage of every opportunity in the stock, debt and money markets.

Table 4.1 Characteristics of Money Funds

Risk	Extremely Low (similar to bank savings, the lowest risk in funds)
Yield (Annual)	Relatively low (3%-5%)
Investment Target	Money market instrument such as treasuries and bills
Purchase and Redemption Fee	0 Commission Charge
Redemption Time	Redemption at any time, T+0
Target Group	Those seeking investment solutions in lieu of bank reserves

Source: China Knowledge Mutual Funds Database

ADVERTORIAL

HSBC Jintrust RMB Money Market Fund——*High Security, High Liquidity*

As a result of its holdings of bonds that are internationally rated and with ample liquidity, HSBC Jintrust Money Market Fund is one of the three domestic MMFs to have attained an AAA (CHN) Fitch rating. In order to obtain a Fitch rating, a fund would have to adhere to stricter duration and credit risk regulations and controls than local industry standards.

"The money market fund by nature is a cash management tool; the primary aim is not to seek exceptional returns, but to achieve security and liquidity. HSBC Jintrust Money Market Fund adheres to this philosophy and will not deviate from it to take up more risk than it is set out to."

— HSBC Jintrust Fund Manager , Li Yuanyuan

Domestically in China, many investors see money market funds as capital guaranteed fixed income products, hence neglecting the risks involved. In reality, in the event of a liquidity squeeze or large redemption, money market funds can also suffer losses or even be forced to liquidate.

In June 2013, as a result of policy tightening and liquidity squeeze at the end of the quarter, the short-end rate hiked. For example, the Shanghai Interbank Offered Rate (SHIBOR) rose rapidly to levels high above 10%, reaching for one time as high as 30%. This led to a huge amount of redemption requests in a very short period of time, which put many money market funds in danger zones. These money market funds were forced to sell off securities at a fire sale, with annualized yields falling to below 1%, while some funds suffered losses.

In contrast, with key focus on liquidity and security concerns, the HSBC Jintrust Money Market Fund benefited from the much shorter average maturity of its investment portfolio and conservative liquidity ladder, resulting in a rising annualized yield.

According to the fund manager Li Yuanyuan (Vivian), in terms of risk control, HSBC Jintrust Money Market Fund has established a solid framework and investment guidelines. For example, limits for the proportion of the various asset classes are implemented strictly, especially for assets restricted by liquidity such as time deposits, term repurchases and interest-paying debts. Credit risk controls are adhered to closely; even when a credit possesses investment potential, the internal rating and credit risk management committee must still approve it before it will be included in the Money Market Fund.

The HSBC Jintrust Money Market Fund places high liquidity and high security as its priority, with returns taking a back seat. As a result, in the situation of market turmoil, the fund would not be affected by an abrupt shortage of liquidity. This is also a reflection of HSBC Jintrust's "true to label" philosophy, which avoids unnecessary risks for its investors.

4.1.2 MONEY MARKET FUND DEVELOPMENT

The money market fund industry grew exponentially from 2011 to 2016. In 2012, its NAV grew 139.93% from the year before. As of mid-November 2016, its NAV and total shares issued reached RMB 4.71 trillion (US$ 0.68 trillion) and RMB 4.69 trillion (US$ 0.67 trillion) respectively, an increase of nearly 1,500% over 2011.

The rapid development of China's money market funds in 2012 can be attributed to three main factors.

(1) High Interest Rates

Rising interest rates in 2012 boosted the returns of money market funds. These connected the controlled interest rates of bank deposits with the liberal rates of the interbank market, laying the current macroeconomic foundation for China's interest rate market. Hence, returns on money market funds are closely tied to money market returns. Since 2012, the marketization of interest rates, rapid development of shadow banking and slowdown of foreign exchange inflow has led to higher yields in the capital markets. This is the main driving force for the increased returns of money market funds.

(2) Dividend Policy

Money market funds have a dividend policy that ensures high returns and liquidity.

In 2011, CSRC released the "Notice on Strengthening Risk Management of Money Market Funds". It lifted the restrictions on investing in fixed-term deposits related to money market fund portfolios. The new regulation laid foundation for money market funds' 'excess returns' through 2013, and bolstered these funds' scale.

It also lifted the regulation that money market funds shall not withdraw agreed deposits in advance. Thus, money market funds can realize the interest rate of fixed-term deposits while withdrawing current deposits. Bank agreed deposits now account for more than 80% of the asset allocation of major money market funds.

(3) Rise of the Internet

The exponential growth of e-commerce and third-party payment methods increased investors' demand for financial management, a change in mindset that made it much easier to direct bank deposits into money market funds.

Tianhong Asset Management set up what is now the largest money market fund in May 2013. It leveraged its popularity, vast user base, and established names like Taobao and Alipay to build a 20% market share in just seven months.

Figure 4.1 2011-16 Money Fund Market

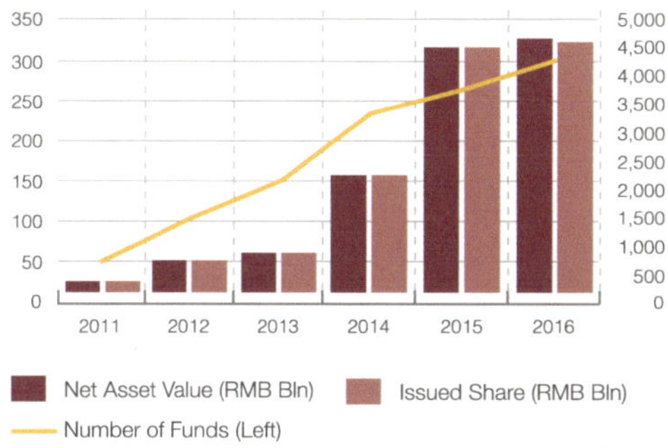

Source: Asset Management Association of China & China Knowledge Mutual Funds Database

As of November 2016, 67% of all money market funds had year-to-date yields greater than 2%, while 14% of money market funds' yields were above 2.5% year to date. Zhong Ou Asset Management, E Fund Management and Minsheng Royal Fund Management had the best performing money market funds in terms of YTD yields. Based on annual returns, 12.46% of money funds generated returns higher than 4%, while 45% earned between 2% and 4%. Another 36% achieved monthly annual returns that were between 1% and 3%. The average size of 45% of money market funds by this time was equal to or greater than RMB 1 billion (US$ 145.85 million).

Table 4.2 Top 20 Money Funds in Terms of Year-to-Date Returns (as of end-Oct 2016)

Code	Name	YTD Returns (%)	Annualized Returns (%)	Latest Size (RMB Bln)	Fund Mgt Company
001211.OF	Lombarda China Gun Qian Bao Initiating Money Market Fund	2.98	3.15	1.72	Zhong Ou Asset Mgt.
110051.OF	E Fund Yueyueli Financial Bond Fund-B	2.97	4.78	8.00	E Fund Mgt.
000090.OF	Minsheng Royal Jiaying Financial Monthly Bond Fund-B	2.96	4.44	185.23	Minsheng Royal Fund Mgt.
202304.OF	China Southern Financial 14 Days Bond Fund-B	2.91	4.43	64.36	China Southern Fund Mgt.
485022.OF	ICBCCS 60 Days Financial Bond Fund-B	2.88	4.70	65.56	ICBC Credit Suisse Asset Mgt.
110053.OF	E Fund Shuangyueli Financial Bond Fund-B	2.87	4.58	16.38	E Fund Mgt.
000902.OF	CDBS Cathay Asset Money Market Fund-B	2.83	3.50	0.58	CDBS Cathay Asset Mgt.
471060.OF	China Universal Financial 60 Days Bond Fund-B	2.80	4.48	3.12	China Universal Asset Mgt.
202306.OF	China Southern Financial 60 Days Bond Fund-B	2.79	4.54	1,007.12	China Southern Fund Mgt.
472007.OF	China Universal Financial 7 Days Bond Fund-B	2.78	4.54	1.06	China Universal Asset Mgt.
000905.OF	Penghua An Ying Treasure Money Market Fund	2.78	4.01	4.47	Penghua Fund Mgt.
001233.OF	JYAH Money Market Fund-B	2.78	3.30	9.34	JYAH Asset Mgt.
730103.OF	Founder Fubon Money Market Fund-B	2.76	4.04	0.30	Founder Fubon Fund Mgt.
000089.OF	Minsheng Royal Jiaying Financial Monthly Bond Fund-A	2.75	4.24	0.50	Minsheng Royal Fund Mgt.
000715.OF	Minsheng Royal Jiaying Financial Monthly Bond Fund-E	2.75	3.87	2.94	Minsheng Royal Fund Mgt.
471030.OF	China Universal Financial 30 Days Bond Fund-B	2.74	4.27	0.06	China Universal Asset Mgt.
270047.OF	GF Financial 30 Days Bond Fund-B	2.73	4.50	803.21	GF Fund Mgt.
000648.OF	E Fund Wealth Express Money Market Fund-B	2.73	3.82	1.22	E Fund Mgt.
001843.OF	JT Ritianjin Money Market Fund-B	2.73	3.09	0.43	JT Asset Mgt.
000621.OF	E Fund Cash Income Money Market Fund-B	2.71	3.31	52.31	E Fund Mgt.

Source: China Knowledge Mutual Funds Database

4.2 EQUITY FUNDS

4.2.1 BASIC INFORMATION ABOUT EQUITY FUNDS

Equity funds invest more than 80% of their fund assets in stocks. Investing in an equity fund is the equivalent of investing in the stock market through a fund manager. They typically carry heavy risks. However, high risks generally translate into higher returns. Relative to other types of industry funds, equity funds are more likely to earn the best returns.

Table 4.3 Characteristics of Equity Funds

Risk	High
Annualized Return	Above 15% (Results vary greatly)
Investment Target	Minimum 80% in equity
Target Investors	Investors with high tolerance for risk

Source: China Knowledge Mutual Funds Database

Advantage Over Investing in Stocks

Investing in an equity fund is a safer and cheaper option than investing directly in the stock market. Equity funds offer widespread diversification for a small initial investment. Each individual stock generally makes up less than 5% of a portfolio, enabling retail investors to spread risk across several stocks in a single investment. To achieve individually the same level of portfolio diversification, retail investors would need thousands of dollars. Another advantage is that equity funds charge low fixed management fees.

Equity Fund Classification

(1) Growth Funds

The main aim of a growth fund is capital appreciation. It is composed of stocks of high-growth companies that expect, and continue to expect, strong earnings, sales, and cash flows. These companies are usually in growing industries such as network technology, bio-pharmaceuticals, and alternative energy.

Although these funds can earn higher returns, they are more suited for investors with a greater appetite for risk. Technology stocks are popular assets for growth funds with their high growth and price-to-earnings ratios.

(2) Value Funds

A value fund holds stocks of high quality companies that are out of favor with the market. They are often in relatively stable industries such as the financial industry and are established blue-chip businesses. These stocks are typically undervalued and pay dividends. Value fund managers focus on finding low-priced stocks that fit these criteria.

Value investing assumes that the market is imperfect and has inefficiencies that result in a stock's undervaluation. The belief is that once the market corrects itself, the company stock will start trading at a price that reflects its true value.

(3) Blend Funds

Blend funds are a hybrid of growth and value funds. The investment strategy of their fund managers is to divide their investments between undervalued stocks and stocks of listed companies in growth industries.

Risk Sources of Equity Funds

Investment risks faced by equity fund managers includes systematic, non-systematic, and management risks.

Table 4.4 Risk Sources of Equity Funds

Systematic Risks	Also known as market risks, these cannot be reduced or eliminated through portfolio diversification such as policy, interest, or currency risks, among others.
Non-systematic Risks	Risks that can be reduced or eliminated through portfolio diversification such as credit, operational, and other risks.
Management risks	Risks that arise from fund managers' active management and fund operation.

Source: China Knowledge Mutual Funds Database

4.2.2 EQUITY FUND MARKET

Overall equity fund risk is equivalent to the risk of investing in equities directly plus fund managers' management risk.

Overview of the 2016 Stock Market Environment

Although market share on the Shanghai Stock Exchange dropped sharply in January, February and September 2016, it saw a substantial growth in March as well as in November. From October to November 2016, major Chinese indices rose sharply. The SSE Composite Index rose 5.69% to 3,277; the Shenzhen SZSE Composite Index was up 3.34% to 11,068.87; the Shanghai-Shenzhen CSI 300 Index up 5.84% to 3,535.08; and the S&P-Hong Kong GEM Index rose 0.03% to 2,166.05.

Figure 4.2 Monthly Change of A-Share Stock Market in 2016

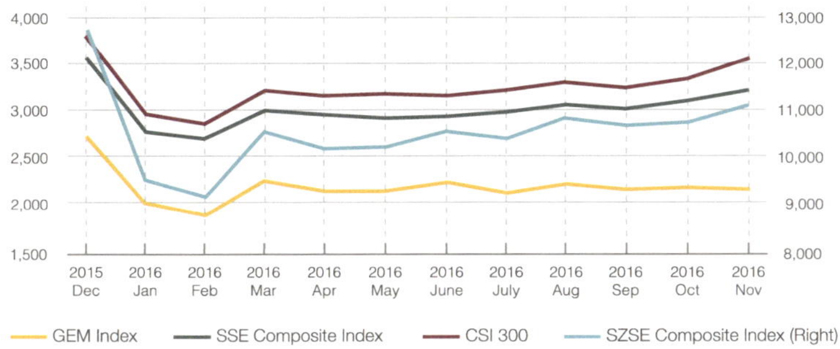

Source: China Knowledge Mutual Funds Database

There is a correlation between the market share and the issuance of equity funds. In January 2016, the SSE Composite and SZSE Composite Index dropped more than 20% from the previous month. Meanwhile, equity funds' total net assets declined 21.17% month over month to RMB 603.59 billion (US$ 91.75 billion). From August to September, the SSE Composite Index rose 3.56% and the SZSE Composite Index was up 4.15%. Equity funds' total net assets increased 5.78% from July to September. In November alone, the total net assets and shares of equity funds reached RMB 659.27 billion (US$ 95.57 billion) and RMB 637.8 billion (US$ 92.4 billion), or 7.32% and 7.38% of the total fund market, respectively.

Figure 4.3 Monthly Market Change of Equity Fund in 2016 (as of mid-November)

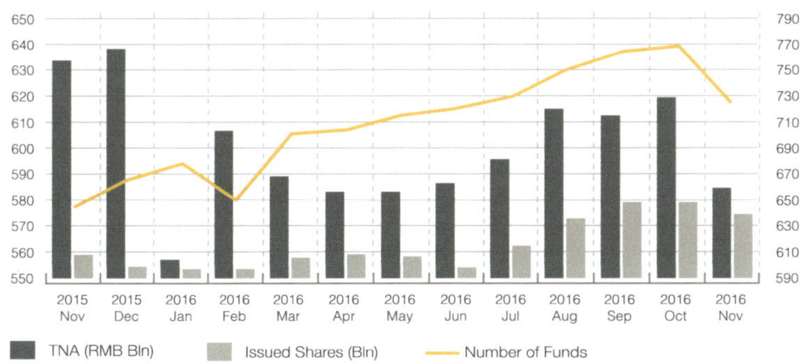

Source: Asset Management Association of China

As of November 2016, 77 equity funds that comprised 12% of the total equity fund market saw their monthly average yield exceed 1%. The average monthly yield of 235 equity funds ranged from 0% to 1%, while another 261 equity funds fell between -1% and 0%, making up 36% and 40%, respectively, of the total equity fund market.

The year-to-date yield of the top 20 equity funds were all above 5%. Among these, two funds saw their yields year to date hit more than 20%; the YTD yield of nearly half these top funds passed 10%. The three top equity funds with the highest YTD yield were managed by ICBC Credit Suisse Asset Management, Golden Trust Sinopac Fund Management, and Harvest Fund Management. The highest annualized returns from among the top 20 equity funds were 34.28%, 29.08% and 28.47%.

Figure 4.4 Monthly Average Yield Distribution of Equity Fund in 2016

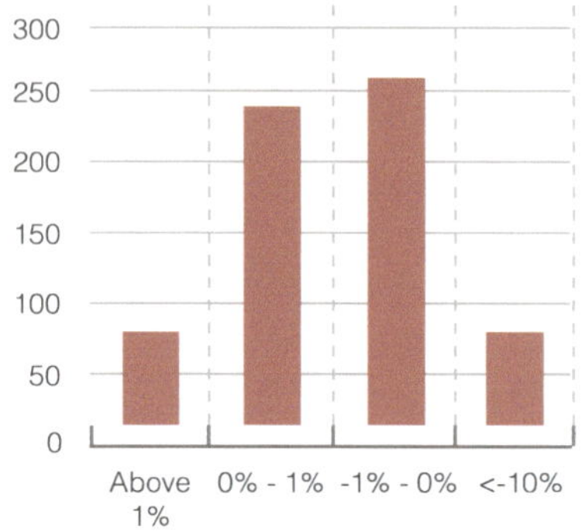

Source: China Knowledge Mutual Funds Database

Table 4.5 Top 20 Equity Funds in Terms of Year-to-Date Returns (as of end-Oct 2016)

Code	Name	YTD Returns (%)	Annualized Returns (%)	Latest Size (RMB Bln)	Fund Mgt Company
001714.OF	ICBCCS Culture Sports Industry Equity Fund	22.92	26.40	0.18	ICBC Credit Suisse Asset Mgt.
001736.OF	Golden Trust Sinopac Youjia Life Equity Fund	21.26	23.60	0.55	Golden Trust Sinopac Fund Mgt.
001616.OF	Harvest Environmental Protection Low Carbon Equity Fund	19.80	22.88	1.19	Harvest Fund Mgt.
001705.OF	Hongde Strategic Transformation Equity Fund	15.67	17.15	0.88	Hongde Fund Mgt.
001938.OF	Lombarda China Times Pioneer Equity Initiating Fund	14.88	29.08	0.09	Zhong Ou Asset Mgt.
001637.OF	Harvest Tencent Self-select Stock Big Data Strategy Equity Fund	11.24	12.60	0.68	Harvest Fund Mgt.
000309.OF	Morgan Stanley Huaxin Quality Life Selected Equity Fund	10.49	23.15	1.03	Morgan Stanley Huaxin Fund Mgt.
001421.OF	China Southern Quantitative Growth Equity Fund	10.41	24.81	0.43	China Southern Fund Mgt.
001178.OF	First Seafront Refinancing Theme Selected Equity Fund	10.09	8.83	0.77	First Seafront Fund
000577.OF	Anxin Value Selected Equity Fund	9.72	34.28	0.13	Essence Fund Mgt.
519975.OF	Changxin Quantitative Mid/Small-Cap Equity Fund	9.64	28.47	1.93	Chang Xin Asset Mgt.
001528.OF	Lion Advanced Manufacturing Equity Fund	9.57	8.89	0.09	Lion Fund Mgt.
001651.OF	ICBCCS New Blue Chip Equity Fund	8.26	7.83	0.20	ICBC Credit Suisse Asset Mgt.
000974.OF	Anxin Consumption Medicine Theme Equity Fund	7.94	7.52	0.27	Essence Fund Mgt.
163110.OF	SWS MU Quantitative Small Cap Equity Fund(LOF)	7.58	20.43	2.08	SWS MU Fund Mgt.
001677.OF	BOC Strategic Emerging Industries Stock Fund	7.30	7.54	0.15	Bank of China Investment Mgt.
519965.OF	Changxin Quantization Multi-Strategy Equity Fund	7.22	22.05	0.15	Chang Xin Asset Mgt.
001521.OF	China Life AMP. Growth Select Equity Fund	6.77	7.77	0.33	Guotai Asset Mgt.
160127.OF	China Southern Emerging Consumption Growth Structured Equity Fund	6.45	14.04	0.21	China Southern Fund Mgt.
110022.OF	E Fund Consumption Sector Equity Fund	5.77	5.47	1.32	E Fund Mgt.

Source: China Knowledge Mutual Funds Database

4.2.3 PASSIVE INDEX FUNDS AND ENHANCED INDEX FUNDS

Passive Index Funds

Passive funds, more commonly referred to as index funds, are designed to mirror market indices. They generally select a specific index as their investment objective and aim not to outperform the market, but rather mirror the index' performance. The returns of such an investment strategy have been higher than most active funds as investors enjoy lower risk through diversification, lower portfolio turnover, and reduced operating expenses.

Enhanced Index Funds

Index funds are passive funds that can be further divided into specific index replication funds and enhanced index funds. The former is a copy of the corresponding index portfolio, while the latter is a modified index fund that includes some active investing designed to outperform the tracking index.

There are two ways to improve the performance of enhanced index funds: adding value or selective stock picking. Adding value includes diversifying investments into financial derivatives such as buying bullish futures. Selective stock picking refers to expanding the portfolio to include stocks that have high potential for capital appreciation or selling stocks that lack such potential.

As of mid-November 2016, 33 equity funds, or 8% of all passive index funds, saw their average monthly yields surpass 1%. The average monthly yield of 144 equity funds, or 34% of total passive index funds, was between 0% and 1%, while that of 192 equity funds, 45% of these funds, fell in the -1% to 0% range.

As of mid-November 2016, 3 enhanced index funds, or 7%, saw their monthly annualized returns surpass 1%. The monthly annualized return of 24 equity funds, or 52% of all passive index funds, was between 0% and 1%, while that of 17 equity funds, or 37% of the total, fell between -1% and 0%.

Figure 4.5 Monthly average Yield Distribution of Passive Index Fund

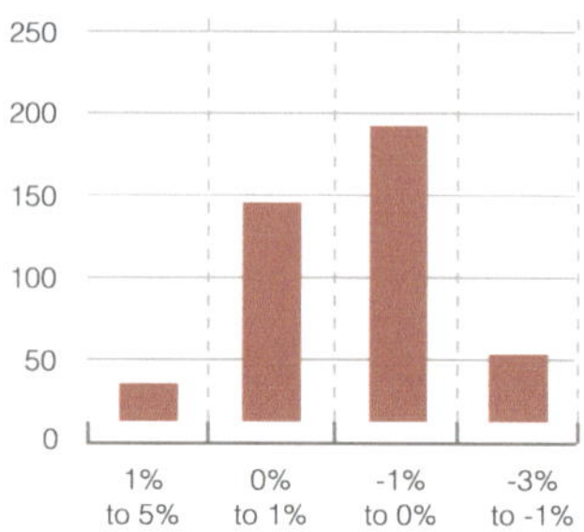

Source: China Knowledge Mutual Funds Database

Figure 4.6 Annualized Yield Distribution of Enhanced Index Fund

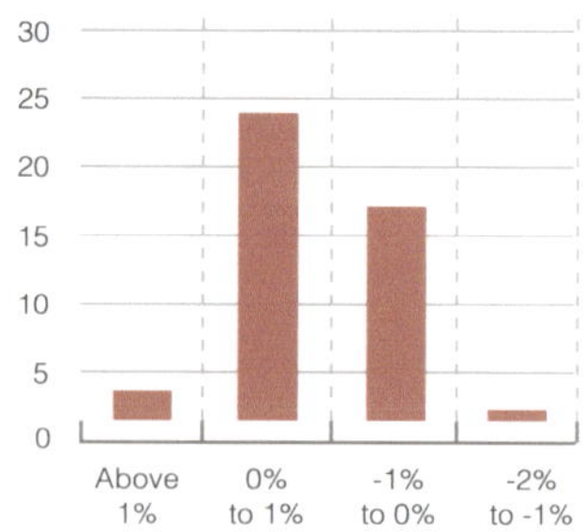

Source: China Knowledge Mutual Funds Database

4.3 HYBRID FUNDS

4.3.1 DEFINITION OF HYBRID MARKET FUNDS

A hybrid mutual fund, also referred to as an asset allocation, target date, or balanced fund, is a portfolio made up of a mix of stocks, bonds and cash. A hybrid fund is classified as either domestic or international and may be aggressive (with a higher equity component) or conservative (a higher-fixed income component) depending on the fund's prospectus. Hybrid funds includes equity-oriented, flexible, core, and bond-oriented hybrid funds.

With the development of China's mutual fund market, most investors who purchase mutual funds tend to favor a one-stop shop approach. As such, hybrid mutual funds have become more and more popular with the investing crowd. Hybrid funds are safer than equity funds, and there are a huge variety of choices suited to different appetites for risk.

4.3.2 HYBRID FUND DEVELOPMENT AND MARKET PERFORMANCE

Hybrid Funds popular while Equity Funds fall behind

In the first ten months of 2016, the most popular type of newly issued fund product in terms of quantity and scale was the hybrid fund. It accounted for 52.05% of all new product issuances and 52.15% by size. Bond funds came in second place, with 33.16% of the total and 32.30% by scale. Institutions' enthusiasm for issuing and investors' passion for subscribing to these products was high.

By means of comparison, equity funds accounted for just 7.27% of new products and only 5.34% by scale, suggesting low investor interest. Qualified Domestic Institutional Investor (QDII) funds totaled 1.72% by quantity and 1.24% by size, while alternative investment funds accounted for 0.79% by number and 0.28% by scale. These remained scarce in the mutual funds industry.

Table 4.6 Different Types of Bond Funds

Hybrid Funds	Number of New Funds	Amount of Issuance Shares (Bln)
Flexible Hybrid Funds	438	187.51
Equity-Oriented Hybrid Funds	18	6.45
Bond-Oriented Hybrid Funds	135	206.93
Core Hybrid Funds	1	0.59
Total	592	401.47

Source: China Knowledge Mutual Funds Database

The Number and Scale of Hybrid Funds Shrank

The internal structure of the hybrid fund market changed in the first half of 2016, as their scale shrank in the wake of the earlier stock market correction. Equity-oriented hybrid funds with high stock positions plummeted and lost scale. Meanwhile, bond-oriented hybrid funds, especially guaranteed funds, were popular, driving their scales up.

Figure 4.7 Number of Funds by Type (%)

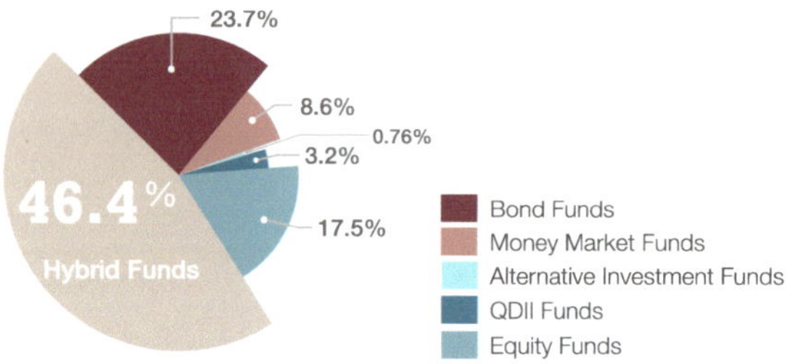

Source: China Knowledge Mutual Funds Database

Although 1,637 hybrid funds constituted 46.35% of all fund types as of November 15, 2016, money market funds' total NAV of 52.64% far outpaced hybrid funds' 23.73% share.

Figure 4.8 Number of Units Traded by Fund Type (%)

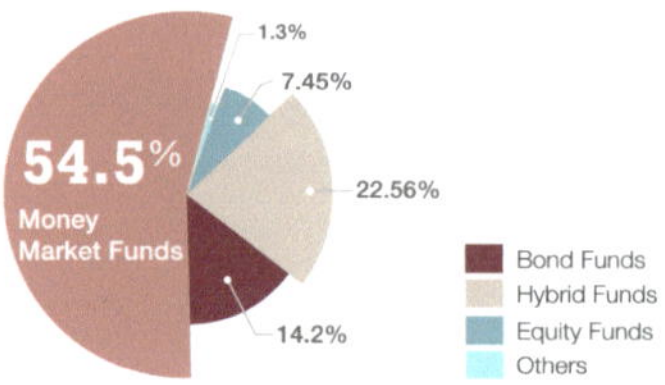

Source: China Knowledge Mutual Funds Database

Figure 4.9 Net Asset by Percentage (%)

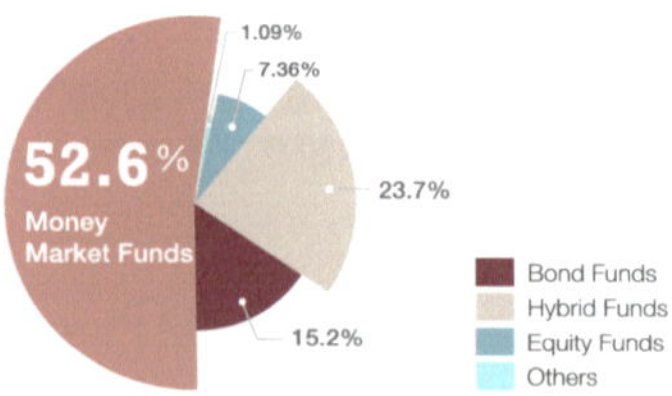

Source: China Knowledge Mutual Funds Database

From 2010 to 2015, the net and annualized growth rates of 26 money market funds, of which 25 were hybrid and 1 bond, were more than 100% and 25.7%, respectively. The China Universal Poes Hybrid Fund offered the highest return during this period. Although hybrid funds offer enticing returns, they face substantial risk in the mutual fund market.

Hybrid Funds Return in 2016

The average return of hybrid funds in the first 10 months of 2016 was –8.08%. A breakdown by fund type indicates that the average returns were as follows: equity-oriented hybrid funds, -13.49%; bond-oriented hybrid funds, -0.59%; flexible hybrid funds, -4.55%; and core hybrid funds, -25.14%.

Only 3% of equity-oriented hybrid funds earned positive returns during this period. The winner, Fullgoal Low Carbon New Economy (001985.OF), returned 6.67% because at the end of 2015, it hedged its positions during the Fusing Policy period. More than 61% of bond-oriented hybrid funds achieved positive returns, the highest of which was 11.00% by GuangFa JuAn A (001115.OF) after its manager reduced its stock holdings to less than 4%, avoiding the sharp stock market decline in January 2016. More than 47% of flexible hybrid funds had positive returns, most notably the E Fund XinYi E, whose large-scale redemptions helped it return a surprising 57.10%. Only 2 of 21 core hybrid funds had positive returns in the first 10 months of 2016. The Orient New Value (001495.OF) came in first place after the market rebound fueled its extraordinary performance.

Table 4.7 Top 20 Hybrid Funds in Terms of Year-to-Date Returns (as of end-Oct 2016)

Code	Name	YTD Returns (%)	Annualized Returns (%)	Latest Size (RMB Mln)	Fund Mgt Company
002059.OF	Guotai Nongyi Dynamic Allocation Hybrid Fund-C	94.76	95.83	466.32	Guotai Asset Mgt.
002061.OF	Guotai Ankang Pension Regular Payment Hybrid Fund-C	89.24	90.61	401.10	Guotai Asset Mgt.
001315.OF	E Fund Xinyi Dynamic Allocation Hybrid Fund-E	62.10	40.55	32.59	E Fund Mgt.
001903.OF	E&P Xinxin Dynamic Allocation Hybrid Fund-A	59.54	63.21	552.05	Everbright Pramerica Fund Mgt.
001380.OF	Penghua Hongsheng Dynamic Allocation Hybrid Fund-C	47.59	32.72	602.06	Penghua Fund Mgt.
001342.OF	E Fund Xinxiang Dynamic Allocation Hybrid Fund-A	40.83	27.03	408.14	E Fund Mgt.
002186.OF	GTJA Allianz Xinxiang Dynamic Allocation Hybrid Fund-C	38.11	39.77	11.73	GTJA Allianz Fund Mgt Limited Company
001272.OF	CIB Juli Dynamic Allocation Hybrid Fund	31.07	30.71	304.43	CIB Fund Mgt.
001302.OF	First Seafront Gold and Silver Jewelry Theme Selected Dynamic Allocation Hybrid Fund-A	30.22	21.14	617.30	First Qianhai Fund Mgt.
001939.OF	E&P Ruixin Dynamic Allocation Hybrid Fund-A	29.94	30.29	157.01	Everbright Pramerica Fund Mgt.
110025.OF	E Fund Resources Sector Hybrid Fund	28.32	1.53	895.53	E Fund Mgt.
240022.OF	Fortune SG Resources Selected Hybrid Fund	28.20	7.77	275.67	Fortune SG Fund Mgt.
002207.OF	First Seafront Gold and Silver Jewelry Theme Selected Dynamic Allocation Hybrid Fund-C	27.66	29.77	184.77	First Qianhai Fund Mgt.
420003.OF	Tianhong Yongding Value Growth Hybrid Fund	23.94	12.68	537.80	Tianhong Asset Mgt.
001314.OF	E Fund Xinyi Dynamic Allocation Hybrid Fund-I	21.14	14.71	1,045.01	E Fund Mgt.
002080.OF	First Seafront One Belt And One Road Theme Selected Dynamic Allocation Hybrid Fund-C	18.28	18.40	0.27	First Qianhai Fund Mgt.
002082.OF	Huatai-PB Excitation Power Dynamic Allocation Hybrid Fund-C	16.62	16.88	0.38	Huatai-Pinebridge Fund Mgt.
001869.OF	China Merchants Manufacturing Transformation Allocation Hybrid Fund	15.87	16.90	283.11	China Merchants Fund Mgt.
001985.OF	Fullgoal Low-Carbon New Economy Hybrid Fund	15.74	17.89	532.63	Fullgoal Fund Mgt.
519983.OF	Changxin Quantitative Pioneer Hybrid Fund	15.17	19.01	7,447.44	Chang Xin Asset Mgt.

Source: China Knowledge Mutual Funds Database

4.4 BOND FUND

4.4.1 DEFINITION OF BOND FUND

A bond fund invests primarily in bonds and related debt instruments. The type of debt the fund invests in depends on the fund's investment strategy. Investments may include government, corporate, municipal and convertible bonds, as well as other debt instruments. In China, the net asset value of bond funds accounts for 12.74% of all funds. Per CSRC's Fund Category Classification, bond funds must invest at least 80% of their assets in bonds.

The following are some advantages and disadvantages of bond funds:

Advantages

(1) Lower Risk

By focusing investors' capital on different bond portfolio investments, bond funds can effectively reduce individual investor risk assumed by investing in bonds directly.

(2) Strong Liquidity

If investors invest in illiquid bonds, they receive cash only at maturity. However, when investors invest in bond funds, they may achieve a higher liquidity and transfer or redeem bond funds at any time.

Disadvantages

When investors hold bond funds for long periods of time, they may earn satisfactory returns. Compared to equity funds, however, bond fund returns are generally lower.

4.4.2 BOND FUND DEVELOPMENT AND MARKET PERFORMANCE

Most Bond Funds Earn Profits With Significant Variations in Individual Fund Performance

According to 2015 statistics published by the Asset Management Association of China (AMAC), China's bond market recorded an annual average net growth of 10%, building on 2014's growth. Furthermore, 686 open-end bond funds and 50 close-end bond funds respectively recorded annual average net growth rates of 9.78% and 11.48%,

Figure 4.10: Average NAV Growth Rate of All Bond Funds

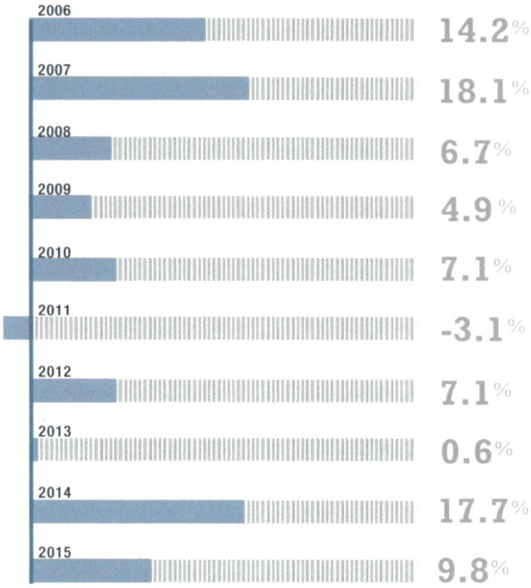

Source: China Knowledge Mutual Funds Database

Figure 4.11 Average NAV Growth Rate of Close-ended Bond Funds

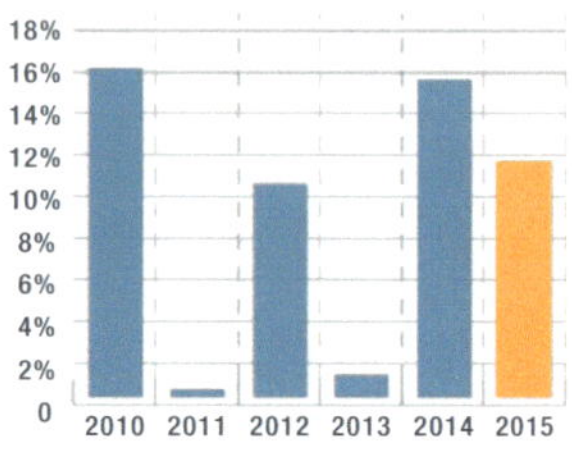

Source: China Knowledge Mutual Funds Database

Figure 4.12 Average NAV Growth Rate of Open-ended Bond Funds

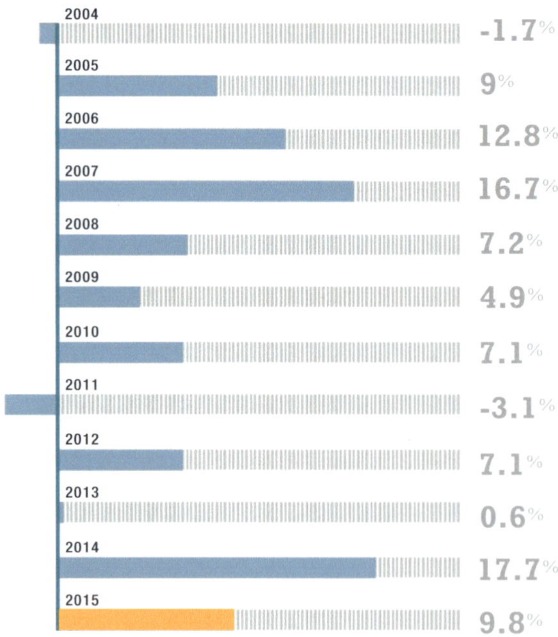

Source: China Knowledge Mutual Funds Database

Bond Market Rebounds After the April 2016 Crash

Capital supply loosened, tightened, and then steadied in 2016. At the beginning of the year, the PBoC increased the frequency and intensity of its open market operations and used a variety of liquidity tools to stabilize capital. With the arrival of the day for deposit payment in the first quarter of 2016, and with the implementation of the Macro-Prudential Assessment (MPA) system, bank financing faced short-term headwinds when the PBoC's willingness to fund it decreased. In April, affected by maturity of the medium-term lending facility (MLF) and changing of the tax form from a business tax to value added tax, the currency interest rate increased. This upward trend eased from late April and almost disappeared by the end of June 2016. The PBoC then continued to increase the frequency and intensity of open market operations in order to maintain capital stability.

After the bull market of 2014-15, the bond market adjusted. For interest rate bonds, the yields of treasury and policy financial bonds rose sharply due to factors such as capital supply, credit risk, tax system changes, rising commodity prices, and concerns over the impact of deleveraging. However, interest rate bond yields declined following the referendum on June 23, 2016, when British citizens voted to leave the European Union (Brexit). As for credit debt, by all measures more bond defaults occurred in the first five months of 2016, including the number of enterprises, bonds issued and total amount, than during the entire year in 2015. Enterprises that defaulted on their bonds in 2016 included: DongBei Special Steel Group, the first local state-owned enterprise to default; China Coal Group ShanXi HuaYu Energy, the first coal SOE to do so; and China Railway Material Group, the first AA+ SOE involved in this kind of event. The concentrated outbreak of these bond defaults made credit risk the bond market's greatest concern and affected both stocks and bonds.

In the first half of 2016, as a result of these events, the China Bond Aggregate Index Net Price Index fell by 0.50%; the China Bond Corporate Bond Index Net Price Index declined by 3.21%; the China Bond Treasury Bond Aggregate Index Net Price Index went down by 0.21%; and the CSI Convertible Bond Index fell by 11.90%.

Table 4.8 Bond Market Quotation

Index Name	Close Index	Changes (%)
Total Net Price Index	119.08	-0.50
Total Net Price Index of Corporate Bonds	91.39	-3.21
Total Net Price Index of Government Debts	120.03	-0.21

Source: China Knowledge Mutual Funds Database

Even though credit debt violations frequently happened during this period, asset shortages coupled with a bear market strengthened the investment value of bond market where investors could still find opportunities. Overall, the scale of bond funds increased from RMB 0.70 trillion at year-end 2015 (8.30%) to RMB 0.92 trillion by the end of June 2016 (11.61%).

Fixed Income Products Taking the Lead Position

In the first 10 months of 2016, 757 fixed income funds launched, exceeding the 658 that went into operation in the first 10 months of 2015. This suggests ongoing institutional enthusiasm of new issuances. Although the number of funds increased, their scale declined because of investors' passion for subscribing to funds cooled down after the April 2016 stock market collapse. The total number of shares of new fund issuance was 727.4 billion, far fewer than 1,437.80 billion issued during the first 10 months of 2015.

The total number of funds issued by category include 55 equity funds with 38.87 billion shares; 394 hybrid funds with 379.32 billion shares; 251 bond funds with 234.94 shares; 13 QDII funds with 9.04 billion shares; and 38 money market funds with 63.19 billion shares.

From among 383 newly issued products, 174 are equity with 83.94 billion shares (0.48 billion shares per product) and 202 are fixed income with 302.77 billion shares (1.50 billion shares per product). Investors clearly preferred fixed income products over alternative investments, of which only 7 with 2.41 billion shares (0.34 billion shares per product) were issued.

Prior to 2011, the market lacked enthusiasm for mutual funds, and fund share and size were small. Aside from a money shortage in 2013, since 2012, the scale of public funds has fast developed. The following table demonstrates that the NAV of the China Securities Index (CSI) and bond funds are now roughly equal.

Figure 4.13 Annual Volatility in Bond Funds

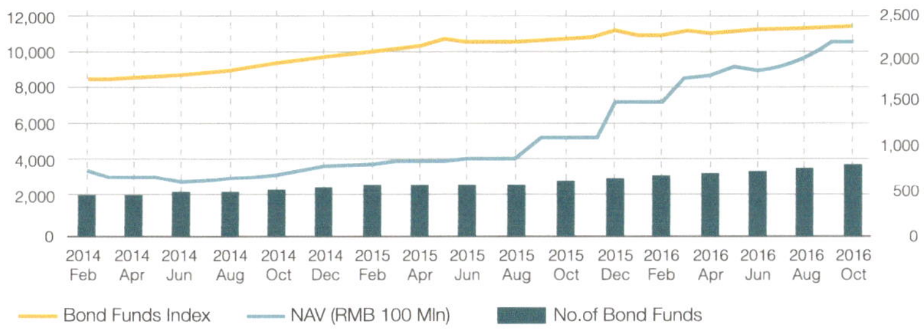

Source: China Knowledge Mutual Funds Database

By of the end of October 2016, 761 bond funds accounted for 22.57% of the all mutual funds. Total bond fund NAV totaled RMB 1,024. 2 billion (US$ 149.28 billion), and the average size of single bond fund was RMB 1.35 billion (US$ 0.19 billion).

Figure 4.14 Number of Fund Types by Percentage

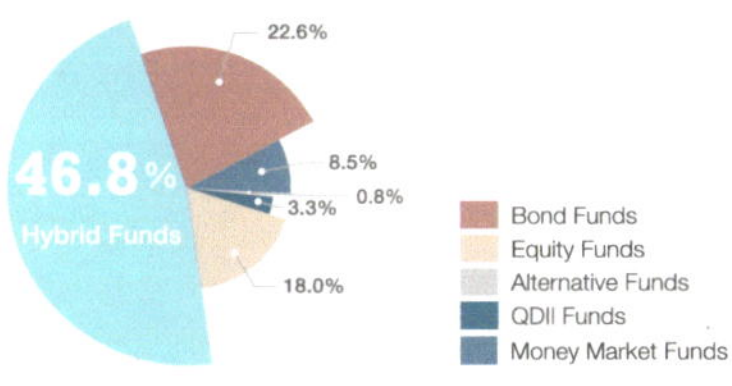

Source: China Knowledge Mutual Funds Database

Figure 4.15 Size of Fund Types by Percentage

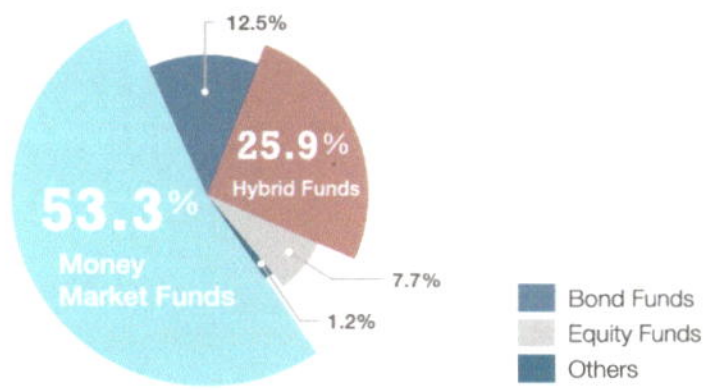

Source: China Knowledge Mutual Funds Database

Medium-and long-term bond funds ranked first among all bond funds based on size and quantity, followed by bond funds (class 2) and bond funds (class 1). By the same measures, index bond funds accounted only for 2% relative to equity index funds. This suggests that investors preferred active funds and more leverage exchange for promises of higher returns.

Figure 4.16 Number of Bond Fund Types by Percentage

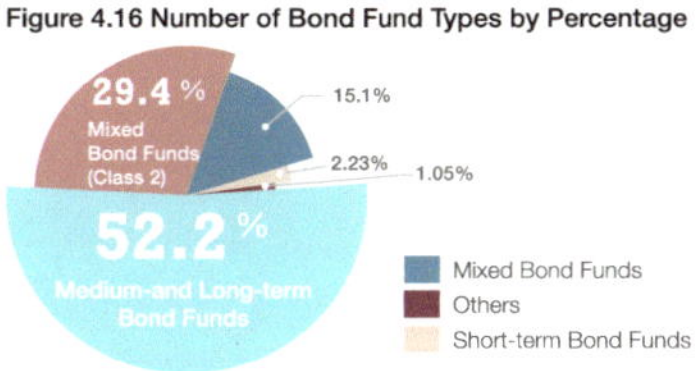

Source: China Knowledge Mutual Funds Database

Figure 4.17 Size of Bond Fund Types by Percentage

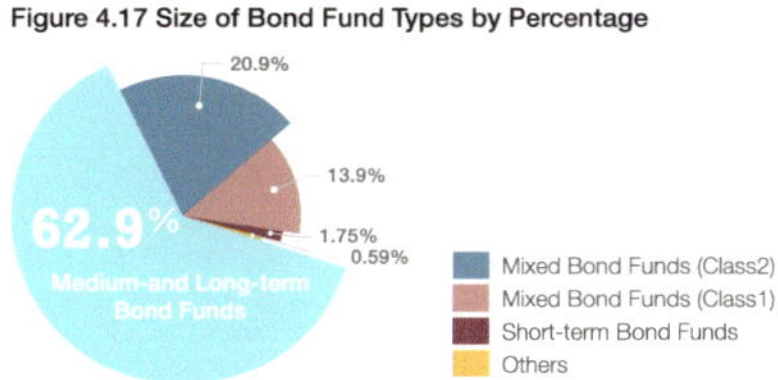

Source: China Knowledge Mutual Funds Database

Table 4.9 Average Size of Bond Funds (RMB Bln)

Fund Type	Average Size
Medium-and Long-term Bond Funds	1.63
Mixed Bond Funds (Class 1)	1.24
Short-term Bond Funds	1.09
Passive Index Bond Funds	1.06
Mixed Bond Funds (Class2)	0.96
Enhanced Index Bond Funds	0.21

Source: China Knowledge Mutual Funds Database

Bond funds are different from equity funds. Bond fund holders are mainly institutional investors. The following chart shows that institutional investors hold 75% of bond funds NAV.

Bond Fund Managers

At present, 330 bond fund managers work in the mutual funds industry, 85% of whom hold a master's degree. Although educated, most lack seniority. More than 60% of fund managers have less than three years of work experience, and most have never been through a bear market.

Figure 4.18 Holder Structure

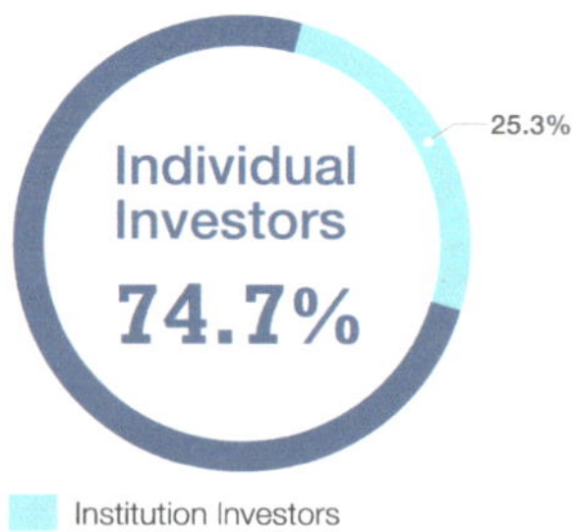

Source: China Knowledge Mutual Funds Database

Figure 4.19 Fund Manager's Working Experience Distribution

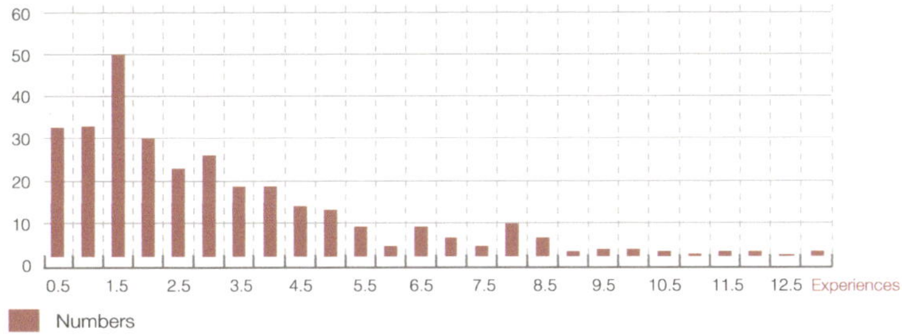

Source: China Knowledge Mutual Funds Database

Figure 4.20 Fund Manager's Degree Distribution

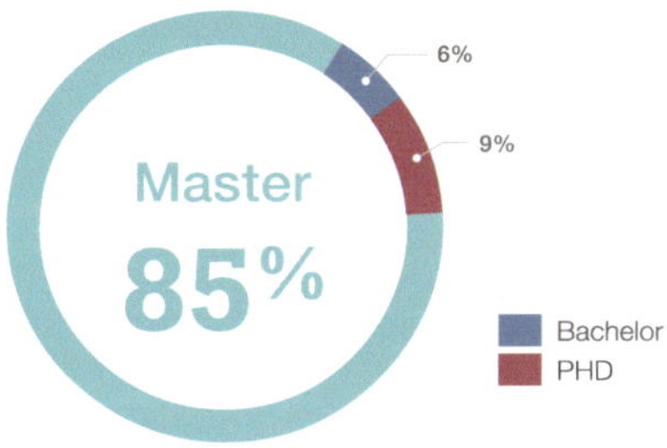

Source: China Knowledge Mutual Funds Database

Nearly 70% of bond fund managers have been working in that capacity for less than two years. Moreover, 23% of bond fund managers' work experience is less than six months. This is partly because bond fund manager turnover is very high. For long-term holdings of mutual funds, replacing a fund manager every half year seems too frequent. It is difficult for a fund to engage in stable long-term investment strategy and support investors when turnover happens so often.

Figure 4.21 Bond Fund Manager's Working Experience Distribution

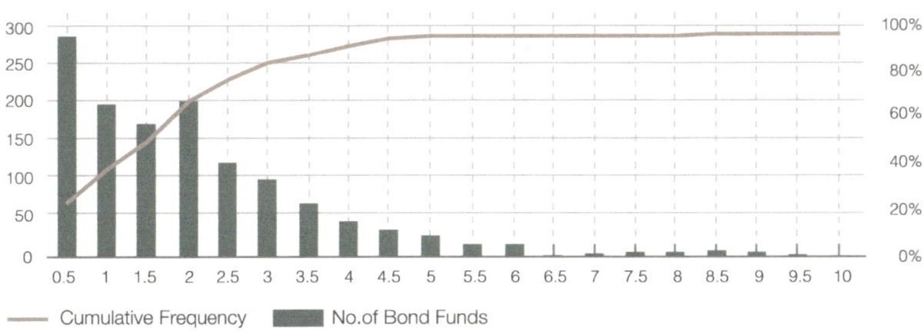

Source: China Knowledge Mutual Funds Database

Asset Allocation of Public Bond Funds

In terms of bond fund asset allocation, the credit debt allocation ratio has gradually increased since the third quarter of 2011. It reached a precarious 90% in the first quarter of 2013, much higher than 8-9% interest rate debt levels. This ratio peaked in the first quarter of 2015, but since declined. This may be the result of the breakdown of rigid payment methods and increased credit risk inherent within markets.

Figure 4.22 Bond Type Configuration in Bond Funds

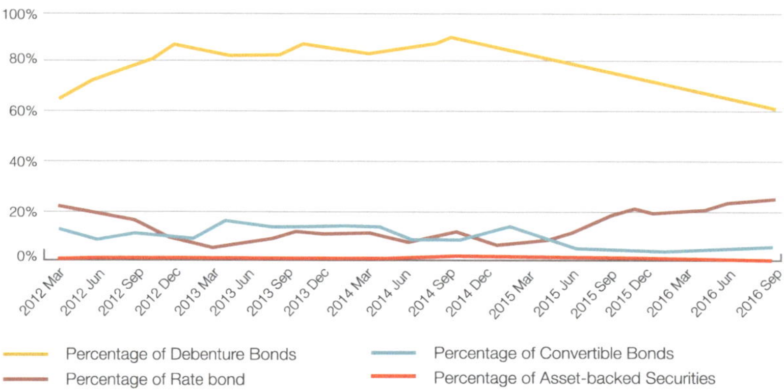

Source: China Knowledge Mutual Funds Database

The figures below depicts the bond market structure. Treasury and municipal bonds comprise more than 34% of the market and enjoy interest rates that far exceed those of public mutual funds. The reason why the net value of public mutual funds is much higher than that of the ChinaBond Composite Index is not limited to leverage factors but also the higher credit risk caused by increased credit debt.

The credit asset allocation of medium' and long-term bond funds is directly proportionate to its annual yield. From 2009 to 2015, with the notable exception of 2011, both metrics shared a positive correlation. Since 2014, however, this correlation diverged. This trend mirrors the change in investment style from asset allocation to more active trading with higher leverage and return. Meanwhile, irregular fluctuations between first- and second-grade bond funds indicate that there is no inherent relationship between them.

Maturity of Public Mutual Bond Funds

The maturity of public mutual bond funds lies within the 3-4 year level, slightly higher than the level of maturity for bonds in the stock market. More than 50% of the bonds in the market have maturities of three years or less. Among them, maturity periods of 1 year or less constitute 23.43%; 1-2 years, 12.55%; and 2-3 years, 13.37%.

Public mutual bond funds lend themselves to credit debt, and treasury bonds have the longest maturity periods in the market. Taking these factors into account, the average maturity of public mutual bond funds is significantly longer than those of typical bonds.

Figure 4.23 Average Duration of Bond Funds

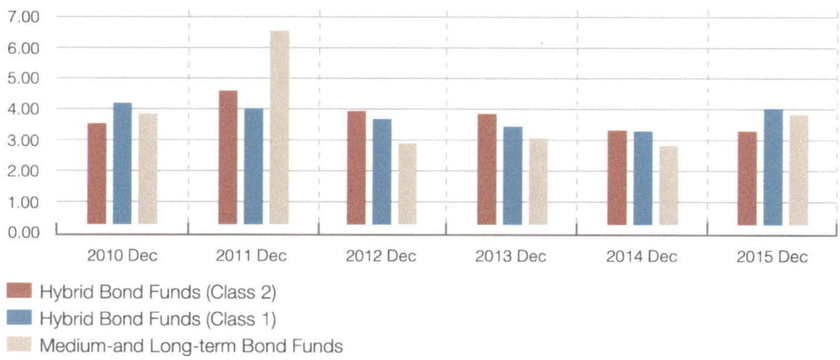

Source: China Knowledge Mutual Funds Database

The maturity of public mutual bond funds changes based on interest rates. In 2010, as bond yields grew, bond maturity remained relatively low. When interest rates began rising in 2011, the maturity of medium- and long-term bond funds increased significantly. In 2013, when bond yields spiked, the maturity of long-term debt dropped drastically. Although the bond market was bullish from 2014 to 2016, it took time in 2014 for the market to adjust. Bond maturity increased significantly from 2015 onwards.

It is evident that the outperformance of public mutual bond against the markets is attributable in part to interest rate trends. As bond funds follow interest rates, they adjust their maturity periods to earn higher yields.

This adjustment carries inherent interest rate risk. If the maturity of bond funds does not make timely adjustments, it is liable to suffer substantial losses.

4.5 ETFS AND LOFS

4.5.1 CHARACTERISTICS AND MARKET OF ETFS

Exchange-traded funds (ETFs) are open-end securities listed on a stock exchange that track other securities. It is a typical open-end fund whose portfolio is generally composed of equities in an underlying index. The performance of an ETF's net value is coincides with the performance of its underlying index.

Unlike funds whose investors own these assets, ETFs divide assets into shares sold on the stock market. They are traded on public stock exchanges and behave like stocks. They can be purchased, redeemed and transferred in the same manner as individual equities. Their transaction price depends on the value of the basket of equities they own, or the Unit Net Asset Value.

Table 4.10 Difference between ETFs and Index Funds

	ETF	Index Fund
Method of Purchase and Redemption	• In both primary and secondary markets • By a basket of shares	Only in the Primary Market By Cash
The lowest limit of Purchase and Redemption	• Primary Market: More than 500,000 shares and above RMB 1.5 million (US$ 0.22 million) • Secondary Market: More than 100 shares	Relatively low Small and medium investors can participate
Transparency	• Daily portfolio review • Real-time calculation of net value per share	Quarterly or semi-annually portfolio review Net asset value calculated at the end of day
Liquidity	Instantaneous transactions in both the primary and secondary markets	Fund share typically enters accounts two days after settlement
Interchange Fees	Do not exceed 0.3%	Purchase: 1% to 1.5% of Commission Charge Redemption: 0.5% Commission Charge

Source: China Knowledge Mutual Funds Database

Table 4.11 Difference between ETFs and Close-end Funds

	ETF	Close-end Fund
Fund Type	Index Fund	Includes both index funds and active funds
Transaction Method	ETFs can be transacted in both primary and secondary markets	Can only be traded in the secondary market
Discount Rate, Premium Rate and Liquidity	• Since ETF funds can be arbitraged in real time, discounting rate is relatively low • High liquidity due to arbitrage	• Relatively high ratio of premium and discount rates • Low fluidity due to discounts
Transparency	Real-time calculation of net value per share	• Quarterly or semi-annually portfolio review • Net asset value calculated at the end of every week with low transparency

Source: China Knowledge Mutual Funds Database

Transaction Model of ETFs in the Primary Market

Investors can purchase and sell ETFs in both the primary and secondary markets. In the primary market, dealers can establish or redeem ETFs if they satisfy the exchange requirements and complete listing procedures with ETF management companies. In the secondary market, investors may regard ETFs as listed shares or listed funds.

(1) Only Participating Dealers can Transact ETFs in the Primary Market

Participating dealers refer to intermediaries who signed participating agreements with ETF issuers to operate the creation and redemption of ETFs on behalf of non-primary dealers and other investors, or themselves. These intermediaries may also trade ETFs in the secondary market as stock brokers.

(2) Creation and Redemption Mechanism of ETFs

Participating dealers can only exchange ETF fund shares through a basket or redeem share baskets through ETF fund shares. The purchase and redemption of ETFs in the primary market offers the smallest purchase and redemption unit and varies by fund. For instance, the smallest purchase and redemption unit of the SSE 50 ETF is 1 million, while that of the SME Board ETF is 500,000.

Figure 4.24 Transaction Model of ETF in the Primary Market

Source: China Knowledge Mutual Funds Database

Transaction Model of ETFs in the Secondary Market

In the secondary market, investors can purchase or redeem an ETF in any stock account opened by legal securities brokers. For retail investors, ETF transactions are similar to close-end funds, since investors can purchase them in the secondary market at any time. With timely price changes, open-end funds may only be purchased or redeemed at the net closing price.

Figure 4.25 Transaction Model of ETFs in the Secondary Market

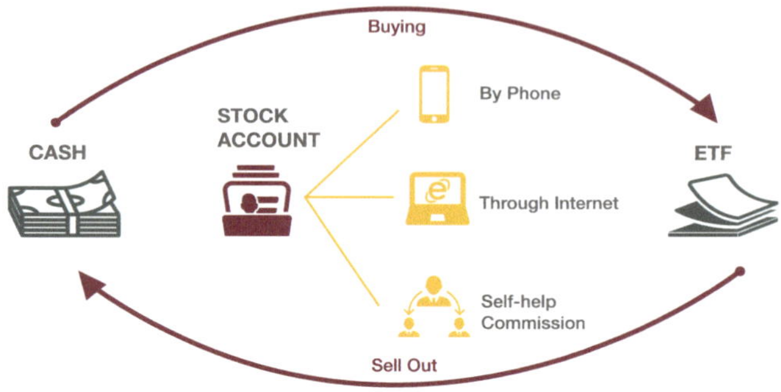

Source: China Knowledge Mutual Funds Database

Unlike steep discounts or premiums characterizing close-end funds, an ETF's market value is intrinsically close to its net worth since its unique purchase and redemption system link the primary and the secondary ETF markets together. When the transaction value of the ETF in the secondary market is higher than its net asset value, investors will buy in the stock portfolio with the same structure as the ETF Index in the secondary market and then purchase the ETF in the primary market. After that, investors can cash out the ETF in the secondary market at a higher value than its net asset value and earn the difference. On the contrary, when the ETF market value is lower than its net worth, investors will buy at the ETF's market price and then redeem the ETF in the primary market in exchange for a stock portfolio. Investors can then sell stocks in secondary market to earn profit.

Figure 4.26 Arbitrage Model of ETFs

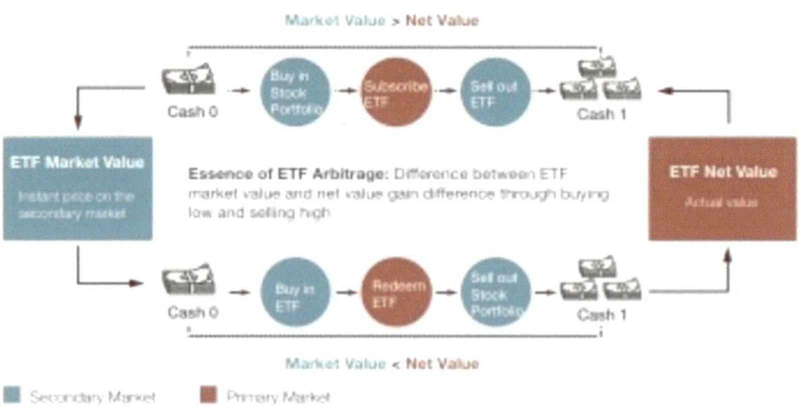

When the discount or premium in prices in the ETF primary and secondary markets occurs, investors will arbitrage and narrow the price gap between two markets, so the real transaction price of ETFs in the secondary market is almost the same as their net value, indicating that ETFs will not trade at such a steep discount or premium as close-end funds. Since the purchase and redemption of ETFs are conducted through the buying and selling of stocks, ETF managers don't need to reserve currency for redemptions, hence keeping the capital flow.

ETF Fund Fees

The operating costs of ETFs in broad terms include administrative fees, trustee fees, index usage fees, registration fees, marketing fees, attorney fees, and audit fees, among others. ETF operational fees are generally lower than those of other fund types.

(1) ETFs Compared to Actively Managed Funds

ETF is a kind of index fund. The administrative fees of index funds are generally lower than those of actively-managed funds. Hence, ETFs operation fees are typically lower than those of actively-managed open-end funds.

(2) ETFs Compared to Open-end Index Funds

Since ETF transactions require investors to purchase or redeem the fund share through a basket of shares, the purchase and redemption process of cash transactions is omitted. Hence, an ETF's operational fee is lower than that of an open-end index fund.

Most ETFs have a combined custodian and management fee of 0.6% and do not charge subscription or redemption fees. This stands in contrast to typical index funds with a combined custodian and management fee between 0.7% and 0.12%, subscription fees ranging from 0.8% to 1.2%, and redemption fees between 0.25% and 0.5%. Active funds charge even more, with a combined custodian and management fee between 1.45% and 1.75%, subscription fees from 1% to 1.5%, and redemption fees between 0.5% and 0.75%.

Figure 4.27 Fund Rate of different Types of Funds

Source: China Knowledge Mutual Funds Database

ETF Risk

(1) Market Risks

The net value of an ETF fund share is volatile and changes as the stock price changes. The economic operation cycle and the short-term volatility in the ETF price can negatively impact investors.

(2) Passive Investment Risks

Since an ETF is closely related to its index, it lacks flexibility and is subject to market risk as its index rises and falls.

(3) Tracking Error

Tracking error refers to the difference between a portfolio position and the tracked index. It is often recorded as the standard deviation of the percentage difference of the return on investment (ROI) and index return. It is used to assess investment performance against a benchmark.

Fund Varieties

Domestic ETFs are classified into different categories according to their investment strategies and asset classes. ETFs adopt active or passive investing strategies. Asset classes tracked by the fund fall into four categories: equities or stocks, bonds, commodities, and money market instruments. The first three are considered passive asset classes while money market instruments are in the active asset class.

Figure 4.28 ETF Fund Classification

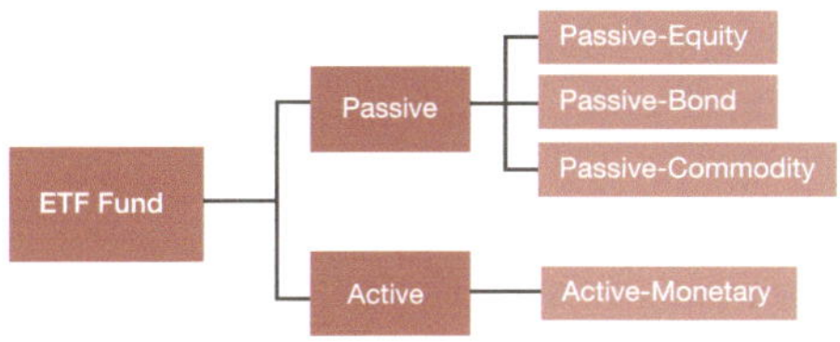

Source: China Knowledge Mutual Funds Database

As of July 2016, there were 132 ETFs in China with a total net asset value of RMB 463.6 billion (US$ 67.21 billion). Among these, 114 were passive funds. The 18 active money market ETFs rivaled their passive peers in size with a net asset value of RMB 187.2 billion (US$ 27.14 billion) compared to the passive funds' RMB 276.4 billion (US$ 40.07 billion) net asset value.

Based on average daily turnover statistics in January 2016, money market ETFs enjoyed higher liquidity than other ETF types. Equity ETFs experienced the greatest volatility following China's 2015 stock market crash and yielded the lowest returns.

Equity ETFs are the most common of the four equity ETF classes. They are classified based on market capitalization, sector, broad based or global. The largest equity ETF class, market capitalization ETFs, has a market share of 84.32%. Following China's 2015 stock market crash, global ETFs were the best performers with the least volatility and highest returns.

Table 4.12 ETFs' Four Major Asset Types (as of end-July 2016)

Variety	Number	Total Asset (RMB Bln)	Proportion	Average Asset (RMB Bln)	Daily Average Trading Volume in the latest Month (RMB Mln)	Average Yield of the latest Year	Volatility of the latest Year
Bond	4	7.18	1.55%	1.80	20.73	5.56%	1.40%
Commodities	4	7.53	1.62%	1.88	136.36	24.47%	15.04%
Equity	106	172.53	37.21%	1.63	27.24	-10.73%	35.33%
Currency	18	276.39	59.61%	15.35	1,898.66	1.76%	0.11%

Source: China Knowledge Mutual Funds Database

Table 4.13 Equity ETF Types (as of end-July 2016)

Variety	Number	Total Asset (RMB Bln)	Proportion	Average Asset (RMB Mln)	Daily Average Trading Volume in the latest Month (RMB Mln)	Average Yield of the latest Year	Volatility of the latest Year
Market Size Index	47	145.47	84.32%	3,095.11	51.25	-10.17%	36.49%
Thematic Indices	18	3.46	2.00%	192.10	0.45	-16.79%	35.23%
Industry Indices	32	9.70	5.62%	303.05	0.72	-10.30%	37.13%
Global	9	13.90	8.06%	1,544.35	52.36	-3.02%	23.07%

Source: China Knowledge Mutual Funds Database

Global ETF Market

In 2015, ETFs reached more than US$ 2 trillion in assets globally and attracted nearly US$ 3 billion in new investment.

Figure 4.29 2000-15 ETF Global Assets (US $ Bln)

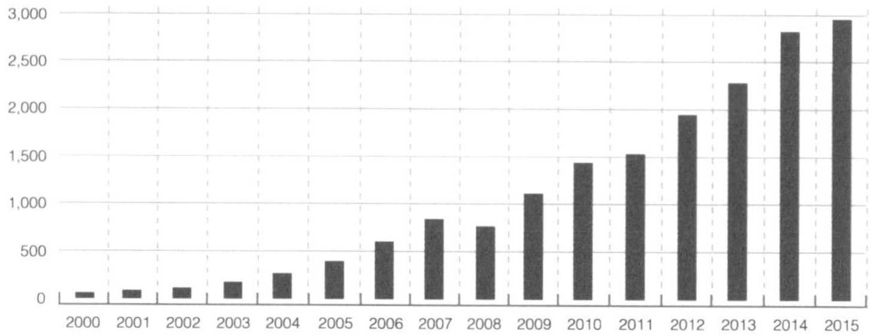

Source: Investment Company Institute

Currently, there are more than 300 varieties of ETFs globally with a wide spectrum of investment scope ranging from industrial, national, and regional ETFs to finance, technology and public utilities ETFs. Apart from traditional instruments like bank deposits, bonds, funds and equities, the ETF industry provides investors with another financial vehicle featuring high stability, low transaction costs, high liquidity and low barriers to entry. This allows them to invest without extensive financial literacy.

Additionally, ETFs enjoy low transaction costs and high transparency, with characteristics mirroring those of their tracked index. This makes ETFs an essential asset for international institutional investors and has led to the widespread approval and recognition of global ETFs. Vanguard, one of the world's largest index fund companies, has not only issued many new ETFs but may gradually convert all of its index funds into ETFs.

The United States introduced ETFs to the financial world and is naturally home to the largest ETF market. In 2000, ETFs pushed aside index funds and technology funds to become the new sweetheart of the U.S. fund market. In terms of the size of issuances and assets, ETFs experienced exponential growth after 2000. At end of 1999, there were 32 ETFs with a net asset value of US$ 35.9 billion. By the end of 2002, there were 116 ETFs with a NAV exceeding US$ 100 billion. In mid-2004, there were 134 ETFs with a NAV of US$ 165 billion.

The U.S. ETF market—with 1,594 funds and US$ 2.1 trillion in assets under management by the end of 2015—remained the largest in the world, accounting for 72% of the US$ 2.9 trillion in ETF assets worldwide.

Figure 4.30 ETF Global Asset as of End-2015

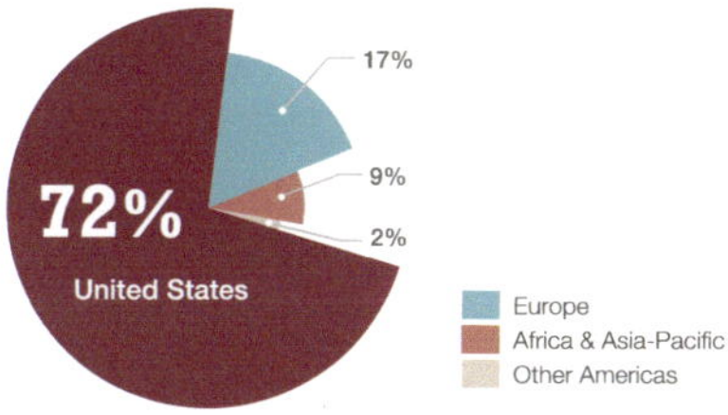

Source: Investment Company Institute

Figure 4.31 ETF Market in the U.S. as of End-2015

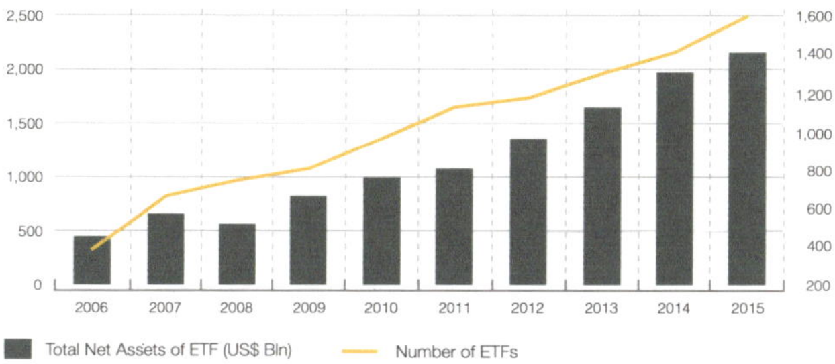

Source: Investment Company Institute

China's ETF Market

Because more than 99% of Chinese listed companies on China's stock markets were originally state-owned enterprises, the decline of state-owned shares has been the biggest factor in the stock market's poor performance. In the second quarter of 2001, CSRC drew up the China National Index System in a bid to resolve the issue of government holdings exceeding US$ 100 billion worth of firm ownership. The index was the result of cooperation between CSRC and State Street Corporation and based on the concept of The Tracker Fund of Hong Kong and the ETF design model.

To prepare to list ETFs, the SSE 180 Index and SSE 50 Index went through several rounds of reforms. In 2004, the Shanghai Stock Exchange finally released the first mainland index ETF, the Huaxia Shanghai 50 ETF, managed by the Huaxia Fund Management Co., Ltd.

Later, in December 2004, the SSE launched the first SSE 50 ETF, marking the official entry of ETFs into China's markets. The Shenzhen 100 ETF, Shanghai Dividend ETF, Small-Mid ETF and Shanghai 180 ETF subsequently entered the market. Two years later, the government launched the Central Enterprises ETF, and shortly thereafter, the SSE Governance 180 ETF. As of December 20, 2012, there were 42 ETF products in the Chinese market, including cross-market ETFs Huatia Borui CSI 300 ETF and Castrol CSI 300 ETF.

By mid-November 2016, China's ETF assets totaled RMB 465.4 billion (US$ 67.88 billion), or 5.17% of total fund assets. From 2010 to 2015, ETF net assets grew more than fivefold from RMB 71.5 billion (US$ 10.43 billion) to RMB 465.4 billion (US$ 67.88 billion).

Figure 4.32 2010-16 ETF Market in China

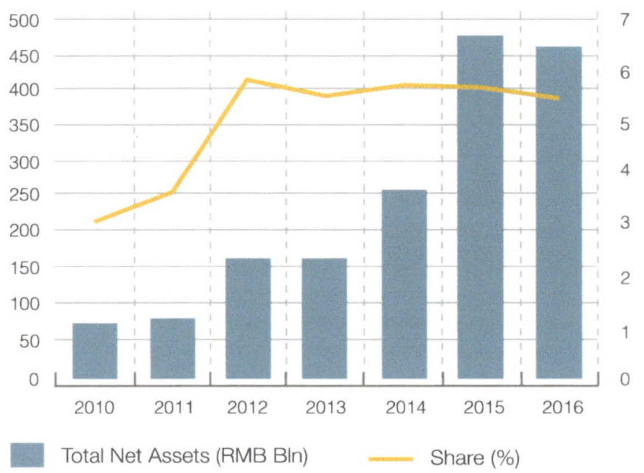

Source: China Knowledge Mutual Funds Database

Since 2010, China's ETF industry has developed rapidly, with the number and size of ETFs increasing almost daily. In 2015, ETFs' net asset value increased 85%, mainly due to the increase in scale of a few but large money market ETFs. By 2009, passive ETFs also bulked up considerably save 2015, when the stock market crash led to a temporary decline.

Figure 4.33 2005-15 ETF Numbers in China

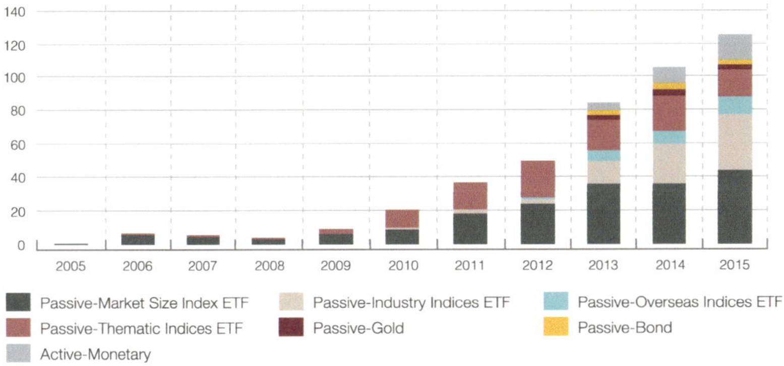

Source: China Knowledge Mutual Funds Database

Figure 4.34 2005-15 Net Asset Value of Passive ETF in China (RMB Bln)

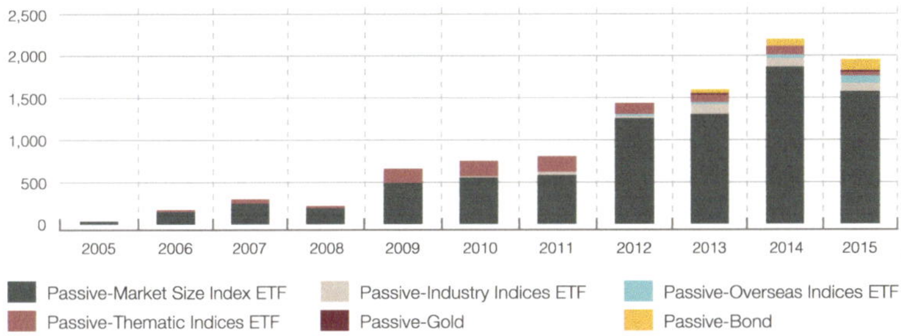

Source: China Knowledge Mutual Funds Database

More than 75% of the top 20 ETFs based on year-to-date returns are listed on the Shanghai Stock Exchange. Only 5% are on the Shenzhen Stock Exchange.

Table 4.14 Top 20 ETF Funds in terms of Year-to-Date Returns

Code	Name	YTD Returns (%)	Annualized Returns (%)	Fund Manager
513500.SH	Bosera S&P 500 ETF	14.67	9.84	Bosera Asset Mgt.
512880.SH	Guotai CSI All Share Investment Banking & Brokerage Index ETF	12.58	30.61	Guotai Asset Mgt.
159920.SZ	ChinaAMC Hang Seng ETF	12.55	16.20	China Asset Mgt.
513100.SH	Guotai NASDAQ 100 ETF	12.08	10.42	Guotai Asset Mgt.
513660.SH	ChinaAMC Shanghai-Hong Kong Tong Hang Seng ETF	11.44	14.68	China Asset Mgt.
513600.SH	China Southern Hang Seng ETF	11.18	14.27	China Southern Fund Mgt.
159941.SZ	GF NASDAQ 100 ETF	11.00	9.23	GF Fund Mgt.
510680.SH	Wanjia SSE 50 ETF	9.67	7.22	Wanjia Asset Mgt.
510900.SH	E Fund HSCEI ETF	8.66	8.87	E Fund Mgt.
512000.SH	Fortune SG CSI All Share Investment Banking & Brokerage Index ETF	7.92	15.31	Fortune SGAM Fund Mgt.
159948.SZ	China Southern ChiNext ETF	7.47	2.21	China Southern Fund Mgt.
512210.SH	Invesco Great Wall CSI 800 Food And Beverage ETF	7.28	20.83	Invesco Great Wall Fund Mgt.
159945.SZ	GF CSI All Share Energy Index EFT	4.03	3.79	GF Fund Mgt.
510810.SH	CSI Shanghai SOEs ETF	3.28	-0.69	China Universal Asset Mgt.
512600.SH	Harvest CSI Consumer Staples ETF	3.27	15.99	Harvest Fund Mgt.
159928.SZ	China Universal CSI Consumer Staples ETF	2.98	14.27	China Universal Asset Mgt.
510630.SH	ChinaAMC SSE Consumer Staples ETF Initiating Fund	2.39	10.11	China Asset Mgt.
512100.SH	China Southern CSI 1000 ETF	2.24	-4.29	China Southern Fund Mgt.
510410.SH	Bosera SSE Natural Resources ETF	2.20	2.27	Bosera Asset Mgt.
510020.SH	Bosera SSE Super Broader ETF	2.17	2.51	Bosera Asset Mgt.

Source: China Knowledge Mutual Funds Database

4.5.2 DEFINITION OF LOF AND MARKET PERFORMANCE

Listed Open-End Funds (LOFs) refer to the issuance, listing and trading of open-end securities investment funds on a stock exchange. LOFs may be issued by a stock exchange and participate in centralized trading through fund managers, banks, and financial agencies. While the operating model of open-end funds do not restrict the amount of shares the fund can issue, listing on the stock exchange increases stock issuances and channels for transactions.

LOFs are essentially open-end funds whereby the total fund amount is not fixed, and fund shares can be purchased and redeemed at the time and place stated in the fund contract.

LOFs combine the sales advantage of distribution agencies such as banks as well as the online sales channel of the Shenzhen Stock Exchange. Distribution agencies such as banks continue to conduct over-the-counter sales, while the transaction system of Shenzhen Stock Exchange carries out online pricing.

After LOFs began to trade on the Shenzhen Stock Exchange, investors had the choice to purchase and redeem their shares in banks according to the fund's net asset value, or buy and sell their shares according to the transaction price listed on the Shenzhen Stock Exchange.

An LOF's valuation in the secondary market is similar to that of a stock on the same market. It is determined by the forces of supply and demand and fluctuates with every interaction between buyers and sellers. LOFs' net asset value represents the total value of financial instruments purchased with raised capital and is set by purchase and redemption transactions. LOF fund managers have the authority to invest fund capital in a variety of investment vehicles.

The share value of LOFs fluctuates continuously during the trading day. The fund's net asset value will be calculated daily after trading ends based on the closing values of the constituent assets in its portfolio. Although only one net asset value figure is released per day, differences often exist between the LOF's share value in the market and its net asset value. Arbitrage opportunities arise when the trading price is greater than NAV and the difference more than transaction costs (usually 1.5% subscription fees plus 0.3% secondary market transaction fees).

Domestic LOFs implement the T+1 trading system in the secondary markets, whereby fund shares can only be redeemed or sold one trading day after purchase. In primary markets, however, LOFs implement the T+2 system through which fund shares can only be redeemed after subscription or sold in the secondary market two trading days after purchase. This is significantly less efficient than ETFs and creates a degree of arbitrage risk for LOFs.

LOFs are similar to ETFs in that both securities can be purchased and redeemed on the primary and secondary markets. Unlike ETFs, however, LOFs cannot be used in barter trade during subscription and redemption. Only cash is allowed during LOF transactions through designated fund channels.

Table 4.15 Comparison between ETFs and LOFs

	ETF	LOF
Purchase and Redemption Method	Through a basket of shares	Through cash
Minimum purchase and redemption limitation	≥RMB 1.5 million (US$ 0.22 million)	Relatively small and small- and medium investors can participate
Variety of fund	Index fund	Can be both the index and the active funds
Price discount or premium rate	Relatively low due to real time arbitrage	Purchase and redemption settled according to the closing price
Liquidity	Good liquidity	Poor liquidity
Transparency	• Release the portfolio everyday • Release the unit net value in real time	• Release the portfolio every quarter or every half-year • Release the net value of previous date everyday
Trustee Fee + Administrative Fee	0.6%	1.25%
Purchase Fee	N.A	1.50%
Redemption Fee	N.A	0.50%

Source: China Knowledge Mutual Funds Database

Types of LOF

Domestic LOFs can be divided into different categories according to their investment strategy and asset classes. LOFs adopt one of two investing strategies: active or passive investing. Asset classes tracked by the fund can be divided into four categories: stocks, bonds, commodities, and money market instruments.

As of July 2016, there were a total of 175 LOFs with a total net asset value of RMB 178.8 billion (US$ 26.93 billion). Of these, there were 122 and 53 active and passive funds, with net asset values of RMB 136.2 billion (US$ 20.51 billion) and RMB 42.6 billion (US$ 6.42 billion), respectively. Active funds comprised of stocks, bonds, and commodities are larger in scale and quantity than passive money market funds. ETFs only track indexes, while LOFs include both the index and active funds. Although the LOF offers more investment options than ETFs, most LOFs invest in equities.

As of July 2016, 66.93% of active LOFs and 94.64% of passive LOFs were invested in the Chinese stock market.

In terms of liquidity, commodity LOFs ranked highest, followed by equity, bond, and money market LOFs. It is interesting to note that more commodity LOFs than commodity ETFs are available in China's stock market. Of the seven commodity LOFs, five are active funds that track the Guotai Commodity Allocation Index, London gold prices, S&P Goldman Sachs Commodities Index and WTI, Brent crude oil prices. The remaining two are passive funds that track gold and silver in London. Tracking diverse indexes is more effective for large-scale asset allocation of LOFs.

Although the number of ETFs and LOFs in the market are roughly equal, ETFs' scale far outweighs that of the latter because LOFs are longer term than short-term investments. While ETFs track benchmarks at current interest rates or seven-day notice rates, LOFs use one, two or even three-year interest rates that are certain to float up.

Table 4.16 LOF Types (as of end-July)

Variety	Number	Total Asset (RMB Bln)	Proportion	Average Asset (RMB Bln)	Daily Average Trading Volume in the latest Month (RMB Mln)	Average Yield of the latest Year	Volatility of the latest Year
Bond	4	1.53	3.59%	0.38	0.05	6.78%	1.41%
Commodities	2	0.75	1.76%	0.38	8.11	17.27%	14.81%
Equity	47	40.31	94.64%	0.86	3.08	-8.98%	31.44%

Source: China Knowledge Mutual Funds Database

Passive equity LOFs are classified like ETFs according to market capitalization, subject, sector, and whether they are global. In terms of scale, market capitalization LOFs are the largest, accounting for 70.64% of market share. In terms of yield, the volatility of the stock market in 2015 has resulted in global LOFs being the most stable and profitable LOF class.

Table 4.17 Equity LOF Types (as of end-July)

Variety	Number	Total Asset (RMB Bln)	Proportion	Average Asset (RMB Bln)	Daily Average Trading Volume in the latest Month (RMB Mln)	Average Yield of the latest Year	Volatility of the latest Year
Market Size Index	20	28.48	70.64%	1.42	0.29	-10.20%	35.89%
Thematic Indices	8	2.75	6.83%	0.34	0.41	-14.04%	34.77%
Industry Indices	11	2.73	6.78%	0.25	3.70	-6.41%	29.65%
Global	8	6.35	15.75%	0.79	13.19	-4.39%	19.44%

Source: China Knowledge Mutual Funds Database

Development of the LOF Market

The first mainland LOF, the Southern Active Allocation Fund established on October 14, 2004, marked the launch of China's LOF market. Over the next two years, LOFs developed gradually until growth exploded in 2007, when their NAV grew 20 times year over year as a result of the 2007 bull market. They dropped 50% the following year, weighed down by the bear market. From 2009 on, volatility left the LOF scale in a state of disarray even as their number steadily increased.

Figure 4.35 2005-15 Number of LOFs in China

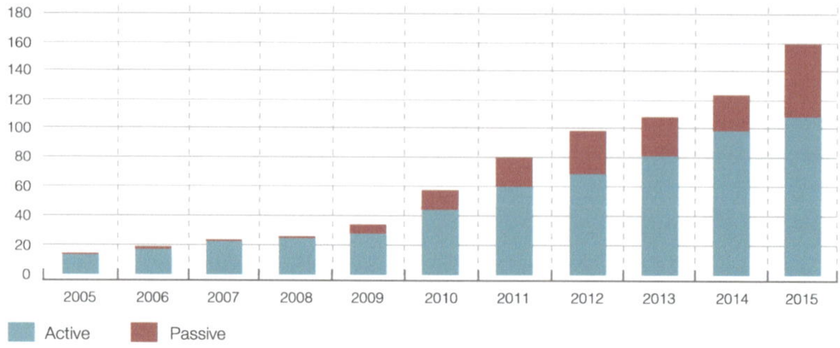

Source: China Knowledge Mutual Funds Database

Figure 4.36 2005-15 Total LOF Assets in China (RMB Bln)

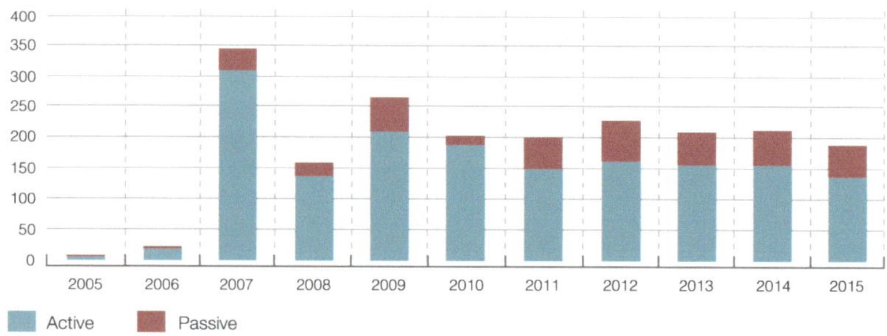

Source: China Knowledge Mutual Funds Database

In terms of YTD returns of the top 20 LOFs, 53% are QDII funds, 32% equity funds, 10% bond funds, and 5% hybrid funds.

Table 4.18 Top 20 LOF in Terms of Year-to-Date Returns (as of end-Oct 2016)

Code	Name	YTD Returns (%)	Annualized Returns (%)	Fund Manager
162411.OF	Fortune SG S&P Oil & Gas Exploration & Production Select Industry Index Fund (LOF)(CNY)	32.53	8.15	Fortune SGAM Fund Mgt.
163208.OF	Lion Oil and Gas Energy Equity Fund (LOF)	24.93	9.34	Lion Fund Mgt.
164815.OF	ICBCCS S&P Global Resources Index Fund (LOF)	21.75	16.74	ICBC Credit Suisse Asset Mgt.
165525.OF	Citic-Prudential CSI Construction & Engineering Index Fund (LOF)	20.80	68.21	Citic-Prudential Fund Mgt.
160416.OF	Huaan S&P Global Oil Index Equity Fund (LOF)	20.74	11.41	HuaAn Fund Mgt.
161229.OF	UBS SDIC China Value Discover Equity Fund	20.69	29.97	UBS SDIC Fund Mgt.
161116.OF	E Fund Gold Theme Fund (LOF)	19.05	27.05	E Fund Mgt.
164701.OF	China Universal Gold and Precious Metals Fund (LOF)	18.76	28.18	China Universal Asset Mgt.
160719.OF	Harvest Gold Securities Investment Fund (LOF)	18.50	27.31	Harvest Fund Mgt.
161225.OF	UBS SDIC Ruiying Dynamic Allocation Hybrid Fund (LOF)	14.91	25.01	UBS SDIC Fund Mgt.
161714.OF	China Merchants S&P BRIC Index Fund (LOF)	13.12	18.63	China Merchants Fund Mgt.
164908.OF	Bocom Schroders CSI Comprehensive Ecological Improvement Index Fund (LOF)	9.66	46.97	Bank of Communications Schroder Fund Mgt.
160512.OF	Bosera Excellent Brand Hybrid Fund (LOF)	9.39	17.63	Bosera Asset Mgt.
162107.OF	Golden Eagle Quantitative Selected Equity Fund (LOF)	9.19	17.74	Golden Eagle Asset Mgt.
501002.OF	Changxin CSI Energy Internet Theme Index Fund (LOF)	8.80	9.76	Chang Xin Asset Mgt.
163110.OF	SWS MU Quantitative Small Cap Equity Fund (LOF)	7.89	19.74	SWS MU Fund Mgt.
161716.OF	China Merchants Double-Bonds Enhanced Bond Fund (LOF)	6.99	9.20	China Merchants Fund Mgt.
161217.OF	UBS SDIC CSI Upstream Resource Industries Index Fund (LOF)	6.92	6.15	UBS SDIC Fund Mgt.
162415.OF	Fortune SG S&P Consumer Discretionary Select Sector Index Fund (LOF)(CNY)	6.60	6.21	Fortune SGAM Fund Mgt.
167501.OF	Anxin Baoli Bond Fund (LOF)	6.47	8.93	Essence Fund Mgt.

Source: China Knowledge Mutual Funds Database

4.6 QUALIFIED DOMESTIC INSTITUTIONAL INVESTORS (QDII)

4.6.1 OVERVIEW OF QDII

The China Securities Regulatory Commission (CSRC) established the Qualified Domestic Institutional Investor scheme in April 2006. QDII allows financial institutions to raise capital from mainland Chinese investors and convert it into foreign currencies to purchase overseas investments. It allows retail investors to invest in offshore securities by investing in QDII institutions approved by CSRC. This increased exposure to foreign stocks and helped provide a growing number of domestic investors with an alternative to investing on the Shanghai and Shenzhen Stock Exchanges.

A QDII is typically a Chinese bank, securities firm, or other institution that meets specified requirements to engage in overseas securities investment. An institutional investor with QDII status is allowed to invest a maximum 50% of net assets into a list of approved foreign securities, with no more than 5% invested in a single security. Only certain foreign markets such as Hong Kong and the United States are eligible for investment.

A domestic firm may employ a foreign fund manager if they have a minimum five years of fund management experience; own a minimum of US$10 billion in assets under management; and possess a memorandum of understanding with CSRC. At the same time, a foreign fund manager may raise capital from domestic Chinese investors if they enter a joint venture or hold a minority stake in a QDII.

4.6.2 DEVELOPMENT OF QDII

Industry Timeline

On April 13, 2006, CSRC officially announced the QDII scheme and encouraged domestic investors to park their money with approved commercial banks for such overseas investments. However, only investments in fixed income and money market securities were permitted.

On May 11, 2007, CSRC granted 15 QDII commercial banks and funds US$ 14.2 billion and allowed them to expand their investment scope to include equity-related products that were either approved by or have MOUs with CSRC. However, the net value of a QDII product investing in stocks was still limited to a maximum of 50%, with the net value of a single stock capped at 5%. Client had to invest at least RMB 300,000.

In November 2007, Chinese Premier Wen Jiabao cautioned domestic investors to be careful when purchasing Hong Kong shares. He highlighted the need for further examination of the train scheme that allows mainlanders to invest directly in Hong Kong stocks.

On April 8, 2008, the China Banking Regulatory Commission (CBRC) and U.S. Securities and Exchange Commission (SEC) signed an agreement that allowed Chinese investors to enter the U.S. stock market directly.

On May 26, 2015, CSRC announced a second iteration of the scheme called QDII2. This iteration lifted the limitation of allowing only institutions to invest directly overseas and allowed individuals with a minimum of RMB 1 million worth of financial assets to invest overseas within a prescribed quota. The pilot scheme is set to launch in Shanghai, Tianjin, Chongqing, Wuhan, Shenzhen, and Wenzhou.

Product Innovation Development Cycle

Over the past few years, both the quantity and scale of QDII funds have gradually accelerated, leading to improved product innovation within the industry. The entire product innovation development cycle went through three phases.

In the first phase, CSRC issued the first QDII license to a securities company, HuaAn Fund Management, in 2006. With an estimated investment budget of US $500 million, HuaAn collaborated with Lehman Brothers and became the first independent QDII asset management firm to denominate assets in US dollars. This phase concentrated on global equity allocation in order to minimize risks.

The second phase of the cycle occurred between 2007 and mid-2010. During this period, there was an influx of QDII funds issuance, mainly those of equity QDII funds. The investment strategies of these funds typically revolved around a fund's target region, such as investing in Asian markets.

The third phase started after mid-2010, when QDII fund investments increasingly diversified. In a span of four months, Wells Fargo launched its international bond QDII fund in October 2010, Yinhua Fund Management issued its ETF fund in December 2010, and Lion Fund Management established its gold ETF fund in January 2011.

4.6.3 PRESENT DEVELOPMENT

The following overview, statistics and news segments cover QDII industry's current market situation.

Current QDII Overview

An overview of the minimum investment required, investment scope, risk level and methods of issuance and purchase in the QDII industry is covered in the table below.

Table 4.19 Current QDII Overview

Minimum Investment Required	RMB 1,000
Investment Scope	Hong Kong stocks, overseas ETFs, and active funds are the main investment targets. Investments in funds and equities constitute 95% of net asset value, with fund investment making up 60% of fund assets and investment in money market instruments and other financial tools the remaining 0-40%.
Level of Risk	Medium-high. Expected risk and return is lower than that of global ETFs but higher than bond and money market funds.
Issuance and Purchase Methods	Bank purchase, fund company purchase, securities account purchase

Source: China Knowledge Mutual Funds Database

Because QDII funds have a wide investment scope and invest in an assortment of securities, their returns vary greatly. Most of the 69 QDII funds can be classified under equity funds, fixed-income funds, and alternative asset funds. The various orientations of QDII funds is summarized below.

Figure 4.37 Investment Direction of QDII Funds

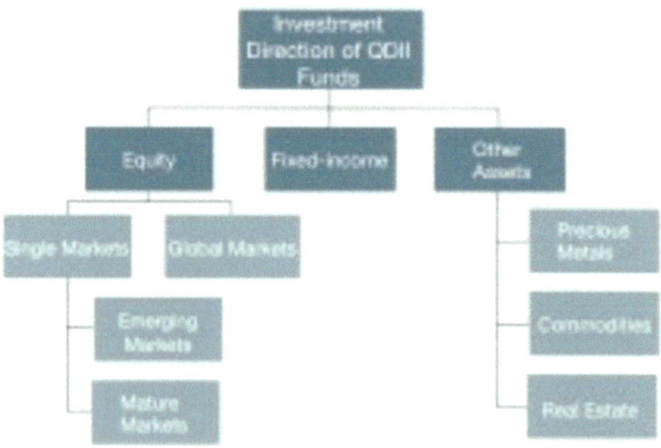

Source: China Knowledge Mutual Funds Database

Current QDII Statistics

Current QDII statistics will cover the proportion of industry funds in terms of asset volume, shares and quantity. It will also present an overview of fund investments by market and geographical segmentation, and give a breakdown of the scale of the QDII quota. Finally, this segment ended with the latest ranking of QDII funds at the end of December 2016.

Figure 4.38 Proportion of QDII Funds

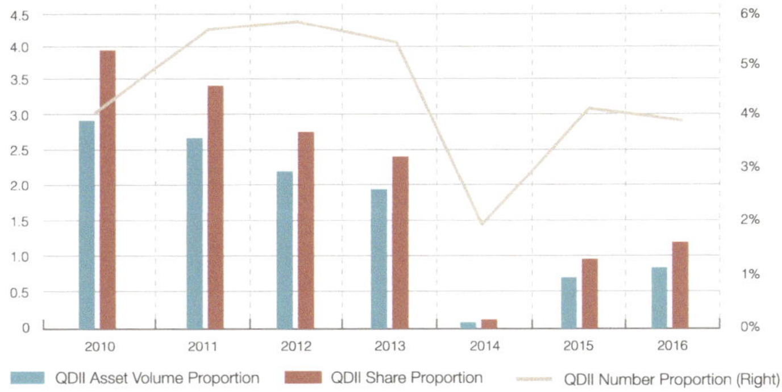

Source: China Knowledge Mutual Funds Database

The number of QDII funds grew 340% from 2010 to 2016. The net asset value and total quota of these funds dropped 17.78% year over year in 2014 and 18.23% in 2015, the greatest decline in seven years. In 2016, net asset value and the total quota of QDII funds rebounded, increasing 40.73% and 39.17% to RMB 79.49 billion and RMB 103.3 billion, respectively.

The volume of QDII funds has notably dropped in proportion to the total volume of Chinese mutual funds. By the end of December 2016, QDII funds constituted just 1.15% of the fund industry.

In 2014, the global economy as a whole experienced a slowdown. With the exception of an economic recovery underway in the United States, other major economies facing low market demand found themselves caught in a structural inflationary environment. That year QDII funds hit a record low of 0.16%, the lowest in the fund industry over the past five years.

Figure 4.39 Market Segmentation and Geographic Segmentation of QDII Funds

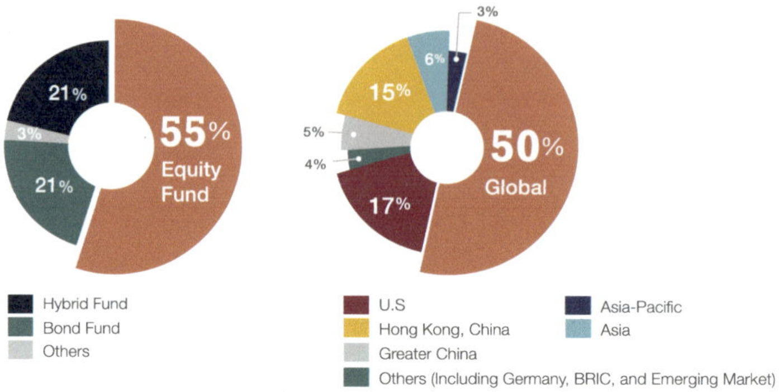

Source: China Knowledge Mutual Funds Database

In terms of market segmentation, QDII equity funds are the most prevalent, making up 55% of the QDII industry. These funds convert capital raised from mainland Chinese investors to foreign currencies and then invest them in overseas stock markets. These are followed by QDII bonds, which invest in foreign debt, and hybrid funds, a mix of debt and equity investment vehicles. Each has a 21% market share. Lastly, QDII funds that invest in other types of securities such as precious metals, commodities and immovable assets like real estate in overseas markets make up 3% of all QDII funds.

Regarding geographical segmentation, 50% of QDII funds invest in global assets. Investment in U.S. securities comes in a distant second at 17% followed by Hong Kong securities with a 15% market share. Meanwhile, investment in Asian, Greater China, others (including Germany, Brazil, India, Russia and other emerging markets) and the Asia-Pacific region make up 6%, 5%, 4%, and 3%, respectively, of all QDII funds invested.

A further analysis of QDII funds' market segmentation is displayed in the table below.

Table 4.20 Market Segmentation of QDII Fund Types

Fund Types	Quantity	Ratio (%)	Quota (RMB Bln)	Ratio (%)	Ratio (%) NAV (RMB Bln)	Ratio (%)
QDII Funds	122	3.22	100.22	1.15	76.44	0.84
International QDII Equity Funds	65	1.72	59.29	0.68	46.18	0.50
International QDII Mixed Funds	25	0.66	20.07	0.23	14.82	0.16
International QDII Bond Funds	17	0.45	16.03	0.18	11.89	0.13
International QDII Other Funds	15	0.40	4.83	0.06	3.46	0.04

*Statistics are accurate as of end 2016

Source: China Knowledge Mutual Funds Database

Figure 4.40 Scale of QDII Quota

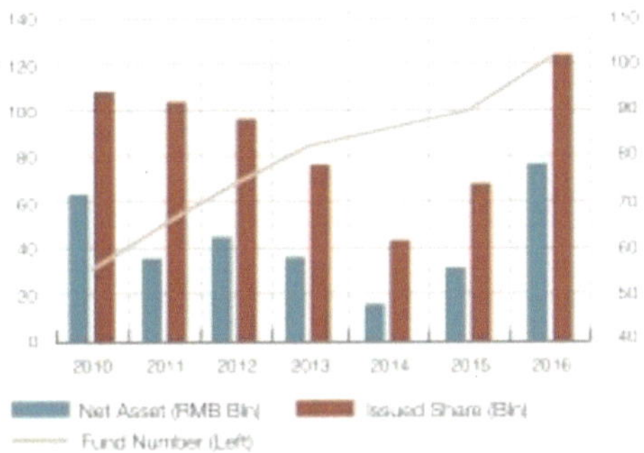

Source: China Knowledge Mutual Funds Database

As of end 2016, there were 189 QDII products in the market. 105 were equity-related products and out of this, only 13 were focused on investing in global markets. The remaining products were split between targeting the Hong Kong and Taiwan stock markets, and investing in US and emerging markets.

Among them, 5 products were invested in overseas REITS and property stocks, 13 were invested in foreign natural resources stocks, funds and options, 9 were invested in domestic companies that listed on the Hong Kong Stock Exchange (denominated in US dollars), 2 were invested in US and European bond funds, 4 were invested in gold ETFs and 1 was invested in a FOF product.

This is a list of the 20 top-performing QDII funds in the industry in 2016. It is accurate as of Jan 2017.

Table 4.21 Top 20 QDII Fund in Terms of Year-to-Date Returns (as of end-Oct 2016)

Code	Name	YTD Returns (%)	Annualized Returns (%)	Latest Size (RMB Mln)	Fund Company	Invest Type
000049.OF	BOC S&P Global Resources EW Index Fund	41.83	41.61	35.53	Bank of China Investment Mgt.	Global Equity
378546.OF	China International Global Natural Resources Hybrid Fund	37.53	37.59	137.18	China International Fund Mgt.	Global Hybrid
162411.OF	Fortune SG S&P Oil & Gas Exploration & Production Select Industry Index Fund	32.53	8.15	2,509.78	Fortune SGAM Fund Mgt.	Global Equity
002230.OF	ChinaAMC Greater China Enterprises Selected Dynamic Allocation Hybrid Fund	27.20	35.39	177.92	China Asset Mgt.	Global Hybrid
001481.OF	Fortune SG S&P Oil & Gas Exploration & Production Select Industry Index Fund	25.20	2.38	375.84	Fortune SGAM Fund Mgt.	Global Equity
163208.OF	Lion Oil and Gas Energy Equity Fund	24.66	9.34	206.05	Lion Fund Mgt.	Global Equity
161229.OF	UBS SDIC China Value Discover Equity Fund	21.85	29.97	157.15	UBS SDIC Fund Mgt.	Global Equity
164815.OF	ICBCCS International Crude Oil Fund	21.33	16.74	29.60	ICBC Credit Suisse Asset Mgt.	Global Equity
160416.OF	Huaan S&P Global Oil Index Equity Fund	20.61	11.41	658.99	HuaAn Fund Mgt.	Global Equity
161116.OF	E Fund Gold Theme Fund	18.06	27.05	420.81	E Fund Mgt.	Global Alternative Investment
320013.OF	Lion Globle Gold Fund	17.95	27.81	739.79	Lion Fund Mgt.	Global Alternative Investment
160719.OF	Harvest Gold Securities Investment Fund	17.33	27.31	351.61	Harvest Fund Mgt.	Global Alternative Investment
164701.OF	China Universal Gold and Precious Metals Fund	17.21	28.18	258.57	China Universal Asset Mgt.	Global Alternative Investment
160121.OF	China Southern BRIC Index Fund	17.15	22.72	88.84	China Southern Fund Mgt.	Global Equity
096001.OF	Dacheng Equal Weight S&P 500 Index Equity Fund	15.28	9.64	97.89	Dacheng Fund Mgt.	Global Equity
150170.OF	China Universal HSI Structured Fund-B	13.81	27.50	1,433.49	China Universal Asset Mgt.	Global Equity
161714.OF	China Merchants S&P BRIC Index Fund	13.70	18.63	45.56	China Merchants Fund Mgt.	Global Equity
513500.OF	Bosera S&P 500 ETF	13.62	9.84	217.51	Bosera Asset Mgt.	Global Equity
000103.OF	Guotai Chinese Enterprises' Overseas High-Yield Bond Fund	13.38	15.18	801.14	Guotai Asset Mgt.	Global Bond
050025.OF	Bosera S&P 500 ETF Feeder Fund	12.84	9.11	170.31	Bosera Asset Mgt.	Global Equity

Source: China Knowledge Mutual Funds Database

Current QDII News

(1) Surge of QDII funds following the launch of the Shenzhen-Hong Kong Stock Connect

In May 2016, a record number of upcoming QDII funds were announced in anticipation of the Shenzhen-Hong Kong Stock Connect launch. This trade link would provide Chinese investors direct access to at least 100 more Hong Kong-listed shares unavailable on the existing Shanghai-Hong Kong Stock Exchange.

About 30 QDII products were expected to raise RMB 20 billion in capital for offshore equity investment. According to a survey conducted by asset management companies, 75.6% of mainland investors contemplated shifting part of their portfolio into overseas-listed shares, while 55.8% planned to use the QDII scheme to access overseas stocks.

(2) Abuse of QDII Quota

China's authorities recently discovered that some financial institutions holding QDII licenses lease out their QDII quotas to non-mainland asset managers. They do this by investing in a fund sponsored by a Western investment manager or retaining the Western manager as a sub-manager in order to invest in foreign markets.

This is a common phenomenon because Chinese investment managers often exploit regulatory ambiguity. This 'delegation' of QDII quota comes on the heels of widespread 'renting' of Qualified Foreign Institutional Investors (QFII). In the latter situation, a fund that is unqualified for QFII approval and quota 'borrows' quota from a QFII license holder so that it can nonetheless invest directly in Chinese markets.

4.7 MUTUAL FUND OF FUNDS

Fund of Funds (FOF), also referred to as a multi-manager investment, is a strategy of holding a portfolio of other investment funds rather than investing directly in stocks, bonds or other securities.

Per regulations, an FOF must invest at least 80 percent of its assets in mutual funds. Management and custodian fees cannot be charged twice.

On July 17, 2016, CSRC published a draft on publicly offered FOFs that officially broke the ice and brought FOF to the stage. CSRC-issued "Public Offering of Securities Investment Fund Operational Guidelines No. 2 – Fund of Funds Guidelines (Draft)", which addressed long-anticipated publicly offered FOFs, will be officially published soon.

CSRC stated that these rules will strengthen supervision of the business and protect the interests of investors in FOFs.

It is worth noting first that the draft clarifies the definition of FOF as a fund that invests more than 80% of its assets in sub-funds approved or registered by CSRC. Second, the draft sets restrictions on underlying fund investments. Market value of a single underlying fund cannot be higher than 20% of the net value of FOF. Moreover, FOFs cannot hold other FOF products and complex or derivative fund shares such as structured funds. Third, the draft mentions problems with double charging. FOF managers cannot charge the underlying funds they manage, and FOF custodians cannot charge underlying funds that they host. Further details of the official guidelines are pending and may differ from the draft version.

With publicly offered FOF on offer, fund management companies have adjusted their product layout structures actively to meet investors' needs. Publicly offered FOFs have diversified management modes and product categories as follows:

Table 4.22 Prospective Types of FOF in Mutual Funds

Classification Criterion	Types of Products
Fund Manager & Investment Scope	Internal FOF Managers + Internal Funds
	Internal FOF Managers + Funds in the Whole Market
	External FOF Investment Advisors + Internal Funds
	External FOF Investment Advisors + Funds in the Whole Market
Type of Investment Fund	FOF Investment in Open-ended Funds
	FOF Investment in Exchange Traded Funds
Strategy of Investment	FOF Investment in Well-selected Funds
	FOF Investment in Allocation of Largest Category Assets

Source: China Knowledge Mutual Funds Database

Advantages

Fund of funds can invest in mutual funds with different risk and return characteristics, FOF build a specific investment strategy with ideas or products such as lifecycle funds in order to spread risk. A mutual fund itself can reduce the risk through portfolio investment in assets such as equities and fixed income products. FOFs offer a higher level of investing by focusing on different investment fund strategies that more effectively spread or reduce risk.

Disadvantages

The most significant disadvantage of a FOF is that management fee rate is higher. Although FOFs don't need a lot of management and research costs and the management fee rate is low, total fund management fees after the double charge rate is relatively high.

Each fund management company has a different strategy for promoting FOF development as a broad new business. Statistics suggest that American FOF products now account for 10% of all mutual funds. Hence, it is estimated that China's FOF products market size is at least RMB 800 billion. There is no doubt that china mutual funds industry has a bright future.

American FOF

In the United States, FOF is a highly-concentrated market dominated by a few players. U.S. FOF assets managed by the top three fund management companies, Vanguard, Fidelity Investments, and T. Rowe Price, accounted for 25%, 15% and 12%, almost half of total FOF market share.

Most FOFs in United States are diversified, internally managed funds. Because their management fee is almost zero, fund companies profit by passing the fee on to subsidiary funds. This model solves the problem of double charging FOFs and ensures that fund management companies maximize market share at lower prices.

As a result of the growth of the mutual funds industry and retirement assets, the United States ushered in a period of rapid development of its FOF market from 2001 to 2010, a 'golden age'of sorts for FOFs. The ratio of newly formed FOFs to the broader mutual fund market gradually increased from 3.5% in 2001, to 29.9% in 2005, leveling out at approximately 20% in later years.

The United States' fund of funds market concentrated mainly on pension funds, which are primarily used to meet pensioners' income needs. The rise of FOFs in the United States reflects maturation of the American pension system. FOF became a cheap and convenient tool for risk diversification and gradually won over pension managers.

Current development: Preferential policies offer opportunities for allocation of private equity and venture capital FOFs

China's private equity (PE) and venture capital (VC) FOFs are in full-on expansion because of the country's economic reform and transformation. PE FOFs in particular have experienced explosive growth since 2015, when the government carried out mass innovation and encouraged entrepreneurship. By the end of June 2016, there were 1,175 FOFs on the Chinese private equity market with nearly US$ 375 billion under management. The implementation of investor-friendly policies has created a better policy and market environment for venture capital funds. Moreover, China is in the midst of a technological revolution with Internet-based innovations coming out in a seemingly endless flow. In addition, a continuously expanding, multi-layered capital market system has widened avenues for PE/VC funds to exit positions. In the context of this structural transformation, emerging economic sectors and industries have caught the attention of the capital market. Behind the mass entrepreneurship are the increasing PE/VC funds that invest in the market. This is an historic opportunity for the growth of PE/VC FOFs.

The 676 government-guidance FOFs accounted for 66.7% of the total 1,013 RMB FOFs. The 109 market-oriented FOFs launched by state-owned enterprises and 228 private capital FOFs respectively accounted for only 10.8% and 22.5% of the total. A total of 617 or 81.4% of government-guidance funds managed US$ 174.47 billion in investible capital; 151 or 10.8% private capital FOFs had US$ 18.64 billion in assets. A total of 57 or 9.9% of market-oriented SOE FOFs stood at US$ 21.29 billion, far less than that of government-guidance funds and privately-run, market-oriented FOFs.

In terms of average investible capital, government-guidance funds lagged market-oriented SOE FOFs but were slightly ahead of privately-run ones. Thanks to their substantial AUM, market-oriented SOE FOFs averaged US$ 373.56 million per fund. In comparison, market-oriented FOFs funded by private capital averaged US$ 123.47 million. Government-guidance funds, which aim to encourage more social capital to engage in industry improvements using small amounts of money, reported US$ 282.76 million per fund.

Figure 4.41 Comparison of RMB FOFs on Chinese PE Market by Type (By No. of Funds)

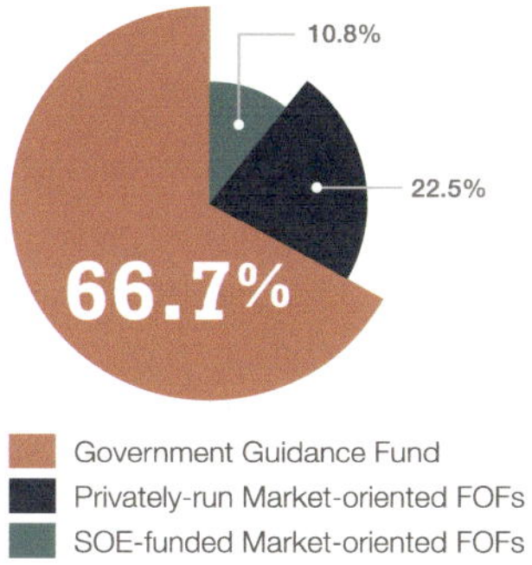

Source: China Knowledge Mutual Funds Database

Figure 4.42 Comparison of RMB FOFs on Chinese PE Market by Type (By Assets under Management, US$ Mln)

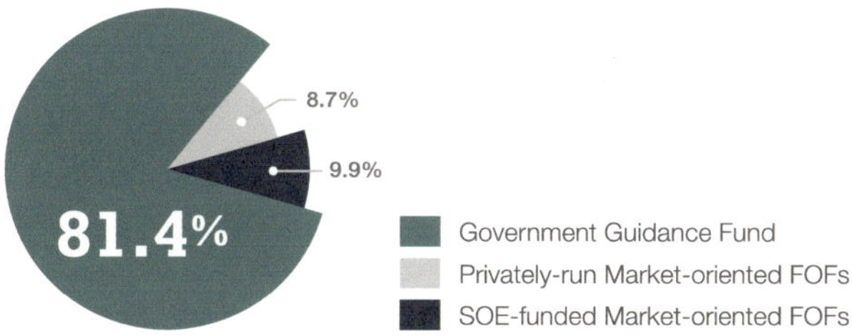

Source: China Knowledge Mutual Funds Database

The Outlook of Mutual Fund of Funds

The foundation for current FOF demand has formed. The number of mutual funds has reached more than 4,000. It is difficult for ordinary investors choose mutual fund products suitable to them. FOFs help can solve this dilemma. Nowadays, the rapid development of differentiated products lends itself to customized service, a trend that will ultimately lead to maturity.

FOF is in its infancy in China's mutual fund market. With the advent of company branding, resource allocation, scale of its products and other inputs, internal FOF funds will definitely mainstream in time.

FOFs are good long-term investment tools. In the long run, China's mutual fund of funds market is potentially large, and FOFs are expected to serve as substitutes to bank deposits and help investors save for retirement, tuition, and big ticket items. China's capital market has had far less time to grow than developed countries. Its investment philosophy has had less time to mature and focus on the long term, given that individual and institutional investors alike have been accustomed to chasing short-term benefits.

The development of FOFs may go through a period of adjustment at the outset. Because China's pension system still needs time to mature, long-term investments such as FOFs lack clout and are relatively weak. Investors do not have accounts for individual endowments and are unaware of options such as FOFs. These unfavorable factors will limit the short-term growth of FOFs.

4.8 OTHERS

4.8.1 GUARANTEED FUNDS

A guaranteed mutual fund is a combination of the best of bonds and stocks. A portion of guaranteed funds is invested in an index fund while the rest is put into zero-coupon bonds. As a result of China's 2015 stock market crash, the explosive growth of guaranteed funds was undoubtedly the biggest highlight in the first 10 months of 2016. A total of 88 guaranteed funds were issued versus 32 in 2015 and 40 in years prior. The number of new guaranteed funds and the 147.34 billion shares they issued is at an historic high. Considering that there were only 61.21 billion shares of guaranteed funds issued prior to 2015, and 71.06 billion shares issued in 2015, the scale of guaranteed mutual funds almost doubled in the first 10 months of 2016.

It is worthy to note that 15 guaranteed mutual funds issued more than 4 billion shares. The largest was GF Wenyu Principal Guaranteed Hybrid Fund with 5 billion shares, followed by CCB Principal Guaranteed Ⅶ Hybrid Fund with 4.99 billion and Lion Hexin Principal Guaranteed with 4.98 billion.

Among 88 guaranteed mutual funds, only 15 had a scale totaling more than RMB 4 billion (US $0.59 billion). Another 35 guaranteed mutual funds was less than RMB 1 billion (US $0.15 billion). Some were only RMB 100 million.

Table 4.23 Top 20 Guaranteed Funds in Terms of Year-to-Date Returns (as of end-Oct 2016)

Code	Name	YTD Returns (%)	Annualized Returns (%)	Latest Size (RMB Mln)	Fund Mgt Company
001317.OF	Orient Yingjia Principal Guaranteed Hybrid Fund	7.55	5.87	573.32	Orient Fund Mgt.
202212.OF	China Southern Guaranteed Fund	7.31	8.90	605.65	China Southern Fund Mgt.
000318.OF	Zhonghai Huili Pure Bond Structured Fund-B	6.73	10.50	8061.69	Zhonghai Fund Mgt.
020022.OF	Guotai Principal Guaranteed Fund	6.23	8.34	267.66	Guotai Asset Mgt.
001292.OF	Tianhong Puhui Pension Principal Guaranteed Hybrid Fund-A	5.90	6.39	481.30	Tianhong Asset Mgt.
001293.OF	Tianhong Puhui Pension Principal Guaranteed Hybrid Fund-B	5.76	6.24	6.99	Tianhong Asset Mgt.
000610.OF	New China Ali-1 Principal Guaranteed Hybrid Fund	5.70	22.41	860.87	New China Fund Mgt.
163411.OF	Industrial Guarantee Securities Investment Fund	5.13	8.22	1043.38	Aegon-Industrial Fund Mgt.
121010.OF	UBS SDIC Ruiyuan Principal Guaranteed Hybrid Fund	5.04	8.79	1519.44	UBS SDIC Fund Mgt.
202211.OF	China Southern Hengyuan Principal Protected Hybrid Fund	4.90	14.16	495.97	China Southern Fund Mgt.
001531.OF	China Merchants Anyi Principal Guaranteed Hybrid Fund	4.67	5.54	1472.72	China Merchants Fund Mgt.
400013.OF	Orient Guarantee Hybrid Fund	4.37	6.26	517.19	Orient Fund Mgt.
001486.OF	Tianhong Xinanbao Guaranteed Hybrid Fund	4.21	4.77	777.26	Tianhong Asset Mgt.
002220.OF	China Southern Ruili Principal Guaranteed Hybrid Fund	3.70	4.05	1500.42	China Southern Fund Mgt.
000327.OF	China Southern Fenghe Principal Guaranteed Hybrid Fund	3.55	3.34	2443.38	China Southern Fund Mgt.
000676.OF	Zhonghai Huixiang Structured Bond Fund-B	3.50	7.99	9981.75	Zhonghai Fund Mgt.
001977.OF	Truvalue Jucai Principal Guaranteed Hybrid Fund	3.46	4.76	293.84	Truvalue Asset Mgt.
001238.OF	Bosera Lucky One Big Data Principal Guaranteed Hybrid Fund	3.44	1.40	1382.16	Bosera Fund Mgt.
001907.OF	UBS SDIC Jingxuan Principal Guaranteed Hybrid Fund-A	3.17	3.83	633.81	UBS SDIC Fund Mgt.
200016.OF	Great Wall Principal Guaranteed Fund	2.97	11.59	1602.30	Great Wall Fund Mgt.

Source: China Knowledge Mutual Funds Database

4.8.2 COMMODITY FUNDS

Gold is an important tool to hedge against domestic currency risk, especially in the case of QDII quota limits. Buying gold is close to buying dollars or a basket of foreign exchange. Hence, this kind of commodity fund can improve portfolio return. At the same time, it can effectively lower overall risk, especially when the stock market is volatile. Gold holdings can mitigate adverse effects of share price volatility.

Benefitting from the rise in global commodity prices, the average return of commodity funds in the first 10 months of 2016 was 13.76%. Bosera Gold ETF-D (000929.OF) was the winner with a return of 23.38%. Unexpected events such as Brexit muted investors' preference for risky assets, thus contributing to rising gold prices.

The UBS Silver Futures Fund is the only other commodity futures fund in China's mutual fund market with a double-digit return. Its YTD return was 16.13%.

Aside from UBS Silver Futures Fund, the 13 commodities funds invested in gold performed relatively well. By the end of October 2016, their average year-to-date return was rough 26%.

Table 4.24 Top 10 Commodity Funds in Terms of Year-to-Date Returns (as of end-Oct 2016)

Code	Name	YTD Returns (%)	Annualized Returns (%)	Latest Size (RMB Mln)	Fund Mgt Company
000929.OF	Bosera Gold ETF-D	23.38	11.42	0.03	Bosera Fund Mgt.
159937.OF	Bosera Gold ETF	23.19	3.28	0.96	Bosera Fund Mgt.
518800.OF	Guotai Gold ETF	22.81	0.83	0.67	Guotai Asset Mgt.
000930.OF	Bosera Gold ETF-I	22.74	7.04	2.01	Bosera Fund Mgt.
159934.OF	E Fund Gold ETF	22.54	3.57	1.77	E Fund Mgt.
518880.OF	Huaan Yifu Gold ETF	22.50	0.98	6.26	HuaAn Fund Mgt.
000217.OF	Huaan Yifu Gold ETF Feeder Fund-C	21.81	0.49	0.41	HuaAn Fund Mgt.
000216.OF	Huaan Yifu Gold ETF Feeder Fund-A	21.76	0.59	0.35	HuaAn Fund Mgt.
161226.OF	UBS SDIC Silver Futures Fund (LOF)	6.28	-1.41	0.35	UBS SDIC Fund Mgt.
000218.OF	Guotai Gold ETF Initiating Feeder Fund	0.00	8.00	0.11	Guotai Asset Mgt.
000307.OF	E Fund Gold ETF Feeder Fund-A	0.00	-3.95	0.96	E Fund Mgt.
002610.OF	Bosera Gold ETF Feeder Fund-A	0.00	-5.93	0.05	Bosera Fund Mgt.
002611.OF	Bosera Gold ETF Feeder Fund-C	0.00	-6.44	0.05	Bosera Fund Mgt.
002963.OF	E Fund Gold ETF Feeder Fund-C	0.00	-11.77	0.02	E Fund Mgt.

Source: China Knowledge Mutual Funds Database

The top-performing commodity fund in 2016 was the Bosera Gold ETF-D with a return of 23.38%, followed by the Bosea Gold ETF Fund with 23.19%. The Guotai Gold ETF came in third at 22.81%

PART FIVE:

2016 OVERVIEW

2016 Top 10 Events of China's Fund Industry

1. Official release of FOF guidelines for retail investors

On September 23, CSRC published the fund of funds (FOF) guidelines for retail investors. FOF allows investors to hold a portfolio of different funds, rather than the conventional strategy of investing directly in equity, bonds and other securities. According to the new rules, a minimum of 80% of FOF assets must be invested in registered mutual funds, each mutual fund cannot exceed 20% of the FOF's net asset value, and management and custodian fees should only be charged once. CSRC approved a total of 27 FOF products between the end of November and early December.

2. CSRC tightened regulations for subsidiaries of fund management companies

On December 2, CSRC officially announced its "Provisions on the Management of Subsidiaries of Fund Management Companies" and "Interim Provisions on the Risk Control Index for Asset Management of Specific Customers of Subsidiaries of Fund Management Companies". The new provisions state that a subsidiary's net capital cannot fall below RMB 100 million or less than 20% of its liabilities.

3. CSRC sought public opinion in its revision of "Guidelines for Capital Preservation Funds"

On August 8, CSRC released a notice seeking public opinion on revisions to its "Guidelines for Capital Preservation Funds". It made six revisions. The three most important are:

1. *Tightened requirements for capital preservation fund management and setting experience criteria for fund managers.*

2. *Increased risk monitoring for earlier detection of hidden risks.*

3. *Tightened risk control index for investment strategies in terms of investment scope, remaining maturity and risky assets.*

4. Increased threshold for fund investment classification

On November 25, CSRC issued its "Guidelines for Grading of Fund Operation Management". It classified investment requirements for the secondary fund market, revising the minimum threshold to RMB 300 million and advising investors to sign risk disclosure documents.

5. Massive influx of outsourced funding and more than 1000 new mutual funds established

As of December 9, there were more than 1,000 newly-established domestic mutual funds, making it the first time in 19 years that new funds hit this level. However, this phenomenon is expected to cool as authorities tighten industry regulations.

6. Revamp of private equity regulations

On June 15, CSRC released its "Interim Provisions for Management of Private Equity Asset Management Operated by Securities and Futures Companies". The interim provisions heightened restrictions on the sale, leverage ratio and structure of asset management products. This included reducing the leverage multiples of structured asset management products and increasing emphasis on information and risk disclosure.

7. Official launch of the Shenzhen-Hong Kong Stock Connect

On December 5, the launch ceremony of the Shenzhen-Hong Kong Stock Connect was held concurrently in both Shenzhen and Hong Kong. As of December 23, there were 59 "Shenzhen-Hong Kong Stock Connect" funds. First Seafront Fund Management Company was the most active fund management company with 15 new "Shenzhen-Hong Kong Stock Connect" funds.

8. AMAC increased transparency over private fund operations to crack down on 'shell companies'

On February 5, the AMAC released the "Announcement on Certain Issues Concerning Further Regulation of Manager Registrations for Private Funds" requiring that all managers register their first fund product within a given period of time. It mandated that fund managers disclose information such as a fund's due incorporation, business scope and the shareholder structure of fund managers. Consequently, on May 1 and August 1, respectively, 1,901 and 7,800 'shell companies' closed.

9. New rules to standardize the development of private equity funds

In 2016, the AMAC released seven management provisions and two guidelines aimed at improving the regulation of fund filings, risk, information disclosures, contracts, investment management, custodian activities, and outsourcing. This '7+2' package became the self-regulatory framework for the private equity industry, prompting firms to abide by the law and act honestly in order to foster trust.

10. The SAC's second First-Member Congress convened

On December 3, the SAC's second First-Member Congress convened in Beijing. After several rounds of campaigns, recommendations and special invitations, 508 members were chosen from among 2,117 who had joined since the end of 2015. According to new SAC rules, asset management product managers must join the SAC. The new congress has been tasked with amending the "Provisions for Member Management" to further strengthen industry support and regulation.

2016 Fund Market Overview

As of December 13, 2016, 113 fund management companies issued 3,820 mutual funds with total assets of RMB 9.18 trillion (US$ 1.32 trillion), up RMB 772.2 billion (US$ 111.12 billion) and 9.19% from 2015. China issued a record high 1,151 mutual funds in 2016; the country's average issuance of single fund shares reached RMB 941 million, a record low. The total share of newly-issued mutual funds reached RMB 1.08 trillion, much lower than RMB 1.64 trillion issued in 2015.

Tianhong Asset Management Co., Ltd. ranked first among the fund companies with RMB 845 billion (US$ 121.6 billion) in assets under management, while ICBC Credit Suisse Asset Management Co., Ltd. and E Fund Management Co., Ltd. ranked second and third. The AUM of Tianhong Asset Mgt.'s Yuebao fund reached RMB 808.3 billion (US$ 116.31 billion), first among individual funds over the past four years.

The average rate of return of QDII funds hit 6.56%, the highest among all types of funds. These mainly benefitted from the stellar performance of Hong Kong and U.S. stocks as well as RMB devaluation. Alternative investment funds and money market funds saw their average rate of return reach 4.94% and 2.61%, respectively.

Market Scale

Market Scale of Mutual Fund

As of December 2016, the market scale of China's mutual funds grew to RMB 9.18 trillion (US $ 1.32 trillion), an increase of RMB 772.2 billion (US $ 111.12 billion) or 9.19% from the previous year. The mutual fund market grew another RMB 1.22 trillion (US $ 175.56 billion) or 15.28% in the second half of 2016. Total assets decreased at the beginning of 2016, and then gradually increased, due primarily to the steady development of the stock market and a boost from banks' outsourced capital.

Figure 5.1 Market Scale of Mutual Fund

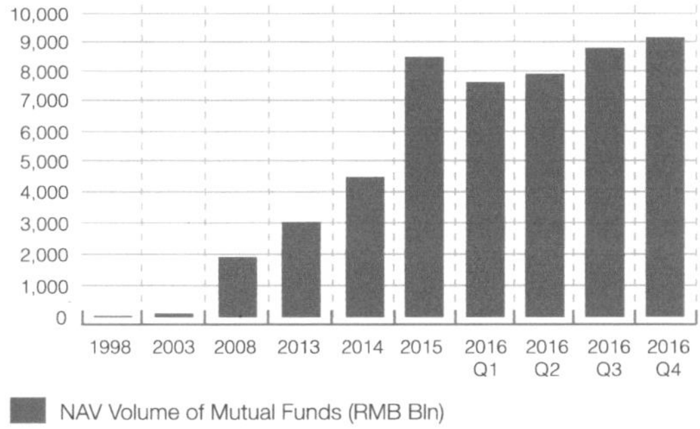

Source: China Knowledge Mutual Funds Database

Change in Fund Scale

In 2016, the total asset scale of bond funds surged 153% from the previous year to more than RMB 1 trillion (US$ 143.9 billion). On one hand, this reflected investors' preference for stable returns following the stock market crash; on the other, it indicated that large amounts of capital from institutions such as banks and insurance companies shifted to bond funds. Meanwhile, QDII funds' asset scale grew 63% year over year. Hybrid and equity bonds saw their asset scale decrease 8% and 7%, respectively, from the year prior due to stock market volatility.

Table 5.1 Change in Fund Scale

Fund Variety	Scale (RMB Bln)	Change	Number of Funds	Change
Money Market Fund	4,464.4	-2%	327	65
Hybrid Fund	2,095.6	-8%	1,771	565
Bond Fund	1,785.6	153%	942	405
Equity Fond	707.9	-7%	630	66
QDII Fond	98.3	63%	123	24
Alternative Investment Fund	25.4	5%	27	6
Total Amount	9,177.2	9%	3,820	1,131

Source: China Knowledge Mutual Funds Database

Change in Scale of Different Types of Funds

Based on their proportion of total fund asset scale, money market funds dominated the market in 2016, while hybrid bonds ranked second. The proportion of equity funds saw a slight decrease, and money market funds were under 50%. Meanwhile, bond funds as a proportion of total fund scale doubled from the previous year. This reflected investors' expectations of higher returns.

Figure 5.2 Change in Scale of Different Types of Funds

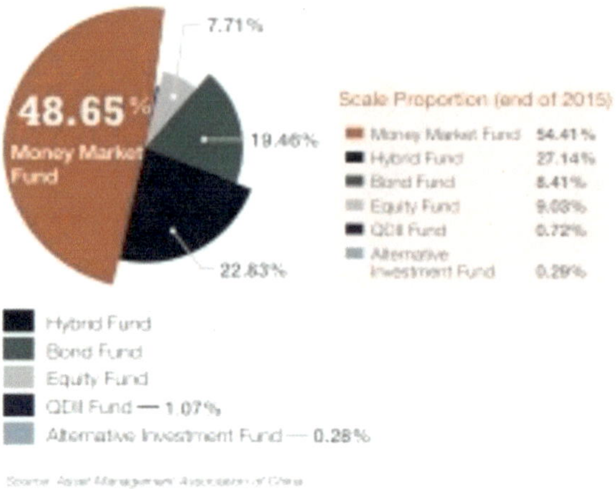

Number of Newly-Issued Funds Broke a Record High

A record high 1,151 mutual funds were issued in 2016. The scale of issuances equaled 1.08 trillion, far below 1.64 trillion in 2015. The average number of shares of a single fund issued reached 941 million, the lowest on record.

Figure 5.3 Number of Newly Issued Funds, 2007-16

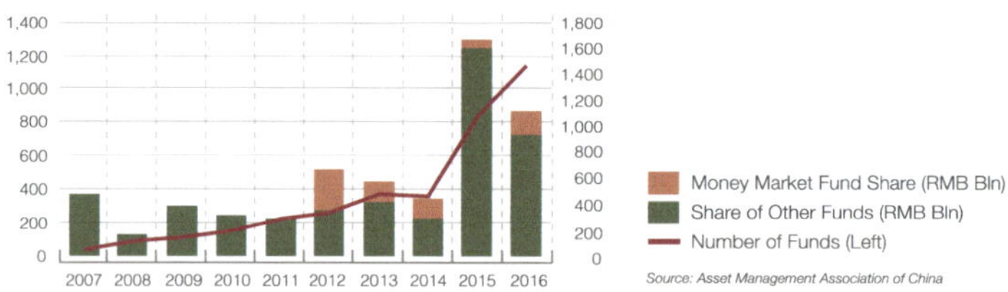

New Issuances Based on Monthly Statistics

Because China's stock market plummeted in the beginning of 2016, the issuance and scale of bonds was relatively small. Benefiting from the rapid development of institutions' outsourcing businesses, the issuance of money market, bond and balanced funds started to accelerate in the second half of 2016.

Figure 5.4 Number of Newly Issued Funds (Monthly)

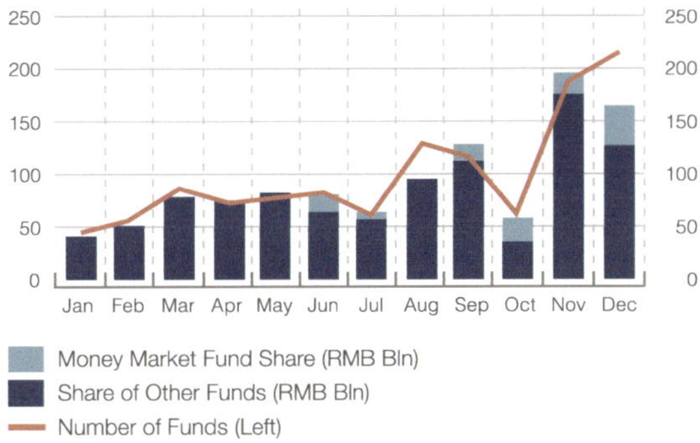

Source: Asset Management Association of China

Average Issuance Scale of Different Types of Funds

Quarterly statistics suggest that in 2016, the average issuance of equity funds was mostly steady, while alternative investment funds stagnated due to the limitation of the number of stock index futures warehouse. In second half of the year, QDII funds became a hot investment. Only two QDII funds were issued in the third quarter, although 13 new QDII funds were issued in the fourth quarter. Due to foreign exchange quota limitations, average issuance shares decreased remarkably in the fourth quarter.

Table 5.2 Average Issuance Scale of Different Fund Types

Fund Variety	Average Issue Share (Mln)			
	Q1	Q2	Q3	Q4
Total Amount	918	1,023	949	905
Equity Fund	354	398	1,178	310
Hybrid Fund	1,035	1,123	847	453
Bond Fund	942	975	965	1,283
Money Market Fund	719	1,483	1,536	1,997
Alternative Investment Fund	-	343	-	-
QDII Fund	695	545	1,071	433

Source: China Knowledge Mutual Funds Database

New Issuance of Different Types of Funds in 2016

Most of China's newly-issued funds are hybrid funds. A total of 569 hybrid funds with 4,555 total shares were issued in 2016. The average issuance scale totaled 800 million shares per fund. Bond funds ranked second with 407 issued for a total of 44.92 million shares. The average issued scale totaled 100 million shares per fund.

Figure 5.5 New Issuance of Different Fund Types in 2016

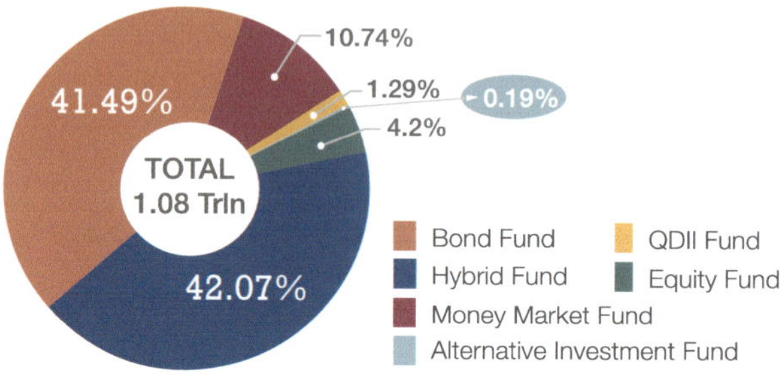

Source: Asset Management Association of China

Fund Size Distribution Range

Most of the funds with a scale more than RMB 10 billion (US$ 1.44 billion) are money market funds. The scale of the 3,820 funds fell mainly between RMB 200 million (US$ 28.78 billion) and RMB 5 billion (US$ 719.5 million), accounting for 70.24% of the total. Funds with a total scale below RMB 200 million (US$ 28.78 billion) accounted for 22%. In addition, a record-breaking number of funds under RMB 50 million (US$ 7.2 million) were issued. This is the one of the after-effects of the mass issuance of new funds over the past two years. Because these products are highly homogenized, they face the prospect of a liquidation crisis.

Figure 5.6 Fund Size Distribution Range

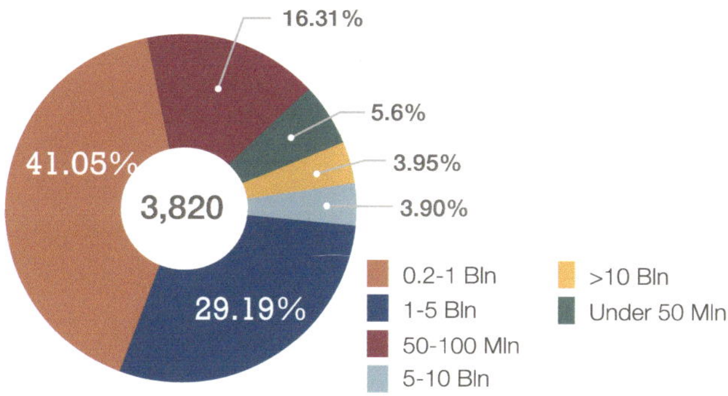

Source: Asset Management Association of China

Fund Management Company

As of December 31, 2016, the scale of the top ten fund management companies accounted for 47% of the total, while the top 20 fund management companies accounted for 68%. Caitong Securities Asset Management Co., Ltd., Changjiang Securities Co., Ltd., Huian Fund Management Co., Ltd., Jinxin Asset Management Co., Ltd., Fortune & Royal Asset, Xianfeng Asset Management Co., Ltd., CS Richland Asset Management Co., Ltd. and BoC International Ltd. were among those included into the ranking.In terms of geographical distribution, most of fund management companies are located in Shanghai, Shenzhen and Beijing.

Figure 5.7 Geographical Distribution of FMCs

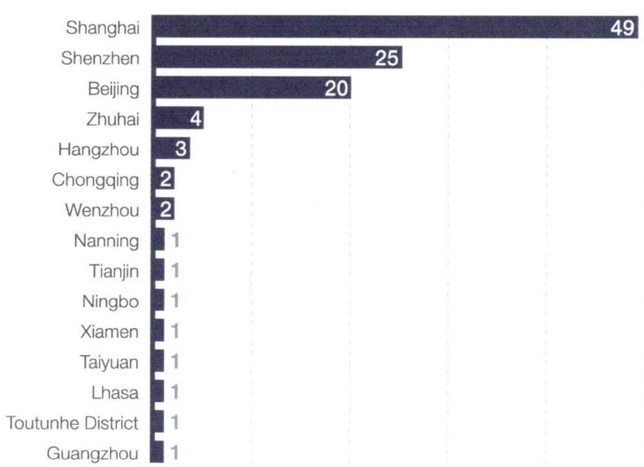

Source: China Knowledge Mutual Funds Database

China Mutual Funds 2017

Rankings of Fund Companies

Tianhong Asset Management Co., Ltd. ranked first among mutual fund companies with a total scale of RMB 845 billion (US$ 121.6 billion). Its service Yu'e Bao grew RMB 13.9 billion (US$ 2 billion) in just one quarter of 2016, double the scale of the second-ranking fund manager, ICBC Credit Suisse Asset Management Co., Ltd. Its total scale was RMB 460.4 billion (US$ 66.25 billion). The total scale of third-ranked E Fund Management Co., Ltd. reached RMB 428.8 billion (US$ 61.7 billion). China Asset Management Co., Ltd. slipped from second to fourth, with its total scale declining to RMB 175.8 billion (US$ 25.3 billion). CIB Fund Management Co., Ltd. climbed from eighteenth to sixteenth, with a total scale of RMB 58.6 billion (US$ 8.43 billion). Among the top 20 fund companies, 4 fund companies accounted for 20% of all assets and saw their total scale surpass RMB 400 billion (US$ 57.56 billion). Seven fund companies accounting for 35% of the top 20 managed between RMB 300 billion (US$ 43.17 billion) and RMB 400 billion (US$ 57.56 billion). The scale of 9 fund managers, or 45% of the top 20, were under RMB 300 billion (US$ 43.17 billion).

Table 5.3 Ranking of Fund Company in Total Assets

Rank	Company	Scale (RMB Bln)	Rank Change	Scale Change (RMB Bln)
1	Tianhong Asset Mgt.	845.0	0	171.0
2	ICBC Credit Suisse Asset Mgt.	460.4	▲2	17.3
3	E Fund Mgt.	428.8	0	-147.3
4	China Asset Mgt.	414.4	▼2	-175.8
5	China Southern Fund Mgt.	389.1	▲1	54.9
6	CCB Principal Asset Mgt.	377.1	▲2	62.4
7	Bosera Fund Mgt.	376.6	▲5	170.7
8	China Merchants Fund Mgt.	360.1	▲3	109.8
9	Harvest Fund Mgt.	354.3	▼4	5.5
10	Bank of China Investment Mgt.	342.1	▼1	64.3
11	GF Fund Mgt.	305.1	▼4	-24.9
12	China Universal Asset Mgt.	274.3	▼2	21.7
13	Penghua Fund Mgt.	248.0	▲2	75.1
14	Fullgoal Fund Mgt.	209.3	▼1	16.9
15	HuaAn Fund Mgt.	163.5	▲1	7.6
16	Yinhua Fund Mgt.	163.4	▲1	11.3
17	China International Fund Mgt.	137.5	▲3	20.8
18	CIB Fund Mgt.	132.1	▲16	58.6
19	Fortune SG Fund Mgt.	119.6	▼5	-63.1
20	ABC-CA Fund Mgt.	113.1	▲5	16.5

Source: China Knowledge Mutual Funds Database

Scale of Top 20 Non-Money Market Funds

Excluding money market funds, E Fund Management Co., Ltd. ranked first in terms of fund scale, with RMB 253.3 billion (US$ 36.45 billion) of non-money market funds. Among the top 20 funds (excluding money market funds), 7 fund companies saw their total scale above RMB 200 billion (US$ 28.78 billion). Another 35% of the top 20 fell between RMB 100 billion (US$ 14.39 billion) and RMB 200 billion (US$ 28.78 billion). Another 6 funds accounted for 30% of the top 20 companies with an asset scale of less than RMB 100 billion (US$ 14.39 billion).

Table 5.4 Top 20 Non-Money Market Fund Size

Rank	Company	Scale (RMB Bln)	Rank Change	Scale Change (RMB Bln)
1	E Fund Mgt.	253.3	0	-23.2
2	Bosera Fund Mgt.	248.8	▲10	150.3
3	ICBC Credit Suisse Asset Mgt.	236.8	▲3	85.6
4	China Asset Mgt.	222.3	▼2	-4.8
5	Harvest Fund Mgt.	220.1	▼2	9.9
6	China Southern Fund Mgt.	206.0	▼2	16.4
7	China Merchants Fund Mgt.	201.3	▲1	85.5
8	Penghua Fund Mgt.	169.1	▲2	58.2
9	Bank of China Investment Mgt.	165.6	▲4	72.7
10	Fullgoal Fund Mgt.	164.4	▼5	-5.8
11	CCB Principal Asset Mgt.	161.4	▲10	101.5
12	China Universal Asset Mgt.	151.4	▼5	31.1
13	GF Fund Mgt.	148.0	▼2	42.0
14	HuaAn Fund Mgt.	130.4	▼5	17.3
15	Yinhua Fund Mgt.	74.9	▼1	-3.2
16	Great Wall Fund Mgt.	72.3	▲14	28.3
17	Guotai Asset Mgt.	70.9	▼2	-4.4
18	Zhong Ou Asset Mgt.	63.8	▲1	1.7
19	CIB Fund Mgt.	62.8	▲22	38.1
20	Lion Fund Mgt.	61.5	▲4	6.6

Source: China Knowledge Mutual Funds Database

Scale of Top 20 Money Market Funds

Taking only money market funds into consideration, Tianhong Asset Management Co., Ltd. placed first with a total scale of RMB 820.1 billion (US$ 118.01 billion). ICBC Credit Suisse Asset Management Co., Ltd. and CCB Principal Asset Management Co., Ltd. oversaw assets worth over RMB 200 billion (US$ 28.78 billion), ranking second and third, respectively. Money market fund China Asset Management shrank RMB 171 billion (US$ 24.61 billion) from the year before, falling to fourth. These money market fund managers mainly expanded their scale by: 1) launching Internet businesses (Tianhong Asset Management, China Asset Management, and China Universal); 2) developing on-site monetary funds (Fortune SG Fund Management, Yinhua Fund Management, and E Fund Management); or 3) linking fund management to banks (ICBC Credit Suisse Asset Management, GF Fund Management, Bank of China Investment Management, and CCB Principal Asset Management).

Table 5.5 Top 20 Money Market Fund Size

Rank	Company	Scale (RMB Bln)	Rank Change	Scale Change (RMB Bln)
1	Tianhong Asset Mgt.	820.1	0	179.6
2	ICBC Credit Suisse Asset Mgt.	223.5	▲2	-68.2
3	CCB Principal Asset Mgt.	215.7	▲2	-39.2
4	China Asset Mgt.	192.1	▼2	-171.0
5	China Southern Fund Mgt.	183.1	▲3	38.4
6	Bank of China Investment Mgt.	176.5	▲1	-8.3
7	E Fund Mgt.	175.5	▼4	-124.1
8	China Merchants Fund Mgt.	158.9	▲3	24.3
9	GF Fund Mgt.	157.1	▼3	-66.9
10	Harvest Fund Mgt.	134.2	▼1	-4.4
11	Bosera Fund Mgt.	127.8	▲2	20.4
12	China Universal Asset Mgt.	122.8	0	-9.3
13	China International Fund Mgt.	96.7	▲5	26.8
14	Yinhua Fund Mgt.	88.6	▲1	14.6
15	Fortune SG Fund Mgt.	80.1	▼5	-58.1
16	Penghua Fund Mgt.	78.9	▲4	16.9
17	Ping An Uob Fund Mgt.	71.1	▲13	39.1
18	CIB Fund Mgt.	69.3	▲5	20.5
19	ABC-CA Fund Mgt.	64.2	▼5	-14.4
20	Aegon-Industrial Fund Mgt.	55.1	▼3	-14.9

Source: China Knowledge Mutual Funds Database

Scale of Top 10 Structured Funds

After the discount tide, the issuance of some structured funds ceased. Still popular with professional investors, existing structured funds did not lose scale.

Table 5.6 Scale of Top 10 Structured Funds

Rank	Company	Scale (RMB Bln)	No. of Funds
1	Fullgoal Fund Mgt.	60.6	11
2	Penghua Fund Mgt.	36.6	18
3	China Merchants Fund Mgt.	33.8	9
4	SWS MU Fund Mgt.	17.3	8
5	Zhonghai Fund Mgt.	17.1	4
6	Yinhua Fund Mgt.	14.3	9
7	Guotai Asset Mgt.	11.8	6
8	First Seafront Fund Mgt.	10.2	2
9	E Fund Mgt.	7.5	9
10	Bank of China Investment Mgt.	5.1	2

Source: China Knowledge Mutual Funds Database

Scale of Top 10 ETF Funds

First-ranked ETF company Huaxia ETF managed assets worth RMB 53.1 billion (US$ 7.64 billion). The scale of its Huaxia SSE 50 ETF totaled RMB 29.3 billion (US$ 4.22 billion).

Table 5.7 Scale of Top 10 ETF Funds

Rank	Company	Scale (RMB Bln)	No. of Funds
1	China Asset Mgt.	53.1	10
2	E Fund Mgt.	25.6	9
3	HuaAn Fund Mgt.	23.9	6
4	China Southern Fund Mgt.	20.0	12
5	Huatai-PineBridge Fund Mgt.	19.1	4
6	Harvest Fund Mgt.	18.9	8
7	China Universal Asset Mgt.	16.2	6
8	HFT Investment Mgt.	6.1	3
9	GF Fund Mgt.	5.5	12
10	Bosera Fund Mgt.	5.4	7

Source: China Knowledge Mutual Funds Database

Fund Performance

Average Return of Different Fund Types since 2016

Due to the influence of stock volatility and fall in bond prices at the end of 2016, the average yield of bond, hybrid, and equity funds hit 0.09%, -7.06%, and -12.20%, respectively.

Figure 5.8 Average Return of Different Fund Types

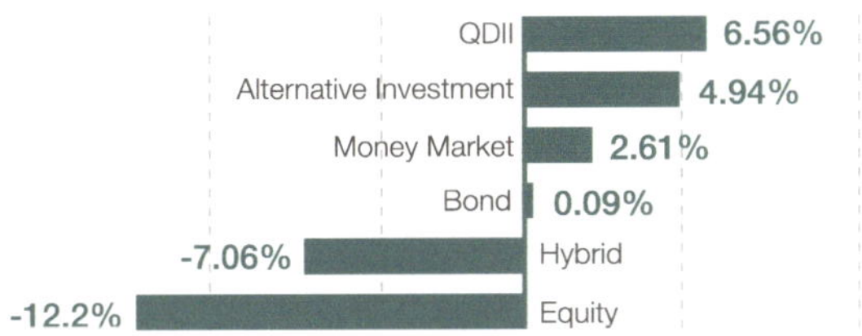

Source: Asset Management Association of China

Interval Distribution of Fund Performance since 2016

In 2016, the interval distribution of fund performance among 35% of all Chinese funds fell between 0% and 5%, while funds that performed below -10% accounted for 30.94% of total funds.

Figure 5.9 Fund Performance Interval Distribution since 2016

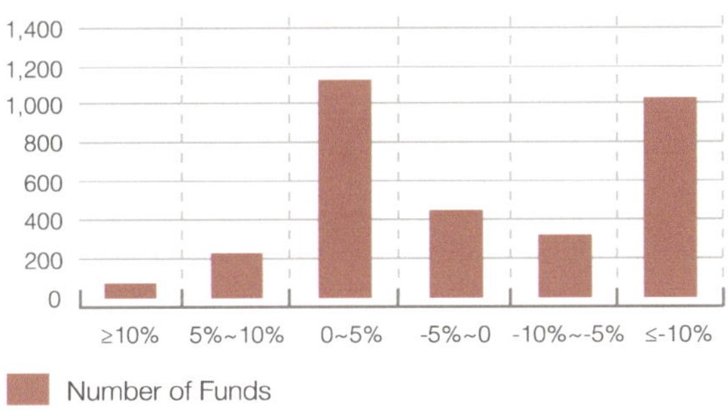

Source: China Knowledge Mutual Funds Database

Average Return of Different Fund Types (Quarterly)

Based on average return, the returns on equity, hybrid, QDII and bond funds were on the rise between the first and third quarters of 2016, benefiting from the solid performance of the equity and bond markets. During the third quarter, the returns of different types of funds was positive and rose significantly quarter over quarter. In the fourth quarter, the equity, bond and foreign exchange markets all dropped, even after bond funds originally with positive performance earned negative returns in the fourth quarter.

Table 5.8 Average Return of Different Fund Types (Quarterly)

Fund Variety	Average Rate of Return			
	Q1	Q2	Q3	Q4
Equity Fund	-14.88%	0.90%	2.64%	-0.26%
Hybrid Fund	-9.21%	2.48%	0.98%	-1.20%
Bond Fund	-0.11%	0.21%	1.91%	-1.51%
Money Market Fund	0.68%	0.62%	0.64%	0.65%
QDII Fund	-2.70%	2.88%	6.17%	0.13%
Alternative Investment Fund	3.94%	3.15%	0.33%	-2.93%

Source: China Knowledge Mutual Funds Database

Performance of Top 20 Stock-Leaning Funds

Among the stock-leaning funds, CIB Juli ranked first with a return of 29.85%, while JT Ruizhi Stable Income ranked second with 27.86%.

Table 5.9 Performance of Top 20 Stock-Leaning Funds

Rank	Name	Return (Recent 1 Year)	Scale (RMB Mln)
1	CIB Juli	29.85%	488
2	JT Ruizhi Stable Income	27.86%	419
3	Golden Trust Sinopac Youjia Life	17.96%	602
4	Tianhong Yongding Value Growth	17.45%	870
5	Harvest Environmental Protection Low Carbon	16.50%	1,287
6	Fortune SG Resources Selected	16.34%	397
7	First Seafront Gold and Silver Jewelry Theme Selected A	15.86%	1,945
8	ICBCCS Culture Sports Industry	15.72%	240
9	China Merchants CSI Liquor Index	15.25%	2,015
10	Lombarda China Times Pioneer	15.03%	138
11	UBS SDIC Ruiying	14.13%	1,008
12	E Fund Resources Sector	13.63%	1,407
13	Guotai Income A	13.37%	2,034
14	Fullgoal Low-Carbon New Economy	13.05%	543
15	GF Anhong Return A	12.60%	508
16	Hongde Strategic Transformation	12.41%	951
17	GF Ju'an A	12.38%	347
18	BOSC ASSET Emerging Value Growth	11.87%	219
19	First Seafront Hugangshen Blue Chip Selected	11.72%	3,460
20	China Merchants Manufacturing Transformation	11.69%	270

Source: China Knowledge Mutual Funds Database

Performance of Top 10 Active Equity Funds

Golden Trust Sinopac Youjia Life was the top-performing active equity fund with a return of 17.96%. Harvest Environmental Protection Low Carbon, ICBCCS Culture Sports Industry, and Lombarda China Times Pioneer saw their returns rise above 15%.

Table 5.10 Performance of Top 10 Active Equity Funds

Rank	Name	Return (Recent 1 Year)	Scale (RMB Mln)
1	Golden Trust Sinopac Youjia Life	17.96%	602
2	Harvest Environmental Protection Low Carbon	16.50%	1,287
3	ICBCCS Culture Sports Industry	15.72%	240
4	Lombarda China Times Pioneer	15.03%	138
5	Hongde Strategic Transformation	12.41%	951
6	Lion Advanced Manufacturing	11.34%	71
7	Anxin Value Selected	8.49%	562
8	First Seafront Refinancing Theme Selected	8.05%	715
9	E Fund Consumption Sector	7.21%	1,284
10	Anxin Consumption Medicine Theme	7.18%	344

Source: China Knowledge Mutual Funds Database

Performance of Top 10 Hybrid Funds

Hybrid funds CIB Juli and JT Ruizhi Stable Income both returned more than 25%. At the same time, the top 20 hybrid funds returned more than 10%.

Table 5.11 Performance of Top 10 Hybrid Funds

Rank	Name	Return (Recent 1 Year)	Scale (RMB Mln)
1	CIB Juli	29.85%	488
2	JT Ruizhi Stable Income	27.86%	419
3	Tianhong Yongding Value Growth	17.45%	870
4	Fortune SG Resources Selected	16.34%	397
5	First Seafront Gold and Silver Jewelry Theme Selected A	15.86%	1,945
6	UBS SDIC Ruiying	14.13%	1,008
7	E Fund Resources Sector	13.63%	1,407
8	Guotai Income A	13.37%	2,034
9	Fullgoal Low-Carbon New Economy	13.05%	543
10	GF Anhong Return A	12.60%	508

Source: China Knowledge Mutual Funds Database

Performance of Top 10 Bond Funds

Aside from a regular open bond fund, the best performing bond fund was Orient Value-Added, with a return of 7.28%. The top ten bond funds boosted their revenue more than 4.5%. Since the leverage requirements for regular open bond funds are different than those of ordinary bond funds, their statistics differ. Although Zheshang Huiying Pure Bond Fund returned 7.32%, mainly due to a large redemption in the second quarter, it was not included in the ranking.

Table 5.12 Performance of Top 10 Bond Funds

Rank	Name	Return (Recent 1 Year)	Scale (RMB Mln)
1	Orient Value-Added	7.28%	444
2	Industrial Stable Income	6.63%	8,138
3	Tebon Xintianli A	6.30%	811
4	China Merchants Double-Bonds Enhanced	6.10%	551
5	Guotai Dual Dividend A	6.02%	375
6	Galaxy Consolidate Income	6.01%	2,764
7	Yingda Pure A	5.93%	365
8	Penghua Credit Enhanced A	4.95%	490
9	Anxin Baoli	4.92%	2,754
10	ICBCCS Dual Dividend A	4.87%	14,584

Source: China Knowledge Mutual Funds Database

Performance of Top 5 Commodities Funds

The market went through ups and downs in 2016. Since July, expectations of rising interest rates increased and led to a stagflation in gold prices.

Table 5.13 Performance of Top 5 Commodities Funds

Rank	Name	Return (Recent 1 Year)	Scale (RMB Mln)
1	Bosera Gold ETF	18.88%	4,870
2	Guotai Gold ETF	18.44%	862
3	E Fund Gold ETF	18.18%	1,972
4	Huaan Yifu Gold ETF	18.15%	6,357
5	UBS SDIC Silver Futures	5.09%	620

Source: China Knowledge Mutual Funds Database

Performance of Top 10 QDII Funds

QDII funds have been an investment hotspot in the mutual funds industry. Due to restrictions on their purchase, QDII funds' average return has been the highest among different types of funds. Among them, BOC S&P Global Resources EW's ranked first with a return of 49.48%. Since QDII funds mainly invest in Hong Kong stocks or overseas assets, they mitigate risk and boost expected returns. Since the RMB is expected to continue its devaluation, investing in QDII funds can hedge by taking advantage of foreign currency appreciation.

Three factors contributed to the outstanding performance of QDII funds last year. First, the USD rose nearly 7% against the RMB, a benefit to the QDII fund industry. Second, Europe and the United States continue to overweight quantitative easing monetary policies to boost their economies, pumping up western stock markets and leading to soaring returns in equity QDII funds. Third, commodities such as oil rebounded strongly last year, driving the surge in the yield of commodity investment QDII funds.

Table 5.14 Performance of Top 10 QDII Funds

Rank	Name	Return (Recent 1 Year)	Scale (RMB Mln)
1	BOC S&P Global Resources EW	49.48%	36
2	Fortune SG S&P Oil & Gas Exploration & Production Select Industry (CNY)	45.25%	2,510
3	China International Global Natural Resources	44.59%	137
4	Lion Oil and Gas Energy	34.55%	206
5	Huaan S&P Global Oil	31.63%	659
6	ICBCCS International Crude Oil(CNY)	25.83%	30
7	China Southern BRIC	20.50%	89
8	UBS SDIC China Value Discover	18.91%	157
9	Dacheng Equal Weight S&P 500	18.65%	98
10	Bosera S&P 500 ETF	18.34%	218

Source: China Knowledge Mutual Funds Database

Performance of Top 10 Guaranteed Funds

The registration of guaranteed funds was suspended in May. A guide notice was released in August 2016, which set restrictions on the scale and mechanisms of guaranteed funds. This resulted in a cooling of guaranteed funds. Among the remaining ones, China Southern Guaranteed performed best, with return of 7.08%.

Table 5.15 Performance of Top 10 Guaranteed Funds

Rank	Name	Return (Recent 1 Year)	Scale (RMB Mln)
1	China Southern Guaranteed	7.08%	591
2	New China Ali-1 Principal Guaranteed	6.10%	864
3	UBS SDIC Ruiyuan Principal Guaranteed	4.41%	210
4	Industrial Guarantee Securities Investment	3.80%	996
5	Guotai Principal Guaranteed	3.64%	255
6	China Southern Ruili Principal Guaranteed	3.40%	1,474
7	China Southern Hengyuan Principal Protected	3.37%	1,972
8	Bosera Lucky One Big Data Principal Guaranteed	3.14%	1,379
9	China Southern Fenghe Principal Guaranteed	3.06%	2,316
10	Tianhong Xinanbao Guaranteed	3.01%	768

Source: China Knowledge Mutual Funds Database

Performance of Top 10 Quantitative Funds

Under conditions of low market turbulence, quantitative funds with big data search and analysis capabilities performed well. Among these was Changxin Quantitative Pioneer A, which returned 10.52%.

Table 5.16 Performance of Top 10 Quantitative Funds

Rank	Name	Return (Recent 1 Year)	Scale (RMB Mln)
1	Changxin Quantitative Pioneer A	10.52%	10,944
2	Manulife Teda Reverse	10.13%	1,876
3	Harvest Tencent Self-select Stock Big Data	7.06%	694
4	JT Jiusheng Quantitative Pioneer	5.96%	318
5	China Southern Quantitative Growth	5.77%	1,295
6	China Southern Strategy Enhancement	5.37%	1,496
7	SWS MU Quantitative Small Cap	5.11%	2,646
8	Orient Qiming Quantitative Pioneer	4.49%	52
9	Changxin Quantization Multi-Strategy	4.19%	209
10	Manulife Teda Reform Power	3.84%	2,136

Source: China Knowledge Mutual Funds Database

Performance of Top 10 Open-Bond Funds

Regularly open-bond funds saw steady performance. In 2016, New China Anxiang Huijin A, Lion Pure Bond A, and Bosera Shuangyuexin were the three best-performing regularly open-end funds in 2016.

Table 5.17 Performance of Top 10 Open-Bond Funds

Rank	Name	Return (Recent 1 Year)	Scale (RMB Mln)
1	New China Anxiang Huijin A	7.48%	223
2	Lion Pure Bond A	6.54%	434
3	Bosera Shuangyuexin	6.54%	1,705
4	Great Wall Enhanced Income A	6.00%	10,884
5	Morgan Stanley Huaxin Pure Bond Stable Income	5.29%	3,735
6	Changxin Futai Pure Bond One-Year A	5.09%	2,399
7	Minsheng Royal Stable Increase Income A	5.08%	2,813
8	Morgan Stanley Huaxin Pure Bond Value-Added A	4.99%	4,888
9	China Universal Jijihong	4.77%	419
10	Bank Of Beijing Scotiabank Pure Bond One-Year A	4.77%	3,771

Source: China Knowledge Mutual Funds Database

Top 10 Active Equity Fund Companies

Essence Fund Management ranked first in terms of the performance of active equity funds, with average rate of return of -0.08%.

Table 5.18 Active Equity Fund Companies

Rank	Company	No. of Equity Fund	Average Rate of Return	Average Scale (RMB Mln)
1	Essence Fund Mgt.	3	-0.08%	310
2	Guotai Asset Mgt.	3	-2.35%	1,359
3	First Seafront Fund Mgt.	4	-4.51%	717
4	Harvest Fund Mgt.	12	-5.14%	2,113
5	Morgan Stanley Huaxin Fund Mgt.	3	-5.60%	961
6	Lion Fund Mgt.	4	-5.65%	841
7	China Southern Fund Mgt.	5	-7.18%	921
8	Invesco Great Wall Fund Mgt.	6	-10.45%	1,249
9	HSBC Jintrust Fund Mgt.	6	-10.86%	662
10	CCB Principal Asset Mgt.	8	-13.00%	841

Source: China Knowledge Mutual Funds Database

Top 10 Bond Fund Companies

Bond funds feature steady returns. New China Fund Management performed best, followed by the Morgan Stanley Huaxin Fund Management and Galaxy Asset Management, ranked second and third, respectively.

Table 5.19 Performance of Top 10 Bond Fund Companies

Rank	Company	No. of Equity Fund	Average Rate of Return	Average Scale (RMB Mln)
1	New China Fund Mgt.	5	5.76%	930
2	Morgan Stanley Huaxin Fund Mgt.	7	4.33%	1,956
3	Galaxy Asset Mgt.	6	3.36%	1,775
4	Franklin Templeton Sealand Fund Mgt.	4	3.30%	565
5	Harfor Fund Mgt.	6	2.70%	533
6	Great Wall Fund Mgt.	5	2.49%	4,623
7	China Life AMP Asset Mgt.	3	2.40%	2,587
8	CIB Fund Mgt.	7	2.35%	4,952
9	Essence Fund Mgt.	3	2.25%	1,101
10	AXA SPDB Investment Managers	6	2.16%	674

Source: China Knowledge Mutual Funds Database

Fund Size of Different Fund Types in Different Regions

The following figures show different fund types issued in different regions. Shanghai took the lead position, followed by Shenzhen and Beijing. Money market funds accounted for the largest portion in different fund types.

Figure 5.10 Fund Size of Different Fund Types in Different Regions in 2015 (RMB Bln)

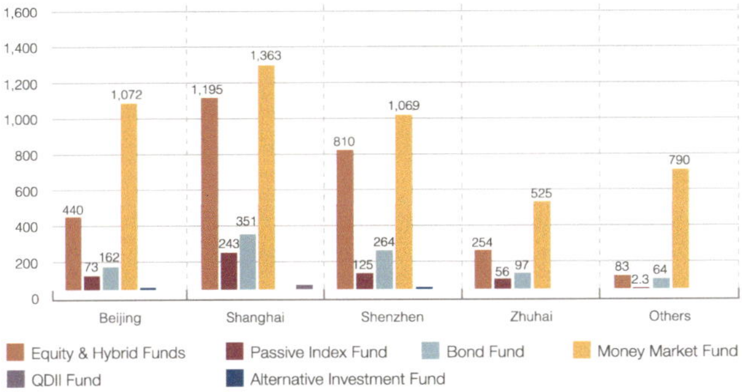

Source: China Knowledge Mutual Funds Database

Figure 5.11 Fund Size of Different Fund Types in Different Regions in 2016 (RMB Bln)

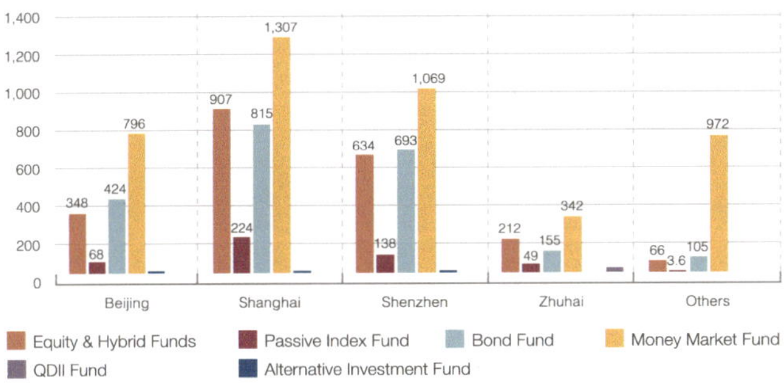

Source: China Knowledge Mutual Funds Database

CHINA MUTUAL FUNDS LISTING

Sample page:

CHINA MUTUAL FUNDS LISTING Page 357

Alternative Investment Funds

Fund Code	Fund Name	Issue Date	Fund Mgt Company	Fund Size (RMB Mln)	YTD Return %	Since Inception Return %	Mgt Fee %
000929.OF	Bosera Gold ETF-D	N.A.	Bosera Fund Mgt.	62.28	19.10	18.71	0.50
159937.OF	Bosera Gold ETF	2014-08-04	Bosera Fund Mgt.	434.90	18.88	3.80	0.50

*To get full 6,100+ China mutual funds, please visit and download at **http://fund.chinaknowledge.com/Download/CMFL.pdf**

Document open password: **ck2017mf**

Made in United States
Cleveland, OH
19 October 2026

46341966R00145